Joan Collins

Passion For Life

Also by Joan Collins

MEMOIRS:

Past Imperfect: An Autobiography (1978)

Katy: A Fight for Life (1982)

Second Act: An Autobiography (1996)

NON-FICTION:

The Joan Collins Beauty Book (1980)

My Secrets (1994)

Health, Youth and Happiness(1995)

My Friends' Secrets (1999)

Joan's Way: Looking Good, Feeling Great (2002)

The Art of Living Well (2007)

The World According to Joan (2012)

FICTION:

Prime Time (1988)

Love and Desire and Hate (1990)

Too Damn Famous (1995)

Infamous (1996)

Star Quality (2002)

Misfortune's Daughters (2004)

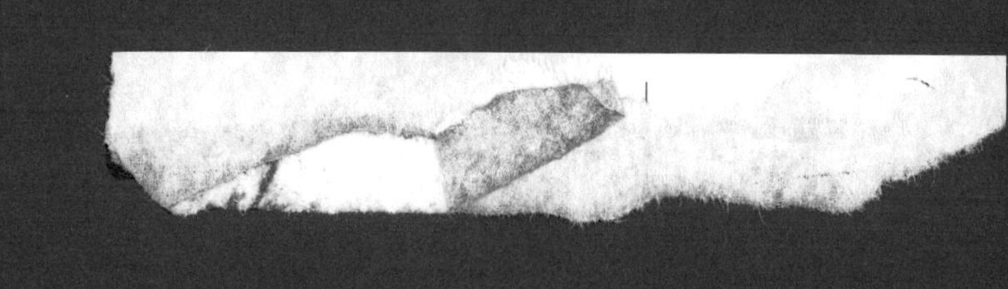

740006527659

JOAN COLLINS

Passion For Life

CONSTABLE

CONTENTS

Chapter One

FAMILY

I blame my grandmother who encouraged me when I wanted to become an actress. She taught me to sing and tap dance and even to do the splits – which I can still do!

'Oh, Grandma, what bendy legs you have!' I squealed as an impressionable five-year-old to my seventy-year-old grandmother. It was Christmas at the Collins abode and the room was full of singers, comedians and magicians. Because my dad, Joe, was a variety agent, our house was always full of performers.

ABOVE: *Rompers and a sun bonnet – well, Mummie thinks I'm cute.*

But none was more theatrical than my grandma, who, not to be outdone amongst the august company of current showbiz stars having a singalong at the piano, decided to perform her famous splits. She had been a dancer and soubrette during the early twentieth century with her two sisters in a performing troupe named 'The Three Cape Girls', so called because they entertained the troops on leave from the Boer War around the capes of South Africa, where my father was born. They toured all around the capes performing highly athletic dances and tricks, of which the splits were the highlight.

'I was doing the splits right up until little Joe was born,' she informed the stunned array of celebrities who were congregated in our living room.

'Can I try?' I asked eagerly, and feisty Grannie hiked up her skirts once again, spread her legs and, in her thick elastic hose, showed me how to do the splits, to my father's embarrassment. I so enjoyed 'splitting' that whenever I did my tap and ballet lessons I usually ended them with a split, much to the mirth of my fellow classmates and the disapproval of my teachers.

OPPOSITE: *Age eighteen, I was voted 'The Most Beautiful Girl in Britain', by the Association of Photographers. Daddy didn't think so!*

Because I always exercised and constantly danced in discos and clubs, I was able to do them whenever I wanted. However, after forty I realized that I definitely needed to 'warm up' before I tried them. At a bacchanalian and very jolly party in Marrakesh, a group of us decided to show off our favourite party trick. We had moved to the bar and some of the guys were standing on their heads or juggling several bottles in a fair imitation of Tom Cruise in *Cocktail*. After one brave individual did six cartwheels in quick succession around the bar where we'd settled in for the night, I jumped up and performed my party trick.

Having imbibed a fair amount of the grape and not having prepared or exercised for several days, I nevertheless performed a perfect split to cheers of approbation, and felt no pain immediately after. However, I couldn't believe the agony of my inner thighs the following morning. I couldn't even get out of bed because my legs hurt so much. Moroccan masseurs were summoned and tended to my soreness but it took a good three days before I could walk without wincing – lesson learned.

OPPOSITE: *Playing Amanda in Noël Coward's* Private Lives *at the Aldwych Theatre in 1990.*

Then, when we were rehearsing Noël Coward's *Private Lives* in London in 1990, the director asked if I would do the splits in the famous drunk scene between Amanda and Elyot. 'Why not?' I said and practised with my trainer Tonya, the tiny torturer, for a few weeks to perfect them before opening night. I must say they worked quite well and the audiences were most appreciative – even the critics grudgingly liked them! In my thirties orange lounging pyjamas they looked suitably effective and I do hope dear Noël would have approved.

I continue to work out because I strongly believe in the 'use it or lose it' maxim. I'm determined to still be able to do physically what I was able to do when I was younger, and therefore exercise has always been of paramount importance to me. It's one thing to get older but I certainly don't want to feel old and I strongly believe that regular exercise, along with a certain amount of clean living, has allowed me to still be lithe and move energetically and youthfully.

I say 'a certain amount' because, after all, like most people I like my wine and my chocolates and love eating, but as Socrates was quoted to say, 'Everything in moderation'. My favourite exercise is simply pushing myself away from the table after dinner and only eating half of what's on my plate.

"Joan Collins is an irrepressibly naughty, adorably sulky, wittily volatile and outrageously provocative Amanda. She not only can feud with disdainful verbal barbs, but throws herself with relish into a wild farcical fracas. It is a most pleasing performance."

MILTON SHULMAN, EVENING STANDARD

"Joan Collins returns triumphantly to the stage. The audience loved it."

REBECCA HARDY – DAILY MAIL

"Joan Collins is an adorably petulant Amanda. She displays a genuinely combative sensuality."

GRAHAM HASSAL – WHAT'S ON IN LONDON

"Cool, extravagant, eternally glamorous, she looks wonderful. She returns to her stage roots with style and assurance."

HILARY BONNER – THE PEOPLE

"She looks great, she sounds great, putting new strength into the Master's brittle dialogue."

JOHN KNIGHT – SUNDAY MIRROR

JOAN COLLINS as "AMANDA"
in Noël Coward's "Private Lives" The Aldwych Theatre, London

"Joan Collins has displays of mischief, outrage, wounded dignity and spitting fury, all timed and perfected to hit the back wall with maximum impact."

IRVING WARDLE – THE INDEPENDENT ON SUNDAY

"A bitchy, witty, wonderful performance. Joan was brilliant."

PIERS MORGAN – THE SUN

"Joan was superb. Triumphant with glamour and verve."

OLIVER WILSON – THE STAR

"A supremely confident performance, sparkling in repartee, superb in the splendidly choreographed fight. She also looks superb and sings with the same endearingly off-key quality as Gertrude Lawrence."

CHARLES OSBORNE – DAILY TELEGRAPH

'If you've got it, flaunt it'

I still do the splits when I feel like it – famously I did them once after the opening night of a movie in New York, in a cocktail gown, when I was trying to make a point about the importance of exercise in the face of getting older – but more suitably I do them when I'm exercising with my trainer. Just a few years ago, when I toured my one-woman show in the UK, I brought the splits back out on public display. I do them regularly in the show now (in November 2010 they caused havoc in New York) when I tell the story of my grandmother and her sisters, and I think audiences appreciate the effort.

'If you've got it, flaunt it,' goes the old adage, so like my grandma I will continue 'splitting' until I can't anymore, and *then* maybe I'll take up knitting.

They didn't go in for the casual look in the 1900s.

My grandmother, Henrietta Assenheim, otherwise known as Hettie, was a feisty Renaissance woman full of life, laughter and fun, and certainly ahead of her time. Born in the late nineteenth century, she took to the stage at an early age, a profession considered by many to be quite risqué.

While still a teenager she played principal girl in panto at the Bristol Theatre Royal. Since Henrietta Assenheim was considered too much of a mouthful to be up in electric lights, she changed it to Hettie Collins when she married my grandfather.

ABOVE: *Hettie at nineteen and Lottie at twenty – there's a definite resemblance.*

My grandfather's real name was Isaac Hart. He lived with his family in Petticoat Lane, East London, and at seventeen he became fascinated by vaudeville when he saw Lottie Collins, the lovely, coquettish star, considered the Madonna of her day, perform her hit song 'Ta-ra-ra-boom-de-ay' at the Tivoli Theatre on the Strand. She was wearing a short, red dress, huge hat and outrageous stiletto boots. Young Isaac became so smitten that he decided to change his name to Will Collins. He started his showbiz career soon after and worked his way up to becoming the business manager of a small theatrical touring company, which became quite successful. Soon Will and Hettie travelled to Cape Town, South Africa, where he mounted variety tours all over the country, one of which featured Hettie.

By 1900, Hettie had enlisted the support of her two sisters, Minnie and Hannah. At the height of the Boer War, they travelled around the capes by bullock wagon, entertaining the British troops. The young soubrette had great charisma and verve and usually garnered excellent reviews. For example, 'Miss Hettie Collins takes the bun for singing and dancing and everything she does.'

Will also believed in the power of publicity, which was not then an accepted thing, but he made sure everyone knew Hettie's worth.

Their cheeky and slightly salacious routines also included performing in 'blackface', which was considered quite normal in those days, but today would get them condemned!

Hettie and Will Collins were married in Port Elizabeth, South Africa, and as an emancipated woman, she continued her uninhibited performances right up until a month before my father, Joseph William Collins, was born in December 1902. Hettie must have had a strong constitution to have sung, danced and performed the splits while pregnant, which was unheard of then.

My father with his mother Hettie. He was voted the most beautiful baby on board the boat taking them to England from South Africa in 1903.

Eventually, when they moved back to England, Hettie gave up her career to devote herself to full-time motherhood and being a good wife. Women of that era were trained to become good wives and mothers, and to continue a stage career, showing off her legs and ample bosom in semi-revealing costumes, would have been considered extremely shocking.

On the boat back to England, my father was voted the most beautiful baby on board, which Grandma and his two younger sisters teased him about unmercifully. But he was very pretty, particularly wearing a dress.

Lalla Collins was born a couple of years after my father. Always coy about her age, none of us were quite sure how old she was. By 1924, when still a teenager, Lalla had followed in her mother's footsteps and was starring in the West End in *André Charlot's Revue* of 1924.

Pauline Collins was born two years later, so Hettie and Will's little family was now complete. But sadly, Will Collins died in 1915 at the age of thirty-nine. Young Joe had to become the breadwinner in the family and, following in the theatrical footsteps of his father, he became a call-boy at variety theatres at fourteen.

When Hettie remarried Jack French, also a theatrical agent, he employed young Joe and they worked together from a tiny office above the fire station in Shaftesbury Avenue.

By the late twenties, both Joe's sisters were on the stage and had achieved considerable success as ingénues and comediennes.

Lalla became the bigger star with the lead in *Sunny*, a top musical comedy. She soon become involved in a 'hot 'n' heavy' romance with the leading man, Jack Buchanan, a cross between debonair Fred Astaire

Tatler

Vol. VIII.—No. 94

Miss LALLA COLLINS, Miss ETHEL STEWART and Miss NELL S…
three of the ladies who play leading parts in the twice-nightly musical comedy

ALHAMBRA THEATRE

THE
FLYING TRAPEZE

MISS LALLA COLLINS
will play the
part of
"Marie Louise"
at this performance.

ABOVE LEFT: *Hettie, Lalla, Pauline and the family dog.*

ABOVE: *Joe, Lalla and Pauline in their party clothes.*

Lalla followed in her mother's footsteps and became a West End star.

The Collins sisters circa 1920s. Pauline wasn't averse to showing a touch of décolletage. Lalla was more refined.

LEFT: *Lalla had a passionate affair with the matinee idol of the day, Jack Buchanan. She treasured this signed picture for years.*

BELOW: *With Pauline looking chic – she looks good too.*

ABOVE: *Happy family snap of the Assenheim-Collins clan on the beach. LOVE the mob caps!*

ABOVE: *On Brighton beach. Young me with Grandma and her sisters Hannah and Minnie.*

RIGHT: *With Hettie feeding pigeons.*

and Cary Grant, who made the ladies swoon in the thirties. When Jack travelled to New York on the *Queen Mary*, he and Lalla exchanged romantic correspondence and he sent her constant, loving telegrams.

Pauline was rather racy, and although not as beautiful as Lalla, she was a typical fun-loving flapper, and was also known as a bit 'fast'. She often posed for publicity photos semi-nude. Perhaps that's why I had no such

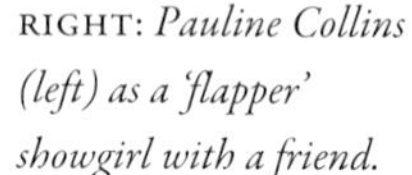

RIGHT: *Pauline Collins (left) as a 'flapper' showgirl with a friend.*

ABOVE: *Elsa Collins with her favourite poodles.*

qualms when I posed for *Playboy*! She gave up her career quite early and also became an agent.

My father's adoring mother and his equally adoring sisters spoiled him rotten. He grew up expecting women to do whatever *he* wanted. In other words, he was a typical male chauvinist of which the early twentieth century abounded.

When he met and married my beautiful mother, Elsa Bessant, he expected her to give up her career as a champion ballroom dancer and gold medallist, and become a good wife and mother like Hettie. This she dutifully did.

My mother was docile, gentle and sweet. She didn't have a mean bone in her body and she worshipped my father, which he took as his due. Elsa loved being a wife, mother and homemaker. She had a wicked sense of humour, though, and such great legs that she was nicknamed 'Marlene' after Dietrich.

When they married, Mummie was earning more money than Daddy (does the apple fall far from the tree . . . !) so it was she who bought all the furniture for their small flat in London's Maida Vale, whilst he spent what he was making as an agent on his car, buying the lease of his new office and putting a down payment on a typewriter.

But Daddy soon became a very successful agent and some of the acts he booked were legendary. He discovered Flanagan and Allen, two brilliant comics who were famous for their songs 'Underneath the Arches' and 'Run Rabbit Run'. He was asked to represent a thirteen-year-old singer, Vera Welch, but turned her down. A few years later, she became the fabled Vera Lynn, the 'Forces' Sweetheart' of the Second World War.

My parents, Bill and Pauline at my first wedding. No wonder they look worried!

He represented Dorothy Squires, a flamboyant singer who was married to a young Roger Moore. When I first saw Roger Moore as a very young schoolgirl, I thought he was the best looking man I'd ever seen! Daddy went on to represent Roger as well.

My father also discovered a young tap dancer called Lew Grade and eventually they went into business together as The Collins and Grade Agency.

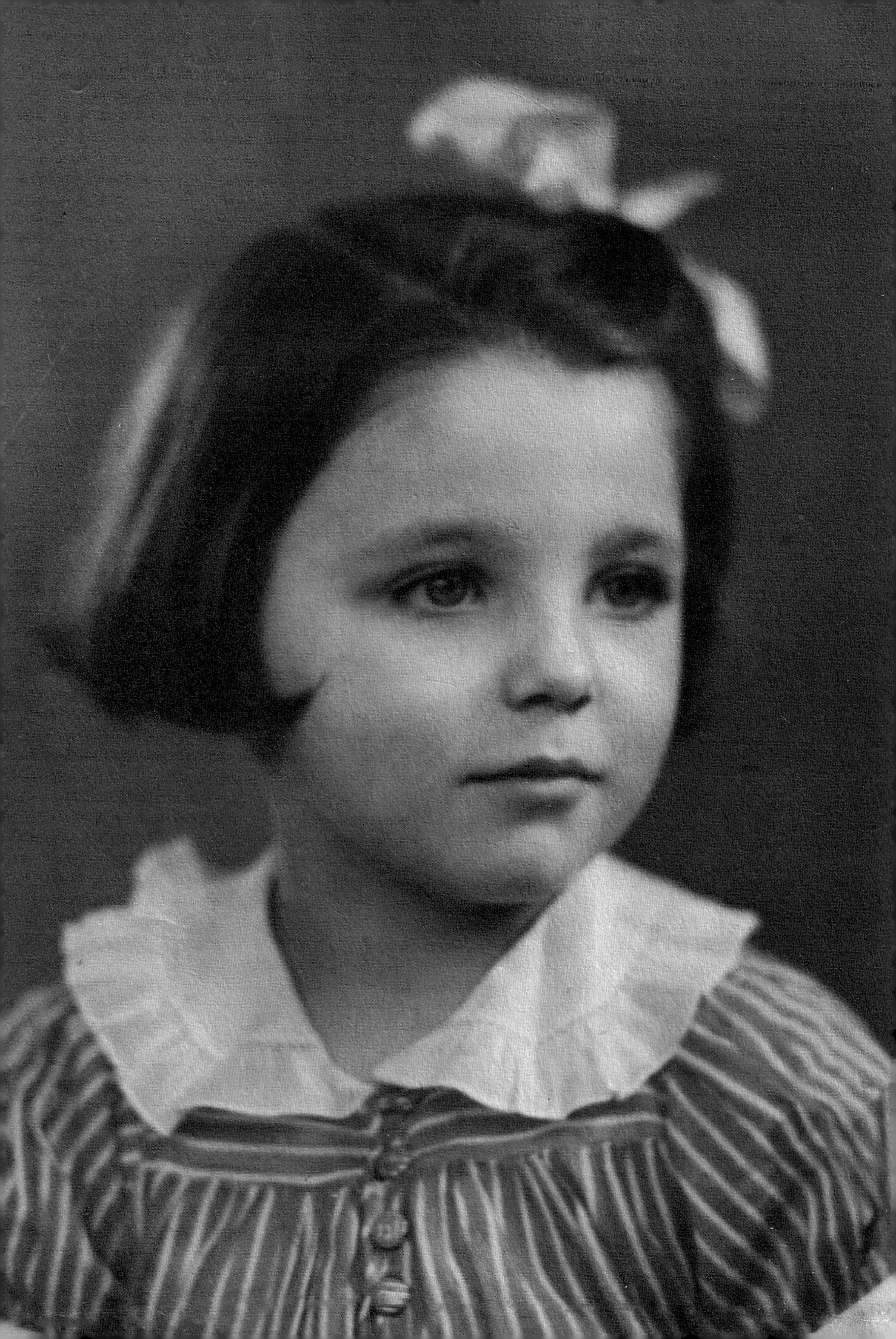

Chapter Two

CHILDHOOD

Mine was an idyllically happy early childhood until everything was turned upside down when war was declared.

I'll never forget asking my mother what a television was, shortly after the war ended; we were walking down Baker Street away from Oxford Street, on our way home. 'It's like a little theatre with tiny people in it,' Mummie said hesitantly. So that's what I believed until, a few years later, we bought one of the first televisions and I saw tiny men running around on the stamp-size football field. 'How boring,' I thought. 'No one will ever be interested in watching that.' So I spent most of my time entertaining myself. I loved designing fashions for my aunts and my mother. They sometimes even had them made by their dressmakers!

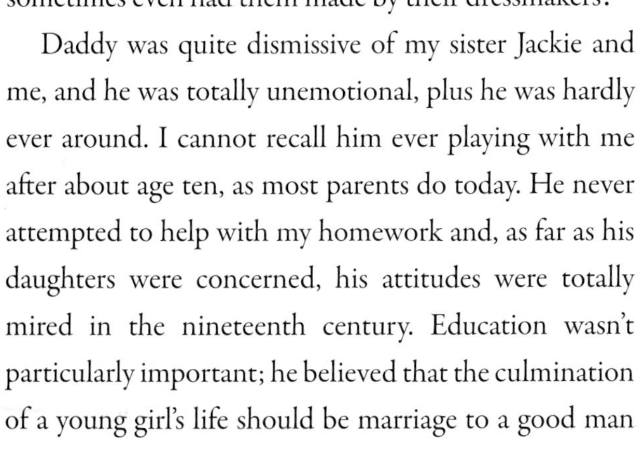

Daddy was quite dismissive of my sister Jackie and me, and he was totally unemotional, plus he was hardly ever around. I cannot recall him ever playing with me after about age ten, as most parents do today. He never attempted to help with my homework and, as far as his daughters were concerned, his attitudes were totally mired in the nineteenth century. Education wasn't particularly important; he believed that the culmination of a young girl's life should be marriage to a good man

Daddy in a homburg, Jackie and me in bonnets on the Brighton Downs. A rare affectionate picture.

OPPOSITE: *The first time I was ever told I had beautiful eyes, by the hairdresser who was trimming my bob.*

(ha!) and motherhood. My mother epitomized this; her role as domestic goddess and Mother Earth were the most important things in her life.

My mother was a bit of a health nut before many people understood fully about nutrition or diet. During the war, every morning Mummie spoon-fed us Virol, a disgusting syrup which, according to her, was 'full of goodness'. We also had to stomach cod liver oil from a massive spoon; how ghastly was that? And she insisted on us drinking a bottled mixture consisting of compressed oranges, which she diluted with water, so

LEFT: *Brighton on the rocks. Mummie cuddles her firstborn.*

BELOW: *Elsa was a devoted mother and adored her two daughters. Jackie is smart in smocking and I had started my ongoing love for stripes.*

My favourite picture of Mummie and me.

'It was like having your own little dolly!'

we could get our vitamins – whatever they were. We were also not allowed sweets or chocolates until after we'd eaten, which wasn't too hard to comply with as, in any case, they were rationed. We were also forced to eat everything on our plate because 'the children in India are starving'. Since there was never much on our plate anyway, that was also easy.

In fact, when I was a child growing up, portions were about a quarter of what is considered a normal serving today, hence hardly anyone was fat then, let alone seriously overweight. Because Mummie knew that too

Mummie loved going out on the town and always looked glamorous.

much sugar and biscuits were bad for you she hardly gave us any, so when she gave me my first banana, after the war, I thought it was the most heavenly thing I had ever tasted.

Mummie also taught me to do exercises. She'd put on her slacks, sometimes even shorts, and do leg bends, 'bicycles', little sit-ups and toe-touching on the rug by our flickering electric fire.

She was, like all of our family, a chocoholic! She adored that delicious treat and could devour a box of Cadbury's Milk Tray in one sitting. She also loved butter, too much I think, as she put on quite a few pounds after the war ended.

Daddy, meanwhile, was thin as a reed, smoked a pack of Player's each day and liked the occasional whisky. Sadly and ironically, it was my darling mother who died of cancer in her early fifties whilst Daddy lived to a ripe old eighty-five. Mummie had never smoked and drank little, which just goes to show that if the Grim Reaper wants you early, it's all in the cards you're dealt. They say the good die young and it was certainly true in Mummie's case.

She was extremely naive, especially about sex, which no one ever discussed then. She never told me about the facts of life, procreation or menstruation, so when the latter occurred it was a huge shock.

I only heard her raise her voice in anger towards my irascible father a couple of times. She was sweet, placid and docile – just what the perfect wife was supposed to be in the mid-twentieth century and what I was determined *not* to be.

My father, however, did instigate some wise adages for his kids to live by: 'No one will ever do anything for you; you have to do it yourself'; 'Don't ever ask or depend on anyone for anything. It's a tough world out there so you're on your own'; and finally, the one which particularly inspired confidence in a young girl, 'You're old enough and you're ugly enough to clear the table and do the dishes.'

Daddy encouraged me – albeit reluctantly – to follow my dream of becoming an actress even if he barked in his brusque way, 'You better

LEFT: *On the Brighton Downs again – boy, we were a healthy lot!*

BELOW: *Obviously not shy about going topless in Bognor Regis but that wooly swimsuit became waterlogged and soggy.*

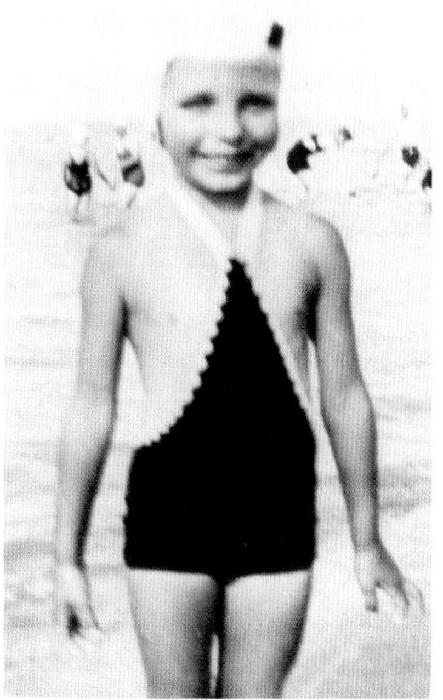

make all the money you can when you're young because by the time you're twenty-three, you'll be all washed up.' This was another prevalent attitude then as the world was extremely ageist towards women, particularly actresses. And the sell-by date for most was age twenty-seven, and after forty you were well past it.

My father didn't believe in debt. He didn't own much either as all our homes were rented, but he did buy a new car quite regularly. Oh, those endless, boring trips every Sunday to the bleak English seaside of either Brighton or Bognor Regis, which were still suffering from post-war blues and austerity. But I had my first real ice-cream cone on the Brighton seafront even though some barbed wire barricades were still up and we couldn't go on the beach because of the possibility of landmines. So we just visited Grandma Hettie in her sunny Brighton flat and Nana, Mummie's terrifying old mother, in her dark and gloomy Bognor house.

'I had my first real ice-cream cone on the Brighton seafront.'

ABOVE: *Bill was the apple of everyone's eye and was even forced to ride a donkey at eighteen months.*

ABOVE: *Katy, my brother Bill, his wife Hazel and Joyce Reuben.*

LEFT: *We all adored little Bill Collins – still do!*

New Year's Eve circa 1950-something. Daddy has a few bevvies, while Mummie pretends not to notice!

Daddy was well liked in the showbiz community in which he moved, though his vile temper often revealed itself, even to his card-playing cronies.

When he played cards – poker or gin rummy – at our house, I was instructed to answer the phone and repeat the name of the caller; if it was a client my father didn't want to talk to, he'd shake his head vehemently and I would parrot, 'I'm sorry, Daddy's out.' So now, whenever I hear an agent's assistant say that to me, I automatically presume they don't want to talk to me!

Daddy had his detractors but everyone loved Elsa Collins. She was sweet and charming, with a wicked sense of humour. My agent, Peter Charlesworth, was a young man when he knew her and he tells fond stories of how she would tease him about the amount of women he dated. Robert Wagner still remembers how kind and friendly she was towards him when we were dating in the early sixties. Mummie's best friend was Lady Kathy Grade. They met when Kathy was a young singer, before she married Lew Grade, who was subsequently given a knighthood and then made a peer. Lady Grade came to see me in my one-woman show recently and lovingly reminisced about the great times she'd had with Mummie on holiday.

Mummie went on holiday with us every year but Daddy never went, as he said he was too busy with work. Later, I came to realize he was probably too busy dallying with various showgirl dollies, as Joe was very attractive to women and I believe that he had his fair share. But I don't think it was blatant. I believe he loved Elsa, even though he often treated her like a slave. Watching him hurl a plate of fish and peas across the dining room and onto one of Mummie's precious Knoll sofas was one of my most harrowing childhood memories. Although he was never physically violent, Mummie would hold over our heads the awful threat, 'If you don't behave your father will give you a good hiding when he comes home.'

Daddy was so emotionally overwhelmed when Mummie was seriously ill, if any friend or acquaintance enquired about her health, he would turn his back and refuse to answer them. When Mummie died in 1962, Daddy was totally grief stricken and wouldn't discuss her death.

Daddy married again but sadly Irene died ten years after he did. He had another daughter, Natasha, who went into the military – not something the Collins family is famous for!

Looking back on my childhood it was like that of most kids of my generation; somewhat of a rocky road because of the war. However, I believe that having a strict disciplinarian father and a loving and domesticated mother instilled in me the values by which I have lived very happily – most of the time!

Rome 1960. I loved playing the pinball machines. Mummie came with me to protect me from an irate ex-husband.

THE ARTS THEATRE GROUP OF ACTORS

During the past three years we have presented at this Theatre plays by the following great English dramatists; **James Bridie, G. J. Chesterton, John Drinkwater, Farquhar, Masefield, Somerset Maugham, Pinero, Shaw, Sheridan** and **Shakespeare,** as well as plays by such well known international authors as **Jean Jacques Bernard, Buchner, Goldoni, Moliere, Odets, Eugene O'Neill, J. M. Synge** and the **Brothers Quintero,** from such various countries as France, Germany, Italy, America, Ireland and Spain.

Also included in our programme have been many first presentations amongst which were :— "THE HOUSE OF REGRETS" by **Peter Ustinov,** "THE OLD FOOLISHNESS" by **Paul Vincent Carroll,** "THE WATCHED POT" by "**Saki,**" two Norwegian plays — "ON LIFE'S SUNNY SIDE" and "THE COPY" by **Helge Krog** and the prize-winning play of our New Play Competition—"THE TWO CHILDREN" by **Peter Powell.**

DETAILS OF MEMBERSHIP

Theatre Membership entitles you to purchase seats for yourself and for your guests at a range of remarkably low prices. Full membership entitles you in addition to full club facilities, including the use of restaurant and lounge.

Theatre Membership, 5/– a Year. (No Entrance Fee)
Full Club Membership, Two Guineas a Year. Two Guineas Entrance Fee.

Theatre Prices :

Stalls 7/6, 5/-, 3/6
Circle 7/6, 5/-

If you want to become a member the Secretary or her assistants will be glad to help you if you apply for further information at the table in the foyer.

G. T. Northover & Son, Printers, Shropshire House, Tottenham Court Rd. W.1

THE ARTS THEATRE GROUP OF ACTORS

Under the direction of ALEC CLUNES

PRESENT

HENRIK IBSEN'S

A DOLL'S HOUSE

ARTS THEATRE CLUB

(*Just by Leicester Square Tube Station*)

6-7, Gt. Newport Street, London, W.C.2

Box Office and all Enquiries : TEMPLE BAR 7544

Programme 6D

ABOVE: *My first job – at the Arts Theatre London playing a ten-year-old-boy in* A Dolls House. *I was attending the Cone-Rysman theatrical school.*

PLEASURE GARDENS THEATRE
FOLKESTONE

Telephone : BOX OFFICE 3227 GENERAL MANAGER'S OFFICE : 3307

Managing Director ... RALPH BIRCH
Licensee and Manager ... G. SPOONER
Stage Manager ... S. COURT

Week commencing MONDAY, APRIL 19th, 1954

BY ARRANGEMENT WITH MARK MARVIN
RALPH BIRCH PRESENTS

"THE PRAYING MANTIS"

Characters in order of their appearance :

Captain Samons, *of the Palace Guard* ... ERIC LANDER
Yolande, *a servant* ... IRENE RICHMOND
Euphrosyne, *a mother to Nicephones and Leo* DAISY BINDLEY
Nicephones, *a eunuch, Minister for Imperial Finance* MICHAEL GOLDEN
Michael, *his page* ... RICHARD MARTIN
Leo, *his brother, a merchant* ... DOUGLAS STEWART
Martina, *Leo's wife* ... JOAN COLLINS
(*By permission of the J. Arthur Rank Organisation*)
Major Philagricus, *of the Palace Guard* ... JAMES SHARKEY
Zoab, *a Jeweller* ... REGINALD SELLICK
Basil IX, *Emperor of Byzantium* ... ELWIN BROOK-JONES
Princess Theodora } *his daughters* ... MARGOT LISTER
Princess Eudocia } ... IRENE RICHMOND
General Lascaris ... REGINALD SELLICK
Slave of the Court ... VIC PATTERSON
Palace Guards } ... DOUGLAS YOUNG, HENRY RAYNER
Lady in Waiting ... FANNY CARBY
Herald ... ROSS REED
Dancer ... MARIGOLD RUSSELL

Settings designed by TOM LINGWOOD
The Play produced by VERE LORRIMER

ABOVE: *My first tour and starring role – J. Arthur Rank gave me permission.*

ON SALE
IN THIS THEATRE NOW...

A UNIQUE PRESENT FOR YOUR "THEATRE-LOVER" FRIEND AND YOURSELF!

"AN
ILLUSTRATED STORY
OF THE
LONDON THEATRES
OF 1851"

CONTAINING

OLD PRINTS, CARTOONS, PLAYBILLS AND STORIES OF THE NINETEEN THEATRES (ONLY EIGHT STILL REMAIN) IN LONDON IN 1851

A LIMITED EDITION 1'6

MAKE SURE OF YOUR COPY

Tuesday, 4th November, to Sunday, 9th November, 1952

THE SKIN OF OUR TEETH

A History of Mankind in Comic Strip

by THORNTON WILDER

Characters in order of their appearance:—

ACT I—THE ICE

Announcer	HENRY WILLIS
Sabina	JOAN COLLINS
Mr. Fitzpatrick	JACK TAYLOR
Mrs. Antrobus	PEGGY LIVESEY
Dinosaur	DAVID HOWARTH
Mammoth	JOHN RUTHERFORD
Telegraph Boy	IAN WHITTAKER
Gladys	JANET REID
Henry	JAMES SHARKEY
Mr. Antrobus	MAXWELL REED
Doctor	HENRY FIELDING
Professor	MURRAY SHAND
Judge Moses	EDWARD MILLER
Homer	CLAUDE HALLIFAX
Muses	JOAN MURRAY, VALERIE RUSSELL, JUNE WARD
Theatre Usher	IAN WHITTAKER

ACT II—THE DELUGE

Announcer	HENRY WILLIS
Mr. Antrobus	MAXWELL REED
Mrs. Antrobus	PEGGY LIVESEY
Henry	JAMES SHARKEY
Gladys	JANET REID
Fortune Teller	JOAN SANDERSON
Sabina	JOAN COLLINS
Defeated Candidate	HENRY FIELDING
Mr. Fitzpatrick	JACK TAYLOR
Broadcast Official	IAN WHITTAKER
Child Conveners	CHRISTINE CALDECOTT, RITA MATTHEWS, BETTY LEASE, KEITH FAULKNER
Chair Pushers	JOHN RUTHERFORD, BRIAN RIDER, TONY LYONS
Female Conveners	VALERIE RUSSELL, NINA NISBET, FRANCES KYSOR, JOAN MURRAY, JUNE WARD, JACQUELINE COLLINS
Male Coveners	EDWARD MILLER, CLAUDE HALLIFAX, MURRAY SHAND, DAVID HOWARTH, HENRY FIELDING

ACT III—THE RESTORATION

Sabina	JOAN COLLINS
Mr. Fitzpatrick	JACK TAYLOR
Mr. Antrobus	MAXWELL REED
Hester	JACQUELINE COLLINS
Ivy	JOAN MURRAY
Mr. Tremayne	HENRY FIELDING
Fred Bailey	IAN WHITTAKER
Assistant Stage Manager	VALERIE RUSSELL
Mrs. Antrobus	PEGGY LIVESEY
Gladys	JANET REID
Henry	JAMES SHARKEY

Directed by PETER DEARING

Furniture by The Old Times Furnishing Co. "Cuebar" Sound Equipment & Effects by Bishop Sound & Electrical Co. Mr. Reed's costumes by M. Berman Ltd. Miss Collins' Act I costume by Charles H. Fox Ltd. Other costumes by H. & N. Benjamin Ltd. "The Eyes & Ears of The World" kindly loaned by Paramount British News. Bedspread by Everwear Candlewick Ltd. Musical instruments by King Street Music Stores, W.6. Watering can & Travelling rug by Goslings of Richmond. Orange boxes and potatoes by Cliffs of Stile Hall Parade, W.4. Electric Torch by E. S. Motors, 325 High Road, W.4. Toys and Lanterns by Galloways, Chiswick High Road, W.4. Fish Bowl by Chiswick Aquaria, 136 Chiswick High Road, W.4. Animal Skins by Barnums, Hammersmith Road, W.6. Cigarettes by Abdulla.

REFER CENTRE PAGE FOR FUTURE ATTRACTIONS

ABOVE: *Maxwell Reed and I starred in this play.*

'The plan was to start as an ingénue in a repertory company, graduate to leading lady roles in the theatre, then, I hoped, the West End.'

ABOVE AND RIGHT: *Illustrating stories in women's magazines. I was usually being threatened by someone – does art imitate life or what?!*

My First Modelling Job

When I was a teenager I never thought of becoming a model; my sights were firmly set on acting, or perhaps becoming a dress designer. The plan was to start as an ingénue in a repertory company, graduate to leading lady roles in the theatre, then, I hoped, the West End, and eventually become a *grande dame* of the theatre à la Flora Robson or Dame Edith Evans.

So when Sir Kenneth Barnes, the avuncular boss of the Royal Academy of Dramatic Art, announced that a famous photographer was coming to the Academy to find a 'new face', I didn't think much about it.

Shortly thereafter a dozen of the female students were asked to line up in the room in which we took fencing and dancing classes to meet the snapper, as we were told that we were considered to be the prettiest girls in

Jayne Mansfield and I comparing cars and cleavages. I couldn't even beat her in the car department!

Early pictures taken by Fox. These were called 'at home' layouts. I guess they couldn't find a real poodle.

the academy. We all giggled nervously, surveying each other critically and commenting rather sweetly and un-bitchily on each other's outfits. I wore the one dress that I possessed: a polka-dotted number with a tight waist and full skirt in which I'd taken my audition for RADA.

The other girls were similarly attired in fifties fashion. We all had tiny waists in those days, probably due to not having had much food during the war. Rationing was still upon us so sweets and chocolates were thin on the ground, as were biscuits and crisps, butter and bacon, and cake and sugar.

The photographer, a cadaverous young man, was wearing grey flannels, a well-worn tweed jacket and an open-necked shirt, quite bohemian for that time as hardly anyone possessed the jeans and leather jackets of later youths. He walked up and down the line inspecting us as though we were today's catch laid out on a marble slab at the fishmongers.

The other girls – who included Eileen Moore, Susan Stephen, Diane Cilento and Yvonne Furneaux (all of whom went on to successful acting careers) – were all quite nervous and we weren't thrilled about being inspected like pieces of meat. After a few minutes we were dismissed and I thought nothing of it until two days later, when I received a phone call from the photographer's assistant saying the photographer had chosen me and would I come to his studio the next day for a sitting. 'And bring a bathing suit,' she instructed. Well, I only had one – a black, boned one-piece, somewhat the worse for wear as I'd worn it constantly on a holiday in Dinard, France, the previous year.

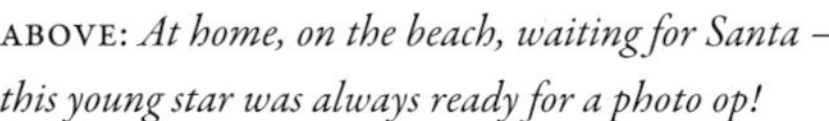

ABOVE: *At home, on the beach, waiting for Santa – this young star was always ready for a photo op!*

RIGHT AND BELOW: *Fox brought out the glamour girl in me, and made me pose patriotically for July 4th celebrations.*

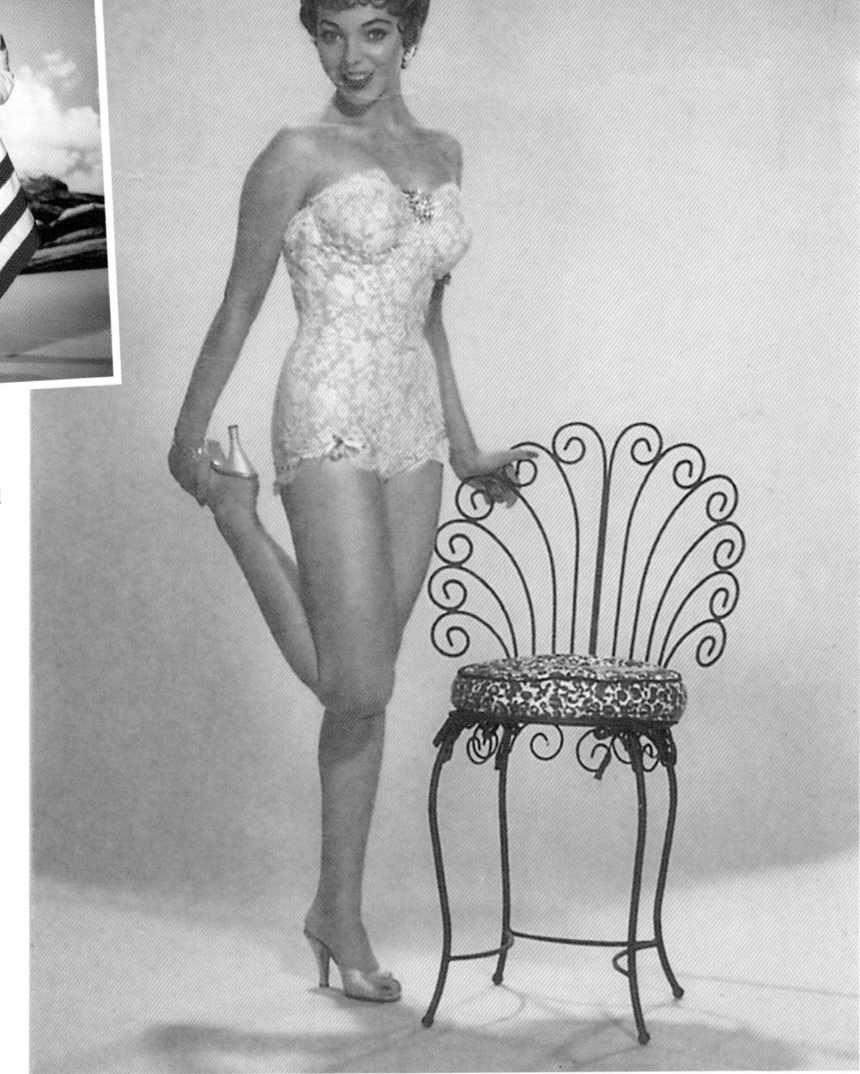

RIGHT: *A glamour still from* Rally Round the Flag Boys *where I made Paul Newman blush the colour of this background!*

OPPOSITE: *Just what the well dressed squaw always wears before returning to her wigwam.*

Good Taste

JULY 1950

9D

Summer Beauty Poise

STORIES BY

John Lastingham
Jean Colombel
Phyllis Hambledon

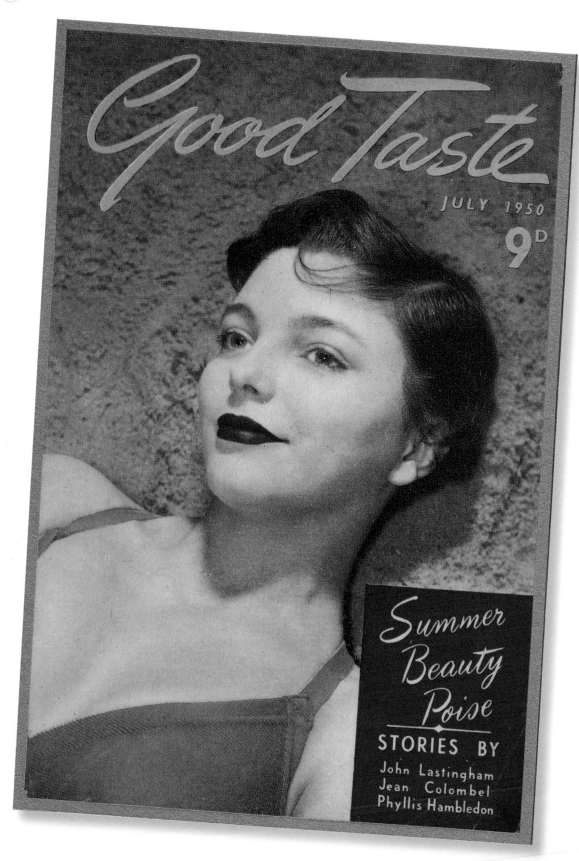

At the studio they bustled around, told me my costume was awful and gave me a blue one to wear instead. They applied thick pan stick on my sixteen-year-old visage, dark red lipstick on my mouth and gelled my short 'urchin cut'.

'What about eye makeup?' I cried.

'Not necessary,' barked the photographer, now in shirt sleeves and with a cigarette dangling from his lips.

'But I always wear eye makeup,' I wailed.

'Now, shut up dear, you're supposed to be on the beach and no one wears eye makeup on the beach. Lie down in the sand. This is for a cover, you know.'

'A cover?' I was impressed. Covers were only for glamour girls like Lana Turner or Ava Gardner, or sophisticated models like Barbara Goalen (the most elegant woman in England and whom we all wanted to look like).

I lay on the freezing studio floor on wet sand, feeling quite uncomfortable as the hot lights burned my face while Mr Snapper told me to turn this way and that and eventually dismissed me.

'You did well – come back next week. We'll have some teenaged clothes for you to model in *Woman's Own*, OK?'

At an awkward seventeen, my attempts at being glamorous were a total disaster.

'OK,' I said, admiring the cheque the assistant gave me – the first cheque I had ever received. But the eventual cover of *Good Taste* magazine horrified me. I looked like a drowned rat but photographers nevertheless seemed pleased, as more work came my way.

I shot quite a few sessions with this photographer. Eventually, one shoot in particular, in which I wore a yellow turtleneck and was being stalked by a murderer to illustrate a story, caught the eye of a theatrical agent called Bill Watts.

Mr Watts summoned me to his office in Dover Street and suggested that I had a good face for 'the films'. At first I demurred, as I was only interested in 'the thea-tah'. Nevertheless he persisted, and the rest is history!

OPPOSITE: *The result of my first day modelling. What I now call my drowned rat look.*

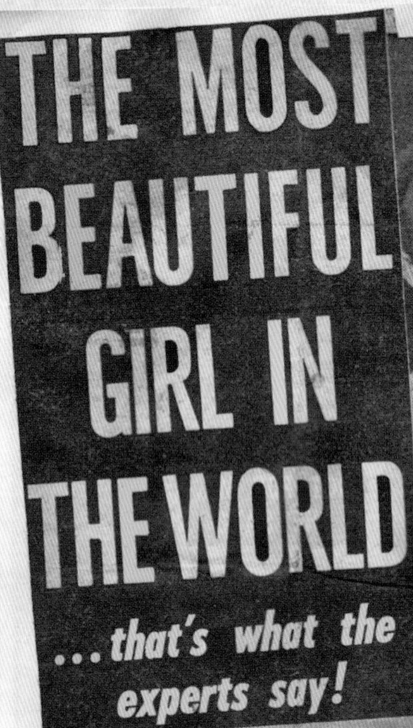

THE MOST BEAUTIFUL GIRL IN THE WORLD

...that's what the experts say!

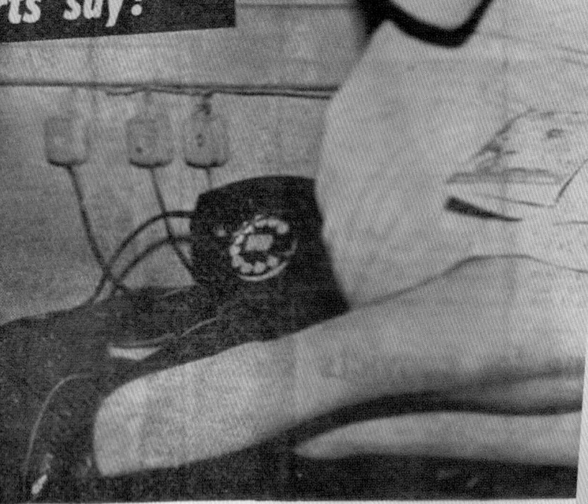

IT was a happy day for British actress Joan Collins yesterday. She had just been called "the most beautiful girl in the world."

And that title was given her by people who know what they are talking about—glamour photographers of 21 countries.

The Professional Photographers' Society Hollywood spokesman said they gave Joan a 75 per cent. vote in a 2,827 poll. He called her the only woman in public life who met the standards of artists like Titian. Which recalls the comment of the New York dockers eyeing Joan in this picture: "That chick sure is some dame."

Una «sconvolgente» espressione di Joan Collins, la bellissima attrice inglese trapiantata a Hollywood

[illegible] I met Joan

SOMETHING, I suppose, to have sat next to the girl they call the Pouting Panther of Hollywood and also the Prettiest Girl in the World, a title she recently won.

But all I can remember about Joan Collins is that she was [illegible] made up rather needlessly because she was so naturally pretty and that she detested leeks and war films.

The lunch was in Manchester with George Baker as host at the Gaumont, to discuss her latest film "Turn the Key Softly."

Only trouble was that she would keep on talking about another film she liked herself in better, "Cosh Boy." Her studio escorts were furious. We talked about war films. She thought women loathed them. Do they?

Joan Collins

Manchester Chron Aug. 13.

They Pick Joan

JOAN COLLINS

The Most Beautiful Girl

Aberdeen Exp.

Joan: la più bella, ma ribelle...

La plus belle fille du monde

Joan Collins proclamée « la plus belle fille du monde »

La Depeche du Midi, Aug 13 1958

Dundee Telegraph

The most beautiful girl . . .

Blackburn Telegraph Aug 12. 1958

WORLD'S "MOST BEAUTIFUL"

Ottawa Citizen, Canada Sept. 14

L'Espoir, Aug. 15. 1958

Acclaimed world's No. 1

PASSED RULER TEST!

Our Joan Collins—'the most beautiful girl in the world'

Rivals for Joan

Empire News Aug 17 1958

Top beauty in world

Joan Collins—world's most beautiful girl

Manchester Evening

Gloucester Echo

NEW LIQUID LUSTRE-CREME IS HERE!

Now you can shampoo... Set with plain water...and have lively, natural looking curls!

Joan Collins starring in Leo McCarey's "RALLY ROUND THE FLAG, BOYS!"

New Rich, Rich Liquid! Lanolin-Blessed!

Lustre-Creme

JOAN COLLINS, beautiful Hollywood star, uses Liquid Lustre-Creme Shampoo to keep her hair soft and easy-to-manage. Why don't You try it, too?

FOR CURLS THAT COME EASY—HERE'S ALL YOU DO:

4 OUT OF 5 TOP MOVIE STARS USE LUSTRE-CREME SHAMPOO!

My sister Jackie lovingly pasted these cuttings into a scrap book and wrote captions.

Chapter Three

NOMAD LIFE

When I was a little girl, one of my favourite games was called 'Travelling the World'. This consisted of a small nursery table being turned upside down, with the legs covered by a sheet, that I would then kneel inside with several dolls and animals and take them on trips to my houses all over the world. I had a 'house' in America, one in Japan, a 'chateau' in France and a 'villa' in India. The Indian one was particularly beloved, as I was able to give my leftover food to what my mother always referred to as 'the starving children of India' – in my case, my dolls.

OPPOSITE: *Always dreaming of fresh fields and pastures new to conquer in Malta 1968, as Tony was terribly busy.*

My other game of choice was moving the furniture around and redecorating my doll's house. As I grew up, I realized that what children love to do when they are very young often mutates into what they love to do as adults.

Therefore, enjoying travelling, moving houses and redecorating is now what I do, and I think by now I have lived in about fifty different abodes.

I was born in a nursing home in Bayswater, London, which no longer exists. My parents lived in a big thirties-style block of flats – Castellain Mansions – at the end of the Edgware Road behind Maida Vale. I remember coming home to the flat in my father's car, after a day visiting my grandma in Brighton, and seeing fire engines and firemen all over the street and the shocked face of my nanny who confessed tearfully that she'd been smoking. Those memories, and her words, 'I can't remember what happened to the cigarette but I think I dropped it on the baby's cot', stay with me still. Everything was destroyed including my few toys and a

Shirley Temple doll I adored. However, kindly neighbours gave me another one, which I kept until I was a teenager.

Although I couldn't have been more than two, the smell of smoke and the sight of fire still scare me. We soon moved to a large, sunny flat in Maida Vale on the continuation of Edgware Road, where I used to dance like crazy to the music of Henry Hall and his big band. They performed every morning on live radio and I enthusiastically practised the steps learned in my ballet and tap classes to their signature tune, 'Here's to the Next Time'.

A couple of years later, my family moved again to Hillcrest Court, on Shoot Up Hill, between Hampstead and Cricklewood. I loved being close to the Heath and enjoyed going for walks with new baby Jackie in her big pram.

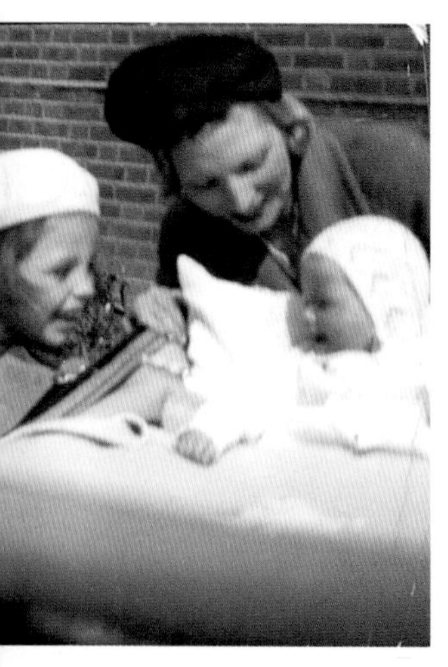

Welcome baby sis Jackie – someone to play with at last!

Then shortly before the war we moved to another big block of flats in Alexandra Court, Maida Vale. Luckily I was too young to understand what 'England at War' meant. I only knew that there was a certain amount of panic in my mother's face in August 1939 as Daddy packed us all up and drove us to a small house in Bognor Regis where Mummie's mother and several of her eleven brothers and sisters resided. We all lived in the house but I was blithely unaware of what being 'evacuated' meant, and I was quite happy being a country girl and frolicking in the fields and meadows bordering the house with some of the other evacuees who lived nearby.

When there was a lull in the bombing, Daddy decided hastily to move us all back to London and Alexandra Court, which was now considered safer than Bognor. German planes had been flying over the coast and there were even rumours that they would shoot people walking on the promenade. However, the night we moved in there was yet another air raid so we all scrambled down to the nearest air raid shelter. We slept for several nights in Marble Arch Underground Station, listening to the shrieks of the bombs falling and the roaring of the planes' engines. It was absolutely terrifying and even today when I hear those air raid sirens in some movie or television show I get the shivers.

After a week of sleeping in the shelters, during which London suffered a horrendous torrent of bombing, we returned to our flat to find it completely demolished. The building had been almost obliterated – nothing left but a jagged ruin, exposed to the drizzling rain. Most of our possessions had been destroyed.

Since my mother was now on the verge of a nervous breakdown, off we went again in Daddy's Ford to Ilfracombe on the Devon coast, which is almost 200 miles from London. Daddy managed to obtain the petrol for the trip from a local farmer by bartering with cheese. For some reason cheese was easy to come by in the open-air London markets, while farmers were allowed extra petrol because they were growing vital food for Britain.

I loved Ilfracombe, where the weather was always summery. We lived in a pretty flat near the seafront and little Jackie and I would spend our days clambering over the rocks, collecting crabs and tiny fish in our buckets and having a whale of a time.

My mother and Lalla, Daddy's sister, decided to open a small dining club called The Odd Spot. It soon became the smartest place in Devon, not only for the locals but also visiting servicemen, many of whom used to hang out at our flat.

I checked it out one afternoon and, at age eight, was impressed by its muted, nightclubby lights and art deco elegance, which I incorporated into some of my future homes.

Holidaying in Ilfracombe. Mummie is chic in forties style, but I just hated wearing clothes!

Then, suddenly, even Ilfracombe was too close to the English coast for my mother's delicate nervous system, particularly when a German bomber was discovered in a field nearby because the Nazi pilot thought he had landed in Occupied France!

So off we went again – first back to London to stay with Daddy for a little while in another flat in Baker Street, next to the station, and where I had to adjust to yet another new school in Bickenhall Street. Then came the flights of Doodlebugs so we were off again. First we went to Chichester; then to Brighton, to a horrible little house that had an outhouse at the end of the garden with torn-up newspaper on a string instead of loo paper; then back to Bognor; and then to Brighton once more. We moved so many times I could hardly keep count and I was constantly going to new schools and leaving again, never having time to make friends.

But at last the war ended and we moved back to London to a wonderfully spacious flat in Portland

Court, Great Portland Street. I loved this flat. The nursery ceiling was painted blue with cotton-wool clouds scurrying across on it and in the hall there was a vast cupboard with six or seven shelves on which we kept our toys and books. I could climb into this cupboard, close the door and perch on the top shelf reading voraciously by the light of a torch. We also had a tiny balcony on which I could sit and watch the cars go by as I read *Girls' Crystal* and movie magazines.

For the first time, I felt settled. I was enrolled in my thirteenth school, Francis Holland in Baker Street, where I remained for four years while the Collins family actually stayed in the same flat. Then, after failing my school certificate at fifteen, I was accepted at RADA. Thank God!

Travel light – what, moi? Louis Vuitton should pay me!

However, the family was to be uprooted again soon after the war, because we had a new addition in our family – my baby brother, Bill. Maybe it was the gipsy in my father's soul but now we relocated to a big, dark, cavernous four-bedroom basement flat in Harley House, a mansion block on Marylebone Road, conveniently opposite the London Clinic. It had a huge front entry hall where Daddy installed a twenties-style cocktail cabinet and entertained his friends in the rather grand sitting room decorated by my mother's Knoll sofas, forties polished wood furniture and various knick-knacks and ceramic statues of dancing ladies she had collected from her thirties dancing days. Jackie and I had our own bedrooms, as did little Bill, who spent most of his time travelling up and down the long hallway of our flat, driving his plastic automobile, and as oblivious to my existence as I was to his.

There was a brief interlude in the early fifties when I married at eighteen and moved to a tiny top-floor flat in elegant Hanover Square. It was decorated by my then husband, Maxwell Reed, in a slightly satanic style: black wallpaper and sheets in the bedroom, sombre lighting, a heavy fake sixteenth-century Spanish tarnished gilt bergère, and tasselled lamps with fifteen-watt yellow bulbs. It had the feeling of a Hammer Horror film. Not to my taste at all.

Then at last, in my early twenties, I found myself in the land of milk and honey: Hollywood, California, where all was sunshine and open spaces, palm trees, fresh new paint and modern furniture. I developed a passion for palm trees and tried to install them, either in ceramic ornaments or in pictures, wherever I put down roots.

My first LA apartment was on Beverly Glen Boulevard, just a stone's throw from 20th Century Fox studios where I toiled under contract. It was heaven – the first place of my own, even if it was a rental and completely furnished in bland LA style: a 'cottage cheese' ceiling, plain white walls and an enormous, dull beige sofa plonked in front of an enormous block of steel, which housed the television. I spent little time there as I was either making a movie or socializing. When I left, the oven still had the plastic wrapping inside it!

My next apartment on Olive Drive was a touch more glamorous. Close to the Sunset Strip, it was across the street from the fashionable nightclub Ciro's. Olive Drive had a bohemian, early thirties Hollywood atmosphere as it was nestled in a tiny courtyard surrounded by olive and palm trees and I finally had a swimming pool – even though I had to share it with all the other residents.

ABOVE LEFT: *My first glimpse of the good old USA. And I was mightily impressed, even though it took almost two days to get there!*

ABOVE RIGHT: *Arriving in London a few years later, by now a seasoned traveller.*

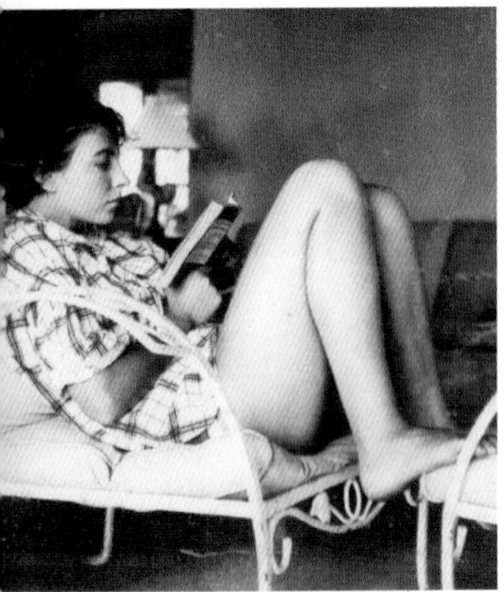

ABOVE: *On location in Barbados for* Island in the Sun. *Studying my script.*

My tenure at Olive Drive lasted a little over a year, during which I was cast in several movies, all of which were on location. When I filmed *Island in the Sun* I gave up the apartment and moved back to London and into my old room at Harley House, back to my parents' house at age twenty-four! I still didn't possess a stick of furniture, any paintings or *objets* or souvenirs from my travels. All I owned was a lot of clothes and several suitcases to schlepp them in!

A year later, back in Hollywood again, I rented my third furnished apartment on Shoreham Drive, just behind Sunset Boulevard. I attempted to do a little decorating by sticking posters on the walls of the bullfighting events I had attended in Acapulco and Tijuana. I hadn't yet developed any serious interest in decorating or furnishing my own home, or collecting antiques, all of which would come later.

Of material possessions I still had none except for many outfits ready for any eventuality. I didn't have family pictures (even of myself) or lithographs, and only a few knick-knacks or *tchotchkes* (as my grandmother would call them). I was ready to roll on location or vacation or promotion at any time. I was footloose and fancy free (more or less), and that was how I wanted it.

BELOW: *For some reason dogs have always been attracted to me.*

In 1960, I moved again to an apartment on Sunset Plaza Drive where Warren Beatty and I lived, rowed, broke up and made up again, but I was paying most of the rent! While the romance was still on the boil, we moved to a small studio apartment at the trendy Chateau Marmont, deep in the heart of Hollywood, where Dennis Hopper, Paul Newman, Jack Nicholson and Marlon Brando were often to be spotted lounging by the pool or smoking in the shabby-chic lobby.

Then, when Warren had to relocate to New York for the duration of *Splendour in the Grass*, I dutifully followed. We rented an utterly charming pied-à-terre owned by Joanne Woodward and Paul Newman on Fifth Avenue. Suddenly, I became interested in warm wall-to-wall thick carpeting, inviting chintz-covered armchairs and attractive pictures arranged in groups on the walls. It was an adorable oasis and one that started to really give me a taste for home-making and collecting.

OPPOSITE: *Will I ever settle down (and stop smoking)?*

Soon after my seven-year Fox contract and my engagement to Warren ended, I told my business manager Eddie Traubner, who at the studio's insistence had handled my financial affairs since the beginning, that I wanted finally to own a property. 'I've seen a sweet little house off Coldwater Canyon, and I'm sure I've saved enough money by now to be able to put a down payment on it. They're only asking $60,000.'

'You can't afford it,' Eddie said brusquely.

'How can that be?' I wailed. 'I've been under Fox contract for seven years – surely you must have managed to save something, Eddie.'

'No,' he said. 'It's all gone on your expenses.'

'What expenses?'

A baby at last! Beautiful Tara is born, and even though she is bald I still adore her.

'Your rent, your car, several trips to London to see your mother . . . and vacations in France and Acapulco. I'm sorry but you haven't enough left to put a down payment on a house.'

Deeply disappointed, I took the first job that I was offered, *The Road to Hong Kong*, and to save money I moved back to Harley House, back into my childhood bedroom. I gritted my teeth and vowed that the next time I moved it would be to a place of my own.

A year later, after a disastrous series of rentals in New York with my then husband Anthony Newley, we bought the most gorgeous penthouse apartment in Manhattan at the grand Imperial House on Sixty-Ninth Street, between Second and Third Avenues. Happily pregnant, I gave full vent to my previously subjugated decorating talents; perhaps my style wouldn't have pleased the aesthetically minded but I loved it! My bedroom was a symphony of pale turquoise silk-padded walls, a turquoise velvet headboard and bed coverings and full-length, swishy silk curtains. I covered the dining-room walls in burgundy flocked velvet wallpaper, hideous in retrospect but it was where every Sunday we gathered together a group of mostly English friends for huge roast lamb and potato lunches (yes, I cooked) and delicious trifle, which everyone adored. The Brits – Leslie Bricusse and his gorgeous wife Evie, Albert Finney, Peter Cook, Dudley Moore, Lionel Bart and Georgia Brown – gossiped and drank with the 'Yanks' Buddy Greco and his lovely wife Dani, Barbra Streisand and Eliot Gould, the Newmans, Eydie Gormé and Steve Lawrence, and, when he was in town, Sammy Davis, Jr.

But all too soon this glorious idyll had to end when beloved President John F. Kennedy was assassinated. Tony, freaked out by the subsequent

horrific events and facing the fact that his Broadway show *Stop the World – I Want to Get Off* was closing, insisted we pack up our family and go back to the UK.

With sadness, and now with baby Tara, again we began a less than desirable nomadic existence: a blur of rented houses in London and, on its outskirts, a sojourn to a Paris hotel where we were almost incinerated by a fire, and a two-month stay in a glamorous hotel in St Moritz, owned by the husband of my gorgeous friend, Cappy Badrutt.

It was while we were living in Hampstead in the rented house of actor Keith Michell, and I was expecting again, that I put my foot down. 'We must

Happy Newley family on the road somewhere.

have *roots*,' I declared. 'We can't go on living like Bedouin gypsies. I've seen a wonderful house in Elstree; it's only £20,000 with twenty acres around it; it will be fabulous for the kids to grow up in.' Reluctantly, Tony agreed. Friar's Mead was indeed glorious, almost like a Georgian chateau, and after Tony had put down a small payment with my friend, the decorator Robin Guild, we started planning the design, renovation and shopping for fabrics and furniture. That mansion today is worth upwards of £25 million.

Then the shit hit the fan yet again. The UK government was cracking down heavily on entertainers – particularly those who often made a great deal of money one year and nothing the next. Tony insisted we must sell Friar's Mead and relocate to America, where the tax laws were kinder. That became a nightmare since I had a two-year-old and was pregnant again. Back in Manhattan, one of the brownstones we rented with the Bricusses was so infested with cockroaches that they were even crawling into the children's cots. The Newmans, Paul and Joanne, came to the rescue again and we moved immediately into their lovely apartment on Fifth Avenue (where I had lived with Warren) and soon after I gave birth to Sacha.

OPPOSITE: *Paris 1963. Could this be a Stepford Wife? I really enjoyed motherhood and could spend hours just cuddling and playing with Tara.*

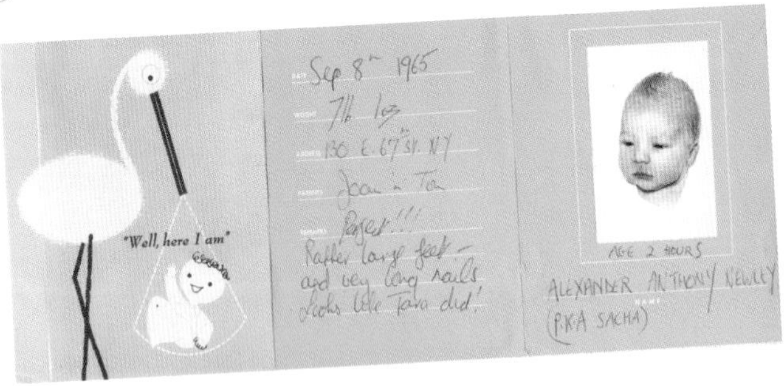

TOP: *Alexander Anthony Newley's birth announcement. We always called him Sacha.*

ABOVE: *Bedtime was always fun time before Mummie went out on the town, just like my mother!*

Suddenly, in 1966, Tony was 'hot' in the movies, having portrayed Matthew Mugg in *Doctor Dolittle*. We relocated to the hills of Hollywood, where we rented a rambling two-storey house on Bel Air Drive in exclusive but (to me) rather spooky Bel Air.

By now I couldn't stand living with other people's possessions, so when eighteen-month-old Sacha became seriously ill from eating some poisoned berries from the garden and I had to drive him to hospital, I insisted we had to buy our own home where our kids weren't going to die from eating toxic fruit, and finally buy our own furniture.

So we bought 1151 Summit Drive, a massive house with a spectacular garden and a huge pool in Beverly Hills 90210. Along with Tony's mother Grace, stepfather Ron, Alice and Humberto Ferrera to help us with two kids, and various assorted pets, we played happy families.

I simply loved Summit. Even though I had been told it was an unlucky house because every couple who had lived there had divorced, I scoffed that it wasn't so unusual. This was Hollywood, after all. Of course, those pundits were correct. Summit Drive had been the pinnacle of my happiness up until that point. It was a gorgeous colonial-type mansion and we turned the whole upstairs floor into a playroom for the children, with separate bedrooms for each of them. We had an enormous Beverly Hills-style living room, which looked out on to the lush green lawn and glimmering pool. The kids had a sandpit, pets and swings and were also in heaven.

The Madonna and Child!

I decorated my bedroom with an exquisite green and white Toile de Jouy on the walls and bed. The white carpet was an inch thick and I had one of the biggest walk-in closets in Beverly Hills. Now that I was a rich Beverly Hills housewife, married to a movie star and retired from acting, I had time to play with my children and take them to school, lunch with the girls and shop on Rodeo Drive in my sleek new Mercedes, to fill my immense closet. We gave many parties at Summit, attended by Peter Sellers, Steve McQueen, Mia Farrow, Samantha Eggar, Jackie Bisset, Natalie Wood and R. J. Wagner, amongst others. My sister Jackie and her husband Oscar Lerman also came regularly.

Jackie and I were always close and she often came to stay with us in Summit Drive.

And life was indeed beautiful. But of course it had to end. After my divorce from Newley in 1970, we had to sell the house to Sammy Davis Jnr and I was forced to return to London and start acting again.

Now a single mother of two, I moved to several more rentals including one in Connaught Street, near the children's school, until I finally married Ron Kass and I gave birth to my third child, Katyana. We found a really great family house at 42 Sheldon Avenue, a quiet neighbourhood street in Highgate, North London. It had a big garden (no pool – this was England!) and enough spacious rooms for all of us to live very well indeed.

I decorated my bedroom with the same green and white toile from LA, and the den with a fashionable paisley fabric that covered the walls, with a huge tan leather sofa placed in front of the fireplace.

There, I entertained Roger Moore, my friend for years, who excitedly told me that he was going to be the next James Bond. His wife Luisa loved the paisley fabric so much that she chose it for the house they were moving into, as did the Bricusses for their guest room in the south of France.

My sitting room was a fantastic and eccentric creation as I was still experimenting with my inner interior decorator. The parquet floor was sanded and painted deep blue, the walls were covered in glittering silver flocked wallpaper, the sofas were sheathed in pale grey silk and – my *pièce de résistance* and homage to my love of California – two huge, almost life-sized, silver lamé palm trees stood on either side of the fireplace!

Naturally, I called this the silver room and it was where I started to display my vast collection of antique silver photograph frames, as well as art deco and art nouveau dancing figurines by Lorenzl and Chiparus, which I had started attending auctions to collect. I found it all fascinating.

I was quite proud of my silver room, even though I know several people mocked it behind my back, but it was my creation and even Patrick Lichfield, the renowned society photographer, was impressed when he photographed me in it.

OPPOSITE: *Patrick Lichfield captured me during my Silver Period. I even had silver palm trees!*

Because we had six kids under the age of twelve living with us, I managed to buy a cheap and cheerful holiday house in Marbella, Spain, where we

would spend Easter and summer holidays, since staying in hotels was too expensive. We also bought a rustic weekend cottage in the little village of Holmbury St Mary, in England.

My sister visited with her three children, as did many other friends. Sadly, I couldn't afford to keep the house when Denis Healey, the Chancellor of the Exchequer, announced his 'Soak the Rich' strategy. Headlines screamed, 'This government is going to squeeze the rich until the pips squeak.' Charming. Along with my husband Ron Kass and my beautiful little children Katy, Tara and Sacha (who like me were now resigned to being nomadic), I moved yet again back to Beverly Hills in 1975.

There we bought a house on Chalette Drive in the Trousdale Estates. It was an enormous modern box of a house, somewhat jerry-built. But it had a tennis court and a pool and enough bedrooms for our six children.

I decorated it with ultra-modern, stark, black-and-white furniture and put in a gorgeous mirrored bar. We entertained a great deal even though

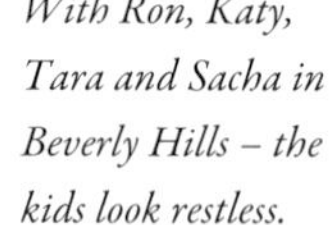

With Ron, Katy, Tara and Sacha in Beverly Hills – the kids look restless.

we didn't have much money. Kirk and Anne Douglas, Leonard Gershe, super-agent Sue Mengers, Sammy and Tita Cahn, David and Dani Janssen, Audrey and Billy Wilder, Tina Sinatra and many other famous and non-famous friends came for drinks, dinners, barbecues, parties and, of course, games of tennis. David Niven, Jr would often pop over to play. I attempted it but my face always turned bright red.

The Bitch *begins. Starring in sister Jackie's steamy sexy saga of a man-eating femme fatale.*

In these years between 1975 and 1979, we had to move three more times and we lived mostly on what we made from the sale of those houses. Since Ron was out of work, I was breadwinning for the whole gang via guest slots on *Batman*, *Beretta*, *Run for Your Life* and assorted others, but each year we had to sell our house and downsize to another smaller one.

After Chalette came Carolyn Way, also in Trousdale, all glass and chrome and Italian modern. I did the dining alcove in modern art deco style, put up loads of mirrored walls to enhance the size, and in the sitting room/den designed an entire wall of bookshelves. After that came Bowmont Drive, a two-storey, mock Tudor house high in the hills off Coldwater Canyon. I didn't particularly like this house but with a young family it was quite suitable and, again, I designed a gorgeous bedroom all in peach with a touch of lime green.

Between 1978 and 1981 I spent much time in London making two notorious movies: *The Stud* and *The Bitch*. During this time we lived at 30 South Street, a house that Ron rented. It was a charming four-storey house on the corner of South Audley Street and although Ron had already furnished it, I completely redid the bedroom, which made the cover of *Homes* magazine.

In the basement, which we used as an office/guest room, we for some reason installed a waterbed and covered the walls of the room in some awful dark blue fabric. The room took on a sinister look, particularly as Ron decided to put in a steam and sauna room. Since this was situated underneath the pavement of the adjacent South Street, right next to a

We called this charming cottage in Holmbury St Mary 'Cheyney', after the role I had played in The Last of Mrs Cheyney. *It was a weekend retreat for all of the eighteen months we had it.*

drain, if ever someone left the sauna on there would be a huge overflow of water – plumbers would arrive en masse while the neighbours complained vociferously.

In 1979 whilst performing *The Last of Mrs Cheyney* at the Chichester Festival Theatre, I fell in love with a little cottage in nearby Holmbury St Mary. It was a charming, traditional thatched cottage with a lovely garden for the six children to play in and we spent as many weekends there as we could.

My next house purchase was in a lovely section of London called Little Venice. It was an imposing three-storey house with high ceilings and large reception rooms, right opposite the canal.

It was a listed house with a blue plaque outside saying that the Poet Laureate John Masefield had lived there. Sadly, I did not live there for very long as, in 1981, I was summoned yet again to Hollywood to work on a little epic called *Dynasty*.

For the first six months Ron, Katy, her nanny Daphne and I stayed in a big, dark, rented apartment in Century City. This complex was on the former grounds of 20th Century Fox, my old stomping ground, and I was amazed to see how all the wonderful buildings, castles, villages and eighteenth- and nineteenth-century sets had been totally replaced by skyscrapers and apartment buildings.

LEFT: *My bedroom at Bowmont Drive – Peach with a touch of jade green, and of course a palm tree.*

BELOW: *Katy learning the piano at Carolyn Way, Beverly Hills.*

Offered at $5,450,000

ABOVE: *The sales brochure for Cabrillo Drive – a fantastic, enormous house, much too big really but I was a star now…*

Then Bowmont Drive (which we had rented) became available again so for the next three years of filming *Dynasty* I lived there. Soon, and with my success in *Dynasty*, I was able to afford a fabulous spread on Cabrillo Drive, off Coldwater Canyon in Beverly Hills. It was a sprawling but elegant white one-storey mansion with magnificent views over the Hollywood Hills. It consisted of an enormous living room, a super-enormous bedroom with two gigantic walk-in closets, a large guesthouse and a basement wine cellar.

I eagerly began the decoration process by placing a giant bar off the sitting room, which featured an aquarium with exotic and expensive tropical fish swimming about on the back wall, and bar stools, which my decorator (I finally had to hire one) insisted were covered in the skin of whale's scrotum! Yuck. But they looked good.

The living room had plenty of room for a full-sized white piano, which could actually play itself. Elton John came to a party one night and, sitting down to play, was astonished when the piano started up, playing one of his hits!

My friend Laurence Harvey had formerly owned this house and, since I sold it in 1989, it has had a variety of owners. Ellen DeGeneres bought up the two houses next door, turned it into a gated, palace-like compound

RIGHT: *The sitting room in Carolyn Way – my art deco phase in full flower now. Note palm tree!*

The dining room in Carolyn Way ready for a dinner party.

and then sold it last year to Ryan Seacrest, supposedly for an unbelievable $34 million. Since I had sold it for under $1.5 million I was slightly miffed to say the least. But that's the real estate market for you – nothing is ever certain and eventually everything goes up in value, if you wait long enough.

Because of my love for the south of France I then bought a tiny *maison de pêcheur* in the new man-made village of Port Grimaud, just a few miles from Saint-Tropez. It was absolutely tiny but at the bottom of the garden was a jetty onto the river which led to the sea and there was moored my boat *Sins*, named after the successful mini-series I had recently finished. By then I was married to 'The Swede', Peter Holm, and we spent much of our time on the boat, although he seldom maintained or cleaned it, which accounted for it breaking down all the time. I realized the truth of the adage that the two happiest days of a boat-owners life are the day they buy the boat and the day they sell the boat. I just didn't realize that the same could hold true for husbands until I married 'The Swede'. I haven't indulged in boating much since, only on other people's yachts.

When I finally got rid of the boat, the house and the husband, all of which I was pleased about, I really wanted to have a bigger and quieter place in the south of France. I looked at several houses but nothing seemed quite right. Then I heard about a divine house for sale on the Saint-Tropez peninsula.

I drove to the house, which wasn't even finished. It seemed extremely remote and I had to drive down a terrible, twisting, bumpy road, but the south-facing view of the Mediterranean was incomparable. Designed by the well-known architect Roger Herrera, it was set in a lush six acres with umbrella pines and oak trees all around the house. Protected by hills and mountains, I fell in love with it then and there. Today, I still never tire of looking out at all the sparkling glory of the rolling hills, the sea and the Poquerolles Island, which is twenty miles away but on a clear day seems very close.

Although it has a fairly small reception room and terrace, the views are so spectacular that it doesn't matter. With five bedrooms and bathrooms and a wonderful covered terrace for al fresco dining, there has not been a year since then that I haven't spent at least two or three months in the summer, savouring the weather, the beauty of the surroundings and the glorious infinity pool. I took great care and gave much attention to detail with the interior of the house. It's perfectly Provençal and exceedingly homey. I called it Villa Destino, as in Destiny, and I hope I never leave it.

Around the same time I needed to relocate to the UK. *Dynasty* had finished and I wanted to be near my children, who were now all living there. I was lucky to find a superb Georgian, laterally converted flat in Belgravia, which I took great joy in transforming into my haven.

PRESQU'ILE DE SAINT-TROPEZ
A 2 KM DE RAMATUELLE

Sur terrain de 2 ha 50 boisé de pins parasol et de chênes, orientation sud. Vue sur mer et îles, collines et montagnes, environnement très protégé. Une maison, conçue par l'architecte Roger Herrera, qui sera disponible en juin 1989, habitable et paysagée.

On the St. Tropez peninsula, this fine house, designed by the architect Roger Herrera will be completed by June 1989. Set in 6 acres of grounds planted with umbrella pines and oak trees, facing south with views of the sea, islands, hills and mountains, in protected surroundings.

The brochure for my villa near St Tropez. The locals call me 'the actress who lives in the middle of the forest'.

Our Manhattan apartment where we can entertain fifty or sixty people. Neil Sedaka always ends up playing the piano.

I did use a decorator for some of the interior, instructing her to 'think Marie Antoinette when you do the bedroom'. It's a mass of peach and cream satin and silk, flouncy taffeta curtains and lots of bows. A bit much for some, but it's deliciously feminine and I love it.

When Percy Gibson and I married in 2002, we decided that since his work was in New York we would buy an apartment there, as well as keeping Destino and Eaton Place. Extravagant maybe, but I had managed to save enough money to do this. Furthermore, I had no faith in business managers and certainly not in financial advisors, banks and fund managers, stocks or shares or any other crazy ways of losing your money. I'd been burned too many times by these. Property was a safe investment.

Our apartment on Fifty-Seventh Street, between Park Avenue and Lexington, is large and airy and it has sixteen closets – perfect for me! Percy had looked at fifty apartments before showing it to me and I simply loved it. We decorated it fairly simply with walls covered in mirrors and much of the furniture from my LA apartment, which I had kept in storage. We have had some fabulous parties there with Neil Sedaka playing the piano and our New York friends singing and dancing on the brilliantly polished parquet floor. Of course, I had to have green and white Toile de Jouy in the bedroom but this time it had more of a Chinese theme than

One of my favourite ways of spending a summer afternoon in the South of France. Lounging in the infinity pool and chatting to Katy.

The South of France is always fabulous, Percy and I with Tara, Sacha and Warren and Susie Todd at their house.

My tiny little dressing room/bathroom in LA – I do all my best work in there!

the others. In front of the window, I placed the amazing dressing table in peach lacquer that I used in *The Bitch.*

After a few years of happiness there, and because I'd always loved LA – it was, after all, my second home for most of my adult life – Percy and I decided to buy a gorgeous apartment in Sierra Towers, on the border between Beverly Hills and Hollywood. Although it's not big, it has the most superb ninety-degree views from all the windows. You can see all the way to the Santa Monica beaches on one side and the snow-capped Santa Ana Mountains on the other.

So now we happily divide our time between the four places. When I think of that little girl all those years ago with the nursery table upside down going on voyages to visit her homes all over the world, I realize I've actually done what I always wanted to do! And when I now think back to my early twenties, when I had no worldly possessions except for my clothes, I think WOW! You've come a long way, baby!

Chapter Four

BOYFRIENDS

Until I was fifteen-and-a-half, I had no interest in boys or men at all – I thought of them as Jack Lemmon opines in *Some Like it Hot*, when dressed as a girl: 'Ugh, men – rough, hairy beasts!' To me, boys were from another planet. Probably even more so since I knew absolutely nothing about them and indeed had never even seen a photograph of a naked man. Therefore, I was quite unaware and frankly uninterested in what men had below the belt.

OPPOSITE: *Waiting for Mr Right while dating a few Mr Wrongs.*

My first boyfriend, in name only and then just briefly, was French so we spent our time together trying to understand each other as I lolled next to his father's ice-cream stand where the young Bernard Gaillot dispensed the goodies, or took discreet walks along the seafront in Dinard where I was holidaying with my mother (she never approved) and brother and sister.

Bernard was very handsome with black, curly hair and dancing blue eyes. At seventeen he seemed quite sophisticated, particularly being French! But my brief holiday fortnight was over far too soon and, with protestations of intended visits to England and a few tears, I went back to school.

We exchanged a few letters but because I became seriously involved in studying for my RADA audition, the little summer romance petered out.

When I first saw sixteen-year-old David McCallum at RADA, I thought he must be related to one of my favourite actors, Richard Widmark. They had the same blond floppy hair, pale complexion and light eyes.

Which handsome stud shall I date tonight?

We dated briefly, nothing too heavy, and then he went on to date and eventually marry Jill Ireland, who eventually left him for Charles Bronson.

I dated John Turner and Ronald Lewis whilst at RADA but nothing salacious happened other than some rather nervous necking. They both became quite well-known actors: John in classical roles, and Ronald in British movies. Strangely enough, the reason I liked Ronald was because he bore more than a passing resemblance to my favourite British actor of the time, Maxwell Reed. John and I used to go regularly to jazz clubs and dance the night away.

Both of these relationships were quite platonic, but then I developed a serious but ridiculous crush on Anthony Livesey, the redheaded son of the celebrated actor, Roger. Unfortunately Tony was gay, but of course I didn't realize he was gay. I didn't know what gay was, in fact. By this time I was seventeen and I was ready to emulate my more worldly RADA classmates and 'do it', as they described it with much girlish giggling. However, twenty-three-year-old Anthony, although he made a couple of valiant attempts on the odd occasion I managed to stay over at the Ebury Street flat he shared with two room-mates, was unable to 'do it'. I didn't understand the physiognomy of the male at all so I had no knowledge or understanding of what a man actually needed to 'do it'.

Crestfallen, I confessed to one of my seasoned girlfriends my failure (of course, I blamed myself) but when she asked, 'Does he have erectile problems?' I didn't have a clue what she was talking about.

Soon after, I was caught up in the glamorous world of movie-making and was lucky enough to get the lead in *I Believe in You*, a stark black-and-white British movie in which I played a juvenile delinquent, as naughty girls were coyly referred to then.

In the stellar cast was the young actor Laurence Harvey. Larry, formerly Laruschka Skikne, was Lithuanian and at twenty-three he was absurdly sophisticated and urbane.

A true man of the world, he smoked cigarettes from a holder with an elegance only rivalled by Noël Coward, frequented the best restaurants and clubs in London, knew all the waiters and maître d's by their first names and had his all his perfectly cut bespoke suits made in Savile Row.

Between boyfriends in the 70s, I went for the Hippy Look.

Larry was extremely knowledgeable about fine wines and gourmet food, and he drove around London in a vintage Rolls. I was fascinated by Larry and watched him on set like a little puppy dog lapping up his witty *bon mots*, his languid aura and his wisdom.

He was a good actor who soon became a good friend – introducing me to the delights of the elegant Caprice and Ivy restaurants and to the couture houses of Madame Rahvis and Norman Hartnell. He encouraged me to dress better, my clothes then being mostly bohemian RADA student with a hint of gypsy and a soupçon of pin-up girl.

Larry had style, bags of it, and he wanted to show me how to enjoy life to the full. So off I trotted to the fabulous Rahvis sisters and spent three weeks' salary on a crystal-embroidered dress.

We dated frequently. I aspired to his sophistication and I also aspired to definitely wanting to 'do it' with him, but alas it was not to be.

OPPOSITE: *My first really naughty girl part in a British film* Our Girl Friday. *She was a spoiled bratty teenager but Kenneth More was smitten.*

'But why?' I wailed in Hyde Park one afternoon after he had – to be blunt – turned down my tentative girlish advances with 'No, you must wait, my darling – you're not ready yet.'

Well, I thought at eighteen I was quite ready enough and since many other men wanted my nubile young body – none of whom interested me enough to give it to them – I was quite hurt by Larry's rejection.

I was even more hurt when a few days later I attended a party given by the character actress Hermione Baddeley. She lost no time in giving me a piece of her mind in front of Larry by informing the guests in a loud voice, 'If this is the new Jean Simmons, as Larry told me, Jean has *nothing* to worry about – you haven't got her looks or her talent and I don't believe anything the newspapers say about you.'

I rushed out in tears and Larry rushed after me and confessed, to my horror, that he was actually living with the old bag! I was humiliated and disgusted by this. He was so contrite that I forgave him but never attempted to 'do it' with him again!

To make up for this, Larry escorted me a few nights later to La Rue nightclub where he introduced me to one of my idols, Maxwell Reed – but that story is for another chapter!

BELOW: *Son of Charlie Chaplin, Sydney was a million laughs. Here we are in Paris. I'm wearing my first mink and it is much too heavy.*

After my separation from Reed, I started dating Sydney Chaplin, son of Charlie and a very funny guy. We met during the filming of *Land of the Pharaohs* in Rome. He played my boyfriend and I played the Princess Nellifer of Egypt, and during our scenes together I found it impossible to keep a straight face as Sydney could make a scurrilous joke out of anything and everything.

The weeks in Rome flew by as we drove around in his high-powered Alfa Romeo convertible, which he loved to race at 120 mph through the leafy roads of suburban Rome, scattering hapless pedestrians heedlessly. With the wind whipping through my hair, I adored the velocity and implicit danger in those mad drives because at twenty-one you think you are immortal and nothing can happen to you. Rome was thrilling. It was the time of *La Dolce Vita* and Syd was a great raconteur and companion.

RIGHT: *My first American starring role as Evelyn Nesbit in* The Girl in the Red Velvet Swing *with handsome Farley Granger as Harry Thaw, a real baddie.*

ABOVE LEFT AND RIGHT: *The clothes were magnificent in* Girl, *and I had a 22 inch waist then.*

DA7

CONGRATULATIONS!

YOU HAVE JUST RECEIVED
A LIMITED EDITION
PERSONALLY AUTOGRAPHED
TRADING CARD SIGNED BY

WILLIAM SHATNER
AS CAPTAIN KIRK AND

JOAN COLLINS
AS EDITH KEELER IN
"THE CITY ON THE EDGE OF FOREVER"

www.scifihobby.com ® & © 2009 CBS Studios Inc. All Rights Reserved.

With William Shatner in one of the most popular episodes of Star Trek: 'The City on the Edge of Forever'. I played Edith Keeler, a saintly missionary worker with whom Captain Kirk falls in love for the first time.

After *Pharaohs*, Syd and I spent that autumn and winter living in a chic but somewhat rundown hotel on the Rue de Trémoille in Paris. We spent our days listening to Frank Sinatra records, eating *pain au chocolat* for breakfast and gourmet meals for dinner, playing pinball machines in all the cafés, and at night dining and drinking with a group of eclectic and amusing friends. These included Anatole (Tola) Litvak, the famous director; Harry Kurnitz, the brilliant screenwriter; Robert Capa, the award-winning war photographer; and Noël Howard, a well-known tennis pro. Syd's best buddy, Norman Mailer, the novelist, was often in the group and we would all usually end up dead drunk in some seedy '*boîte*' or the new discotheque, L'Elephant Blanc, run by the feisty redhead Regine.

In Gene Kelly's yard, George Englund frolics with his three boys – no wonder he couldn't get a divorce.

Adolph Green, the hysterically funny lyricist, playwright, wit and songwriter (one half of the legendary team of 'Comden and Green' who wrote the movie *On the Town*), was often with us, as was a young man fresh out of the US Army called Elliott Kastner. He was determined to make it as a Hollywood producer, and he did!

Sadly, Syd's personality changed when we were by ourselves. He became quite morose and monosyllabic and the crazy sense of humour was nowhere to be seen or heard. I understood why when we travelled with Adolph to Vevey, Switzerland, to visit Charlie Chaplin at his villa.

Charlie was nothing like the vulnerable and funny little tramp of his movies. He seemed cold and distant to Syd, and he ruled the roost in his domain with his other young children, who all seemed quite scared of him, as did Syd.

But in November, our Parisian idyll ended as I was summoned to Hollywood to become a bonded servant for 20th Century Fox.

Syd visited after a while and we lived together in my Beverly Hills apartment, but as my star waxed, his waned and he found it impossible to find work as an actor. He spent the days watching TV or playing golf while I, as a contractee, worked constantly. At weekends we often hung out at Gene Kelly's house on Rodeo Drive, where the group often included director Stanley Donen, Natalie Wood and Oscar Levant, one of Hollywood's great wits. I even chatted to the fabled Marilyn Monroe one night at a party.

Syd and I drifted apart and he went back to the New York stage where he had a good career, eventually starring opposite Barbra Streisand in *Funny Girl.*

BELOW: *Another very funny boyfriend was Arthur Loew Jr, also quite a notorious playboy who liked to date actresses and make them laugh.*

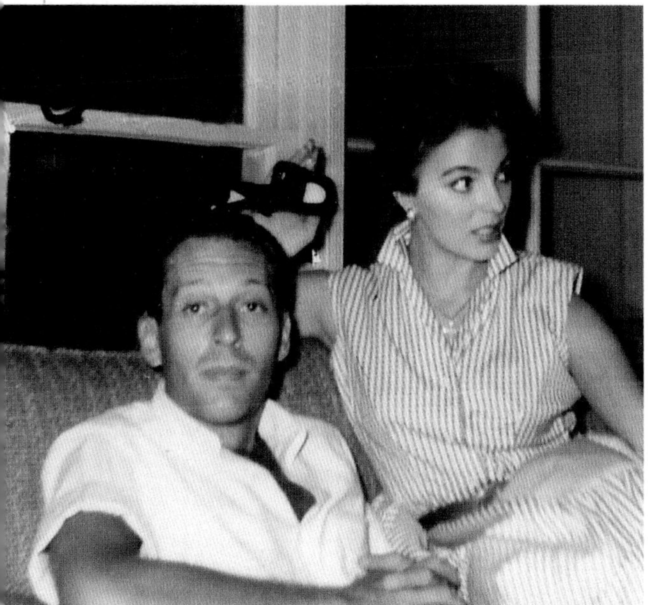

One of Gene Kelly's group was Arthur Loew, Jr, the scion of the founder of Loew's Theaters and MGM. Rich, young and single, Arthur was quite a notorious playboy and party boy. He was terribly funny in a laconic, laid-back fashion and although not classically handsome, he was cute and very eligible!

Not that I was interested in marrying after the Maxwell Reed debacle, but Arthur and I got along so well that he insisted I give up my tiny apartment on Olive Drive and move in with him to his sprawling two-storey house on

They say men are like buses – if you wait long enough one will come along.

Miller Drive, which had spectacular views of Hollywood. Max Reed had started threatening me, and my lawyer Fred Leopold had insisted I get a bodyguard. Remembering Max's threat to 'cut up your pretty little face', I thought the sanctuary of Arthur and Miller Drive an acceptable option.

The group that congregated practically every night in his sprawling living room consisted of Paul Newman and his fiancée Joanne Woodward, the moody and magnificent Marlon Brando and his acolyte James Dean, the brilliant screenwriter Stewart Stern, who had just written *Rebel Without a Cause*, and Jay Kanter, the hottest agent in town who represented Marlon and Paul. Jay was married to the lovely Judy, who became, and still is, one of my best friends.

Then there was George Englund, Marlon's best friend who emulated Marlon in speech patterns, humour and attitude. He was married to the actress Cloris Leachman but I had heard, even though he had three kids, he played around.

OPPOSITE: I learned to waterski in Acapulco and did it all the time in Jamaica and Barbados. But in Marbella I fell off into something really nasty and never skied again!

So did Arthur, as I heard on the grapevine when I went off to Jamaica to film *Sea Wife* with Richard Burton, in which I played a novice nun. Arthur came to visit for a few days and in his typical pithy way announced to all and sundry, 'I fucked a nun!'

ABOVE: *'Nobody ever looks at the face of a nun' I say in* Sea Wife *– oh really!*

RIGHT: *In Jamaica with Burton, Basil Sydney and Cy Grant I went for the full on zero makeup look. When Arthur visited he quipped 'I f****d a nun!'*

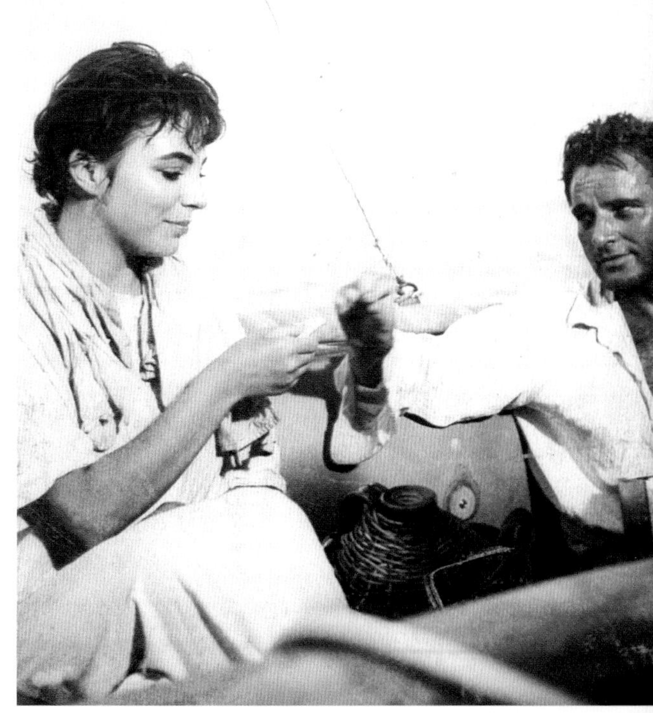

Soon after, our little not-so-hot romance ended on New Year's Eve at a glamorous party. We were dancing together and he suddenly stopped and said, 'You are such a fucking bore.'

Quickly I replied, 'And you are a boring fuck!' And that was the end of that. We remained friends and Arthur went on to date several friends of mine including Natalie Wood.

After Arthur and I broke up I dated the dissolute but handsome Nicky Hilton.

Incredibly rich, incredibly spoiled, Nicky was the heir to the Hilton hotel group who had married Elizabeth Taylor when she was eighteen and he twenty-two. His father Conrad had married a star too – Zsa Zsa Gabor – and he would have been the uncle of Paris Hilton. While he was honeymooning with Elizabeth in Cannes, my aunt Pauline observed him on the beach being verbally abusive to the young actress, often leaving her alone for long periods whilst he gambled away in the casinos.

After Elizabeth, Nick had dated many women; he especially liked actresses and during the time we were dating he also saw Natalie Wood, Terry Moore and various other starlets. He was the definitive handsome playboy and had the definitive equipment to go with it! He was inordinately proud of his manhood and often bragged that between them his brother and father had 'a yard of cock!'

But I was wary of his moods and the fact that he kept a gun next to his bed, which he liked to shoot up into the ceiling as he idled away his time lounging in bed and watching television. I also suspected he was doing drugs.

Nick wasn't a serious boyfriend, so when I went to New York for publicity for one of my Fox movies I met the attractive young son of a Greek billionaire. Peter Theadoracopulos, otherwise known as Taki, was extremely amusing and I found myself beguiled by his dashingly profligate attitude and romantic yet intellectual way with words. He adored dancing, particularly at the unbelievably glamorous El Morocco Club in New York, where being the youngest couple in a room full of middle-aged Manhattanites we created quite a stir. 'From This Moment On', from the musical *Kiss Me, Kate,* was one of our favourites and as we quickstepped across the lustrously polished floor with the joyous nimbleness only possessed by those in their twenties, many green-eyed glances came our way.

Nicky Hilton managed to fit me in between divorcing Liz and dating Natalie Wood.

New York in the late fifties was a glamorous time to be young. Women looked ravishing at night in tightly waisted, strapless cocktail dresses of taffeta, silk or satin, their white or sable brown mink stoles slung casually across their shoulders, pearls or diamonds gleaming on their necks and ears. And the men were equally dashing. No self-respecting bon viveur would dream of venturing into the elegant restaurants and clubs of Manhattan without wearing a well-cut suit, an immaculate shirt and a tie, not to mention highly polished shoes.

Taki, although only twenty-three, was quite a lady-killer and shortly after we met he lavished upon me a beautiful antique diamond brooch in the shape of an anchor. 'It represents my father's fleet,' he joked. I hadn't

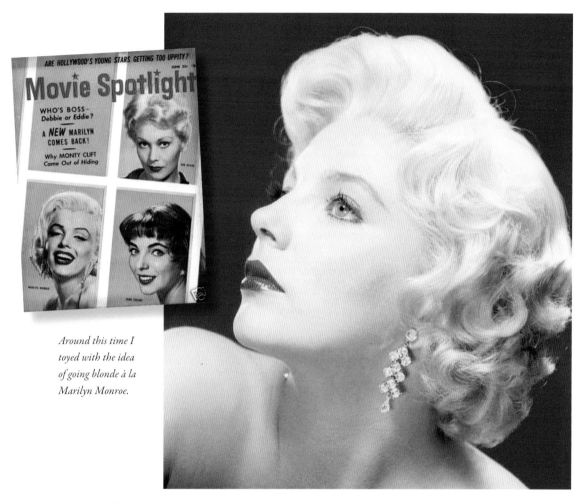

Around this time I toyed with the idea of going blonde à la Marilyn Monroe.

Taki at one of my book launches. He still makes me laugh.

been given diamonds before so I was thrilled. Arthur had bestowed upon me a few gold bracelets and pendants, but nothing of any real value. Sydney, usually being broke, had given me nothing, not even part of the rent for my LA apartment on Beverly Glen; and my ex Maxwell Reed had insisted on me retaining the topaz bracelet and ring he had given me. So I wore my glittering anchor around the *boîtes* of New York until one day Nicky Hilton blew into town.

Although he had been dating a slew of starlets in LA, the rumours of a romance between the rich young Greek and me, whom for some reason he still thought of as his property, infuriated him. One afternoon as Taki and I strolled into the Plaza Hotel lobby, Nicky confronted him and, to my horror and the rest of the people watching, the men started arguing, then brawling. Security guards stopped them from actual fisticuffs but when the gossip hit the boardroom of 20th Century Fox, I was summoned back to Hollywood and to work. 'Give up your playgirl ways,' admonished Lew Schreiber, one of the studio heads, 'or the studio will drop you.' I stopped seeing Nicky but Taki came to visit for a few days and we have remained friends to this day.

Sadly Nicky Hilton died a few years later, his dissolute lifestyle having caught up with him. I believe he was still in love with Elizabeth Taylor as he often remarked that I resembled her, as did some of his other ladies including Natalie Wood.

In the West Indies to film *Island in the Sun*, with a star-studded cast, I was footloose and fancy free. I had no husband and no steady boyfriend. Although I dated quite a bit in Hollywood, I never went 'all the way' as the quaint euphemism of the day went. Nevertheless I was amazed by the number of men who, when rejected by me at the front door of my apartment, would accuse me of being frigid! Men, particularly men in show business, felt a certain divine right to have their way with a girl for the price of a dinner and a dance. Misogyny was rife, not only in Hollywood but everywhere, it seemed.

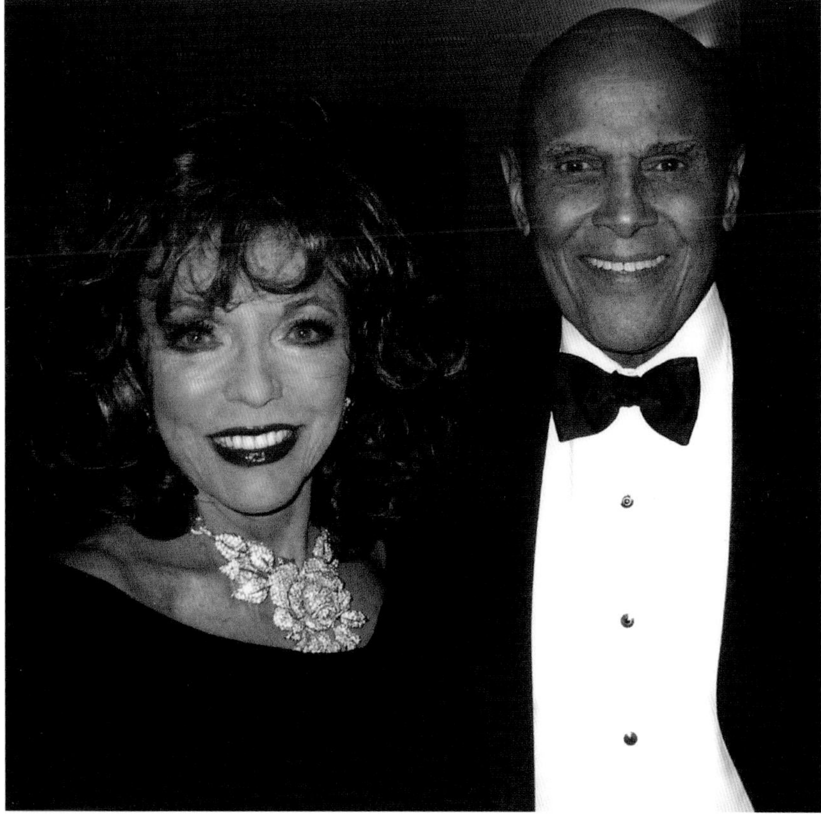

Jackie took this picture of Harry Belafonte and me at a party at her house in 2012.

But when I first glimpsed Harry Belafonte at a cocktail party for the cast and crew of *Island in the Sun* I was impressed by his stunning looks. Women had been flocking to his theatre performances for years, admiring his singing talent and sexual allure, which was always accentuated by tight pants and a shirt open to reveal muscular, caramel-coloured skin.

He was a true folk hero to the people of the West Indies and all of the cast and crew of *Island in the Sun* admired him immensely.

Harry was thirty-one, six foot one and very handsome, with melting brown eyes, a strong nose and close-cropped black hair.

Although we had no scenes together our paths crossed often on the small island and our little unit of actors and technicians socialized every night with each other. The all-British crew, with whom I was pally as we played poker, danced and drank every night, teased me relentlessly as they observed Belafonte often throwing me suggestive glances. 'They say his ambition is to make love with as many beautiful women as he can. Better watch out, you'll be next,' teased Nick Roeg, the camera operator who had married Susan Stephen, my friend from RADA, and who went on to become a very distinguished director.

With Susan Stephen, my best friend at RADA, moaning about boys at Richmond Park.

'No way,' I said and meant it. To have any kind of a relationship with a black man in the moralistic, racist era of the late fifties was totally off limits. But one night in Grenada, after dinner, Belafonte and I took a walk along the beach in the moonlight. I was sorely tempted to invite him to my room as I listened to his articulate and amusing husky voice, which held a hint of forbidden promise. Then he said, 'Now Miss Collins, I'm leaving tomorrow but I'll be at the Grove in April – will you come?'

'Oh yes,' I said, and I did.

In his memoir, *My Story*, Harry Belafonte describes what happened: 'In Grenada, a very beautiful twenty-three-year-old Joan Collins caught my eye. I would be less than honest if I didn't admit there was some heat there. At the Coconut Grove away from prying eyes, our mutual attraction could not be denied. I felt a little escapism was justified and who better to escape with than Joan?'

OPPOSITE: *A lonely little lady on location in Barbados – but the fun is soon to come!*

As I watched Belafonte performing, he was certainly mesmerizing with his spirited calypso songs and spiritual jazz performed in a completely original way, but after a few exciting liaisons in my tiny apartment on

Shoreham Drive we knew we had to cool it. He went on tour and back to his wife and I went back to New York for more Fox publicity.

Recently, we met once more at a dinner party at my sister Jackie's. He was married to a charming woman and he seemed happy to see me and meet Percy. We all exchanged phone numbers and promised to meet up in New York. He has become a brilliant speaker and activist for the National Association for the Advancement of Colored People, for which I respect him immensely.

Always camera-shy!

And then came George Englund. In LA after *Island in the Sun*, I threw myself into work and often socialized at Gene Kelly's house. George was often there and he made no secret of the fact that he was attracted to me and I must admit the feeling was mutual. But he was married and married men were off limits in my book. But back in New York when I was doing publicity for yet another Fox non-blockbuster, Mr Englund reappeared in my life. It started with a simple phone call. 'Hi, heard you were in town. Wanna catch a show and some dinner after?' I said yes, with no foreboding of the eighteen months of misery and frustration that lay ahead for me. After the show, we dined at Billy Reid's Little Club – a swanky saloon whose pianist played the most romantic of show tunes. And, boy, was George romantic! From having been a social friend, sharing trips to Tijuana with him, Sydney and George's wife Cloris and playing volleyball at Gene's and at the beach, before I could say 'Danger. Man working!' I was hooked!

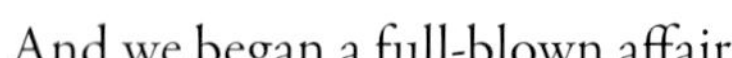

And we began a full-blown affair.

Oh, the horror of falling in love with a married man. Although he vowed his adoration and promised a divorce from Cloris, the latter never happened, and I finally realized that it was just a way of keeping me on the hook. And hooked I was. I had never met a man as fascinating as George Englund, and his wife thought so too as she made no secret that she worshipped the ground he walked on. She had once announced at a party at Arthur Loew's, 'I want to get inside George's body and BE him!'

I certainly should have known the score and I should have ended it before it became too hot not to cool down – which it soon did.

George was a producer at MGM. He was thirty and six foot two, his brown hair was slightly receding and he had intelligent, hazel eyes and a toned, muscular physique from working out in the gym five times a week. But it was his mind and his charm that hooked me. He had a way with words that was inimitable. Only Marlon Brando, his best friend, could match him in witty and original conversation. He dressed beautifully; Prince of Wales checked suits or cashmere jackets looked great on him – and he knew it.

He captured my heart and I became the reluctant back-street wife – waiting for his telephone calls, cooking gourmet dinners served at a candlelit table at my Shoreham Drive apartment only to have to chuck them out when the 10.30 p.m. phone call came. 'Sorry, babe – got caught up. I'll catch you tomorrow.' It was the definitive clichéd scenario.

But the pure emotional torture was worth it when we met up. We managed weekends at various friends' houses at the beach or at our mutual business manager's villa in Palm Springs, and went for secret lunches and dinners in out-of-the-way restaurants.

A jolly jaunt to Tijuana with Sydney, George and Cloris Englund shortly after I arrived in America.

With George Englund at a dinner party in London in 1999. We are still friends. He eventually divorced Cloris and remarried but that didn't work out either.

I never figured out how George did manage to swing all these illicit meetings. Cloris was extremely possessive and she must have suspected because after some months of our relationship she came knocking at my front door one afternoon, screaming, 'Is George there? I know he's in there – I insist on seeing him!' To say George was scared was akin to saying passengers on the *Titanic* were slightly worried.

After I had assured the hysterical wife that I was napping and not receiving visitors, she scurried off. I then asked George the $64,000 question, 'Are you still sleeping with Cloris?' He swore on his children's life he was not. However, I didn't believe he was slumbering in his office at the family abode, as he said. So one night I cruised past the back of their house and saw the two of them in their bedroom getting ready for bed! I was so shattered that I confronted him the next day in his office at MGM, striding past panic-stricken secretaries to beard him in his den.

We had a huge row and he finally admitted that not only was he sharing their bed but also that Cloris was now pregnant! 'But we only did it once!' he said weakly.

'A likely story,' I screamed. I drove home in a fury and called a girlfriend who was going to Acapulco the following day. I asked if I could join her. 'Sure,' she said. So off I went – into hiding from George. In the days before cell phones and the internet, if you wanted to disappear out of someone's life it was relatively easy. Acapulco was marvellous fun but I missed George and after a week I called Judy Kanter in LA, who told me that he was desperately missing me too.

So, silly me, I called him long distance and he instantly invited me to go with him to Eleuthera – a tiny, sun-kissed island in the Caribbean where he promised he would tell me was *definitely* getting divorced.

But of course he didn't and the pathetic romance dragged on for a few more months of misery and broken promises. Finally, I decided it had to end. I was dating several different men who temporarily took my mind off George but he was still under my skin and I was still totally faithful to him. He was fiercely jealous and would often cross-question me about my dates, particularly those with the actor Gardner McKay, who had just been voted the most handsome man in the world by *Life* magazine – and he was!

Then one evening I was dining with Mort and Barbara Viner at La Scala when I caught a young man staring at me from an opposite table. He was with another couple and Jane Fonda, a rising actress. 'That's Warren Beatty,' Mort informed me. 'He's Shirley MacLaine's actor brother, but he hasn't done much other than the Dobie Gillis television show.'

I looked over at Warren, who smiled and raised his glass. 'Cheeky,' I said to Mort. 'He's quite pretty though.'

The following week I went to the beach and when I got home I called my answering service, which told me that Mr Cunningham (George's phone pseudonym) and someone called Warren Beatty had left three messages.

I was surprised that Warren had managed to get my number but, in Hollywood, if you want something badly enough you can usually get it. I soon found out that young Mr Beatty almost *always* got what he wanted, and in the sixties, seventies and eighties he became one of the most successful and popular actors in the world.

I agreed to go out with him. And why not? I wasn't beholden to George Englund even though he thought I was his possession.

Warren was an Aries and at twenty-two insanely ambitious. He was good looking but there were better looking and younger guys out there, as he liked to tell me, which is why he sometimes lied about his age and told people he was twenty!

He was a brilliant piano player and had a youthful zest and enthusiasm that was most appealing to me, an older woman of twenty-six! I enjoyed his company enormously and he was extremely endearing in a boyish way.

He soon moved into my apartment in Shoreham Drive but not before George Englund cornered me outside my doctor's office in Beverly Hills, begging me to meet him to talk and 'work this thing out'.

We rendezvoused at the Cock 'n' Bull, an English pub-like restaurant on Sunset Boulevard which had been one of our meeting places during our affair, and George wasted no time in pulling out all the stops. Still devastatingly attractive and urbane in a pale grey Savile Row suit with a beautifully knotted Charvet tie, at thirty-two he was a huge contrast to young, spotty-faced, twenty-two-year-old Warren with his jeans, sloppy sweaters, shirts and glasses for his myopic eyes. George was a man, not a boy, and I was quite tempted to go back to him to say the least.

A publicity shot for Life *magazine when Warren was filming 'Splendour in the Grass'.*

'Smile for the camera, darling'. Warren is showcasing his James Dean look at the elegant Harwyn Club New York.

I listened to his blandishments and the same old promises to leave Cloris, and then made up my mind. Although I wasn't madly in love with Warren he was a great reason to get me away from George, who I knew would force me back on to his toxic merry-go-round again. I said goodbye to George with a heavy heart because I still had strong feelings for him and at that time Warren was really just a rebound.

Throughout the years I have bumped into George Englund many times. We always enjoy each other's company and he always reiterates that I should have stuck it out and that he would definitely have left Cloris. However, he stayed with her for years, even producing several more children in between having affairs with many glamorous women including, it is rumoured, Jackie Onassis, her sister Lee Radziwill and Leslie Caron. Ah, you know what they say about the leopard!

Warren and I were actually very compatible even if he needed to have sex several times a day, which often wore me out. When I told my friend Joanna Woodward (married to the gorgeous Paul Newman) that I needed to pull the plug as the endless bonking was exhausting me, she warned,

'Don't! If you have a relationship with a libidinous twenty-two-year-old, you better let him. Otherwise he'll look for other avenues, as it were.' So we played happy families and when we moved to New York to stay in Paul and Joanna's apartment, Warren actually proposed!

He was finally shooting his first movie – a breakthrough role in *Splendour in the Grass* with Natalie Wood.

Nat and I had been friends in Hollywood and I had known her husband Robert Wagner, 'RJ', as we always called him, since I had made my first test with him at Fox. For the past year we had become a close foursome in LA, playing poker and going to parties where we would laugh and drink and do the Madison – the hot dance of the early sixties.

Soon after Warren's proposal, I had to go to Rome to make a Fox epic called *Esther and the King*. I didn't want to do it as it was a dull script but I couldn't afford to be put on salary suspension again as I had been when I'd recently turned down a juicy role in *Sons and Lovers* at Warren's insistence.

'I don't want you to leave me, butterfly,' he said sadly. 'And at twenty-six, do you really want to play an older woman opposite that twenty-three-year-old Dean Stockwell?'

Poker time with Vivien Leigh on the set of The Roman Spring of Mrs Stone. *Warren and I seem to have the same noses!*

ONE OF THE GREATEST
LOVE ADVENTURES
OF ALL TIME!
ESTHER
AND THE
KING
JOAN COLLINS
RICHARD EGAN
DENIS O'DEA
RAOUL WALSH

A sand, sex and sandals blockbuster in which I save the Jewish race from extinction – or something like that!

OPPOSITE: *The famous quadrangle of Robert Wagner, Natalie Wood, Warren and me gave the fanmags lots of dirt to dish.*

'Fox docked me three month's pay because of turning down *Sons and Lovers* and the bills are mounting up,' I said.

Warren had presented me with a large gold ring studded with pearls for our engagement, and I wore it all through *Esther and the King*.

While shooting in Rome, during which my mother and brother Bill came to stay with me, I was bombarded with telegrams, calls and letters from Warren. I kept all the letters, along with many from my parents, my sister and my schoolgirl diaries, in a battered, old suitcase. When I came to open it after my divorce from Peter Holm, there was nothing in the case.

But I digress.

Warren missed me so much and begged me to visit him. He suspected I was having an affair, which I definitely was not – I was enjoying taking a rest from that! However, I was seeing, albeit platonically, a devastatingly handsome actor on *Esther* called Gabriele Tinti. My mother totally approved of him. But Warren was very persuasive and during my ten-week shoot in Rome, I flew to New York three times to visit him. After my third visit I started designing my wedding dress as we had thought we would marry the following year. The papers made much of it and I was getting quite excited.

But more rumours were trickling back of a budding romance between Warren and Natalie, which I thought was ridiculous since he was always calling me. But then I realized he was always calling everyone and would make dozens of calls a day, from the moment he opened his eyes. *Splendour* was a huge hit and he then went straight into *The Roman Spring of Mrs Stone*, opposite the fragile forty-five-year-old Vivien Leigh, and soon there were rumours about them too!

In the eighteen months we had been together Warren Beatty had gone from being a total unknown to a hot, rising star.

We rented a sweet house opposite Harrods during *The Roman Spring of Mrs Stone* and Warren became transformed. From the spotty, myopic youngster of eighteen months ago he was now a sophisticated Italian gigolo with a deep tan, exquisite clothes, his sandy hair dyed black and a great haircut. He looked magnificent.

Silver Screen

FEBRUARY • 25c

2/6

The Natalie Wood-Warren Beatty love swap!

★

George Maharis' greatest heartbreak

'Rumours were trickling back of a budding romance between Warren and Natalie, which I thought was ridiculous since he was always calling me.'

Bob and Natalie's obsession with "togetherness" may have been an unconscious vote of no-confidence in their union.

The Natalie Wood-Warren Beatty love swap!

When Natalie and Bob Wagner split up, she turned to Warren Beatty and Bob headed straight for Warren's fiancée, sultry Joan Collins!

Joan Collins and Warren Beatty had been considered "engaged," but when the Wagners split, they changed partners.

By Mark Dayton

It is a fascinating characteristic of life among Hollywood's nobility that some of the most improbable scenarios are played out by movie stars after the cameras stop rolling. While motion pictures increasingly concern themselves with reality, performers often manage to live on levels of unreality that would be considered too far-fetched to put on film.

A notable case in point is the ill-starred romance of Natalie Wood and Warren Beatty in Warner Bros.' current cash register clanger, "Splendor In The Grass," a compelling cinematic slice of life that is providing at least equal splendor in the counting rooms. Audiences being bravely weaned from the pabulum of happy endings chew their handkerchiefs, sniffle and sit on the edges of their seats hoping against what they know to be forlorn hope that somehow the movie's frustrated lovers, Nat and Warren, will get together in the end. Life being what it so often is, they miss their opportunity, prove helpless against the pressures to keep them apart, and they never make it.

But as everyone now knows—Natalie and Warren did get together in *(continued on page 48)*

He was starting to become catnip to women and he knew how to slather on the charm so that few could resist his in-your-face sex appeal. The Warren Beatty the world now knows as a sexual animal was beginning to emerge, which did not help our relationship one bit.

On our return to LA, we lived in my apartment on Sunset Plaza Drive but we had horrible fights about everything – one being the rent, which he said he couldn't afford! My contract at Fox had ended and I needed to work.

The final crunch came when my beloved mother and fifteen-year-old brother Bill came to stay for a week, and Warren deeply resented them being there.

'It's my house,' I would scream, 'and they're my family.' Warren would sulk and go for long drives alone. But maybe he wasn't alone for long.

Natalie was in town with RJ Wagner and the rumours of a romance with Warren were starting again, even though we still went out as a foursome and played cards together.

In my last movie at Fox, I played a stripper in 'Seven Thieves'. 27 was over the hill for leading ladies.

Then I was offered the lead in *The Road to Hong Kong* to shoot in the UK. As usual, Warren said the script was crap. 'Why would you want to do it?' he asked.

'To get away from you,' I replied. It was a sad ending to almost two years of togetherness but ours was a doomed relationship and our marriage would never have lasted because Warren loved the ladies too much.

His list of conquests reads like a who's who of glamour queens of the sixties and seventies, amongst them Natalie Wood, Julie Christie, Leslie Caron, Diane Keaton, Goldie Hawn and many more. Warren became a legend, a joke too, as he was often referred to as a phallus on legs.

However, now that he's happily married to Annette Bening, we kiss and hug and spout protestations of how we must get together for dinner whenever we bump into each other. But since this is Hollywood, where talk is cheap, I doubt this will ever happen. The last time we saw him, at a Hollywood screening, he told Percy, 'I still love this woman.'

'Thanks for telling me,' Percy quipped. 'Wanna duke it out'.

Always nice to have men fighting over you!

Shortly after I started filming *The Road to Hong Kong* in London in

1962, having recently separated from Mr Beatty, Robert Wagner arrived in town to shoot a war movie with Steve McQueen.

Naturally we had a lot to talk about, as both of our exes were the talk of the town, not to mention Hollywood. RJ was totally broken up about his divorce from Natalie, so I did my best to entertain him. We dined at various quiet London restaurants. We didn't want to draw too much attention to our friendship, which had spanned over ten years, because Natalie and Warren were the tabloid fodder of the day. Before Liz 'n' Dick, before Brangelina, they were the hot tabloid couple and Warren loved the attention.

RJ was ever the definitive gentleman. He was and is gentle, sweet and funny, and shows great respect for everyone. A child of Hollywood, he started in movies at age nineteen and quickly became a teenage idol. Tall and handsome, with deep blue eyes and a self-effacing but charming manner, RJ came from a Los Angeles family high on the social register and he was equally at ease with the head of the studio or the postman. Everyone liked him immediately, especially my mother, who absolutely adored him.

But although I was fond of RJ and we got along terribly well, our relationship remained platonic. Needless to say, of all my boyfriends, he is the one who is still one of my closest friends and we see each other often.

RJ with Stephanie Powers, his Hart to Hart *co-star, filming an episode of the show.*

Ryan O'Neal was never a serious boyfriend, more of a 'fling'. Anthony Newley had been having affairs from the moment we married in 1963, and now he had blatantly made a movie about the women he'd bedded; I was deeply hurt. So when Ryan, blond, pretty and very funny, pursued me at the Daisy Night Club and eventually, after several months, laughed me into bed, I saw no reason why I shouldn't even the scales – not to the same extent, however. My marriage was not going well, Tony was away a lot, so I figured, what the hell – it's the sixties!

Our children were around the same age so Tatum and Griffin would often come to our Beverly Hills pool and swim and frolic with Tara and Sacha.

I also had fun frolicking with Ryan, who was full of the joys of young manhood and the success that was on the horizon for him.

He was working on the daytime TV series *Peyton Place* with Mia Farrow, and since Mia was a friend it was not unusual for a bunch of us to hang out together either at a disco or someone's house, often my sister's.

Ryan was a lot of fun but I knew the relationship was dangerous and sooner or later our trysts would be discovered, and eventually they were. Tony was in the UK when this blind item appeared in the press: 'Mr X talented British performer seems unaware that his sexy actress wife Mrs X is doing more than just polishing her dance steps with handsome Mr Z, an up and coming star of one of the US's favourite soap operas.'

Fraught with guilt, I packed my bags, gathered the kids and flew back to the UK. If Ryan and I had been having an affair today it would have hit the gossip blogs, internet and other media almost immediately.

But life was easier then for an extramarital frolic. No cell phones and no sneaky paparazzi, so if you were careful you could pretty much do what you wanted!

As the disastrous Peter Holm divorce fiasco was still going on, I was badly in need of some downtime. So when the *Dynasty* people told me I had a Thursday and a Monday off, my friend Judy Bryer and I quickly booked a trip on the non-stop flight to Acapulco. Within four hours we had left smoggy, damp LA behind us and arrived in gorgeous sunny Acapulco, where we headed straight to my friends Baron Enrico and Baroness Alessandra di Portanova's extraordinary home, the Villa Arabesque.

And oh, what a difference a dose of Acapulcan carefree fun can make to a sad little divorcee-to-be. Ricky and Sandra, as they are less formally known, had a fun group staying and another fun group coming over for dining, dancing and inevitably flirting, as in Latin American countries flirting is almost a hobby. I needed some flirting after the misery I'd been through with 'The Swede' but that was as far as it went. So I left a young Mexican named Pedro at the door with the words of Pamela Kellino, James Mason's ex-wife and the mother of Morgan, ringing in my ears: 'Darling, I'm so tired of having a hard cock brushing against my thigh and a sad

On the town with 'The Bungalow'. He did love the attention and became a big celebrity in the UK.

voice saying, "How can you be so cruel to me?" I'm glad I'm over all that.'

As the weekend of sun, fun and frivolity continued, I had not danced so much, drank so much tequila or felt so free for a long time. The handsome Mexican man's impassioned 'I love you – you're the most beautiful girl in the world' and his constant bouquets of red roses assuaged my bruised ego. The holiday fun was most invigorating and I returned to LA feeling a lot better.

At the di Portanovas I met some English people destined to become lifelong friends – Charles and Pandora Delevingne, Ned Ryan and Davina Phillips. The latter insisted that when I came to London in the spring she wanted to introduce me to someone special.

'I'm not interested in anyone long term,' I said. 'And I never want to get married again. I've done it four times now. I don't need a husband; what I need is a wife!' I joked.

That statement, which made everyone laugh, I announced to the press later, once my Peter Holm divorce was finalized. It became rather famous and even greetings cards were manufactured, with my picture and that quote.

On my next London trip, in February 1987, on a few days off from *Dynasty* to visit Katy, Charles Delevingne and Ned Ryan invited me to a lunch at their office in Chelsea as they had someone they wanted me to meet. My divorce was not yet over. 'The Swede' was being impossible, making ridiculous demands and a complete spectacle of himself by lolling in my swimming pool in a tiny leopard print bikini spouting words like, 'I still love her but I need money.' I was quite fed up and – for the first time in my life – lonely. Tara and Sacha were doing well and living their own lives as young twenty-somethings. Fourteen-year-old Katy was living with me in a rented flat in London and going to the American School, which she loved.

The man who sat on my right at lunch was six foot one with sandy hair, twinkly blue eyes and a muscular sportsman's physique. When we were introduced he stared at me, puzzled, then asked roguishly, 'So what do you do?' As I was now at the height of my *Dynasty* fame, I thought he was quite funny. Bill Wiggins, or Bungalow Bill as he was affectionately known, was ostensibly a property man, but seemed to spend most of his time playing squash or golf, and having four-hour boozy lunches with Charles, Ned, John Chalk and others of his scallywag group, all of whom were exceedingly amusing. Bill would stay up all night telling jokes and drinking. And boy could he drink!

He had just returned from St Moritz where he had done the daredevil Cresta Run toboggan track and he regaled us at lunch with side-splitting stories of that event. He was a great raconteur and a regular good-time guy, and if ever a lady needed a good laugh to cheer her up, it was me!

Bill bore more than a passing resemblance to one of my favourite actors, Jeff Bridges, and was equally attractive in a macho he-man way. He soon made it clear he found me attractive too and although I was fourteen years older, he asked me out and we laughed and joked our way throughout the next three days, closing nightclubs as I batted away his attempts to bed me.

I was sorely tempted but fear of AIDS was rampant then and Davina Phillips had warned me that Bill Wiggins was a ladies' man *par excellence*. 'He's a lovable rogue – don't take him seriously,' she'd warned me.

My miniseries Sins *which I produced, starred in and cast.*

But humour is such a great gift and Bill had it in spades. I spent so much time giggling at his stories that I developed a few more laughter lines! The camaraderie of the seven or eight guys with whom Bill hung out was warm and the badinage with each other was ironic but affectionate. I was extremely flattered to be one of the only women invited to their bawdy lunches, which often finished at past six o'clock, giving me just enough time to change and go out to dinner.

In March, Wiggins came to stay with me in my Cabrillo house in Beverly Hills and we had buckets of fun. I also then discovered what the 'Bungalow' nickname signified. Not much on top but all below!

Since I was now totally disinterested in any kind of commitment, having been so badly burned by Peter Holm, Bill Wiggins was the perfect man for me at the time. After eight days in LA in which he managed to charm all my friends, it was time for him to go back to London. We talked constantly on the phone and when we next met in London the paparazzi went crazy. Wherever we went they followed us and even though we spouted the 'we're just good friends' line they were fascinated by us as a couple. Bill was a regular guy, one of the boys and the press loved that we were an item.

Bill was so attractive to women that they seemed to crawl out of the woodwork to approach him wherever we went. Even at Annabel's – that sacrosanct saloon – they would slink over and ask him to dance. And he loved it! All the attention and the fame and the column inches fed his ego, especially since he was soon offered large sums of money to talk about our relationship. Since this wasn't the first time a man had done that (both Ron and Peter had spilled their guts to the tabloids), I figured that at least Bill's version of life with Joan Collins would be positive.

For the next few months, when I wasn't filming, we travelled around the world – New York, Paris, the south of France, Morocco, Las Vegas and LA – but we kept it light. But when I was away in LA the newspapers delighted in printing that he was seeing other women, but Bill assured me they were platonic – just old girlfriends. Of course, I believed him, because I wanted to.

I usually ignore my own advice to keep out of the sun, as I love it. But I try to avoid face contact!

My kids adored him, especially Katy, with whom he played backgammon – a big change from Peter who had practically ignored her.

We made the cover of *You* magazine and he appeared in a commercial with me and he even got an agent – mine!

Although we both had a fear of commitment, Bill admitted that at forty he definitely wanted kids, which was absolutely not in my future. He did admit that even though our relationship was too hot not to cool down he had never met a woman more amusing and fun to be with than me. He said that our relationship was the best he'd ever had. But I realized that lots of goodbyes, separations and then trips to exciting places certainly helped to keep our relationship vibrant.

Bill also gave me some sweet gifts – a gold bracelet studded with semi-precious stones, an art deco diamond watch and an art nouveau statue of a girl on a swing which he said reminded him of me in *The Girl in the Red Velvet Swing*. Since he was broke most of the time, they were much appreciated. But the drinking and the carousing! How he survived night after night, day after day, without becoming a total alcoholic I couldn't fathom. But his punishing daily regime of squash, running, cricket and golf probably helped.

In late 1987, I had to spend a lot of time in LA on *Dynasty* and I was becoming quite annoyed with Bill Wiggins as he had persuaded me to invest a large sum of money in a property venture. Well, sadly it failed, just as our relationship was doing. Then he did a really spiteful thing. He gave a tabloid a story in which he said I was almost bald! I was in LA and so utterly furious that I refused to speak to him even though he denied saying it over and over again. I didn't believe him and told him he'd do anything for money. I knew our romance, as pleasurable and fun as it had been, would never have lasted, so the halcyon times ended and I bade farewell to the days of wine and roses and wine and wine and wine!

Recently, we bumped into each other at a little beach in Saint-Tropez. Now in his sixties, Bill had barely changed and came bounding up to my table like a happy puppy. He was with the woman with whom he lived and with whom he now has two grown children. 'You never married?' I asked. 'You know I've got a fear of commitment,' he joked. We had a great conversation and when I left with Percy and our group I paused at his table and quipped, 'See you in another quarter of a century!'

Having returned from a great holiday in Acapulco, where I'd reconnected to some old friends and met some new ones, Davina Phillips called to invite me to a dinner saying there was someone she'd like me to meet. 'He's very poetic,' she said. 'And quite in demand as an extra man. He's a perfect gentleman.'

'How old?' I asked.

'About twenty-nine,' she said.

'Good God, I'm over fifty. Isn't that age gap a bit much?'

'I don't think he'll care,' she laughed. 'I think he already likes you.'

When I arrived at Davina's glamorous apartment in Belgravia, several of my friends were there and Robin Hurlstone rose to greet me as we were introduced. He was tall and good looking, with a lanky but languid frame, elegantly dressed with floppy blond hair and sharp blue eyes that seemed to miss nothing as he looked me up and down, greeting me with a charming smile.

Eton educated, he was extremely amusing with a biting and sarcastic wit and seemed older than his age. He also gave some of the best hatchet jobs in town. In that respect, not dissimilar to another friend and confidant to many of the *haut monde* – the interior designer, Nicky Haslam.

Robin and I hit it off well, although he seemed rather shy and had been part of the gay monde. It was common knowledge that some years previously he had been the boyfriend of the notorious John Jermyn, 7th Marquess of Bristol, known drug addict. Robin had been extremely close to him during his late teens, spending many weekends at the stately home Ickworth House, where Jermyn hosted decadent parties and was painted by acclaimed artists of the day. After his death in 1999, it was discovered he had frittered away his £30 million fortune. One day, in the mid-nineties, when Robin and I were waiting at a British Airways desk in Nice, Bristol stood next to us but the two men pointedly ignored each other. Little did I realise that this was Robin's pattern.

Robin was fancy free and we soon started dating. It was somewhat platonic initially. I was still seeing Bill Wiggins on and off although I had become fed up with his womanizing ways. But while Bill was Mr Macho Good Ole Boy, Robin was not. Bill was a wicked mimic and one night, when he and I were in the back of a limousine and Robin was sitting next to the driver, he started mocking him and imitating his mannerisms, which made me giggle but did not go down well with the refined Mr Hurlstone.

We socialized with a group that included the Delevingnes, Theo and Louise Fennell, Tim and Virginia Bell, and we partied in London and the south of France, having some wonderful times.

Eventually Robin and I became lovers and he soon started advising and criticizing me on everything from décor, my clothes and even my hairstyles. Our mutual friend, producer Charles Duggan, nicknamed him the 'Taste Tyrant' as Robin considered himself an expert on everything aesthetic and cultured. I can't deny that he had exquisite taste in the art of decoration and had a commanding knowledge of antiques, pictures and art.

We spent hours exploring quaint antique shops in London, Paris and the south of France, searching for furnishings and pictures for Destino and my flat in London. Although 'hideous' and 'ghastly' were used more ofter than not.

With Robin at Club 55, St Tropez, 1998.

Robin and I were together on and off for a dozen years and although he was officially 'my boyfriend' our lives were very separate and we didn't live together in London – he had his own flat in Kensington and I had mine in Belgravia. He loathed the press, especially the paparazzi who were always quite keen to get photos of me with a man, but at that time most of the photos they were able to shoot were of me with Christopher Biggins, Edward Duke or Didier LeBlanc, all of whom were firmly *not* in the closet. When I asked Robin why he was so averse to the press, he informed me that his mother had told him that a gentleman or lady only appeared in the press three times in their life; at birth, at marriage and at death. I thought that this was a somewhat archaic point of view since this was the nineties and practically everyone was in the newspapers at some time or other. As Andy Warhol said, 'Everyone will be world-famous for fifteen minutes.' Well, Robin Hurlstone didn't want even one minute of fame, which was pretty difficult when he was dating a very famous woman from one of the most popular TV shows in the world.

'Is that a paparazzo I spot? Begone you varmit!'

But he managed to avoid the press to the extent that if we did ever go to an opening (a rare occurrence) or a party, the photographers I knew – Richard Young, Dave Benett and Alan Davidson – would ostentatiously put their cameras down, grinning broadly, and say mockingly, 'Hello, Robin. Don't worry, we'll cut you out of the photo!'

A few rare photographs of us were taken at that time. In 1992 after the opening night of *Private Lives* we were snapped in the back of a limo on the way to my party at the Ivy. And during the tour of *Private Lives*, although he dived and dodged the snappers, several other pictures of us did surface. I asked him once what it was about me that he purported to love. 'You're a beautiful monster,' he said, grinning. 'And I love to collect beautiful monsters.'

Robin was well aware that he could charm people. He had the knack of listening to and talking to individuals and letting them into his confidence, which was very endearing. He often said that if we broke up, he would be 'killed in the rush' and indeed it was true as he was extremely popular with many people and was an in-demand house guest with most of the people he cultivated.

We got along really well for a while. I admired his impeccable eye and his slightly bitchy sense of humour. But he was adamant about what was and wasn't right and that irritated me. Things that I loved like art deco furniture, art nouveau statues and sculptures, silver candelabra and pictures by Dalí, Erté and Cocteau were considered to be in awfully bad taste, but original eighteenth-century armoires, pictures, French red chalk drawings, ormolu credenzas and candelabras were totally acceptable.

I often made fun of his bossiness and insistence on calling the mirror 'the looking glass' or the mantelpiece 'the chimney piece', and as for the word settee: *quelle horreur*! So naff! There was a certain innate Victorianism to his mannerisms and predilections. More of a nineteenth-century dandy than a modern man.

He didn't enjoy socializing other than at small dinners, but he adored hanging out with Valentino, Gianni Versace, his sister Donatella and Elton John, who I introduced him to.

Robin's exquisite taste was often a touch too exquisite for this half-Jewish, gipsy diva from Hollywood via Bayswater and Maida Vale. I was somewhat of a bohemian at heart and even though I enjoyed the high life of private planes and the grand houses of some of our friends, and I had practically grown up attending Hollywood parties and red-carpet events, my favourite times were at home with my family and close friends watching old movies and playing games.

But sadly Robin didn't take to some of my family, most importantly my sister Jackie and my daughter Tara. He made no secret of his dislike for them, so of course, both being Libras, they reciprocated by cold-shouldering him too. Things became so bad that Tara did not want to be anywhere near him, nor he her. I attempted to pour oil on these troubled waters. I had been used to spending Christmas with my three children, Jackie and my brother Bill and his wife Hazel, and various friends, but Robin was adamant that if Tara was at my flat for Christmas Day, he would go to his mother's. When he asked me one Christmas, after we had been together for nearly ten years, what I would like for Christmas, I answered, 'I would like you to spend Christmas Day with my family.'

'That will never happen,' he said firmly. 'And the only time I will ever see Tara again will be at your funeral.'

I was so shocked and deeply hurt by this that my feelings for him started to change radically. Yes, I was fond of him and I admired his charm, humour and his beguiling way, but his insistence on everything being perfectly correct was becoming wearing. He didn't like most of my clothes or my hair when I wore it down, so whenever we went out socially he insisted I wore the short wig from *Dynasty*, which he liked but I didn't. And he was often rude to people who worked for us in the south of France.

Most summers, we spent at Destino and had great fun furnishing and decorating it and entertaining many friends. In the early days, most of the time we were together, we did have fun, but we were like chalk and cheese and his perfectionism and endless disapproval of so many things I enjoyed soon became extremely aggravating. He even criticized friends for mispronouncing words!

1984. A card for Christmas in London with my children. That sweater is sooo 70s!

Tara, Miel and me in St Tropez in 2012 – the Collins girls like hats!

I spent part of the summer of 2000 in Greece and at my house in the south of France with Robin and some friends. I had met Percy Gibson earlier that year, in the spring. I had wanted Tara and her baby daughter, Miel, to stay in France but Robin didn't want her there and announced that if she came he would leave. In fact, as I lay by the pool, gazing out at the sweeping views of Provence, I was reminded more and more of how much I missed Percy!

Both my sister and my closest friend Judy Bryer told me I was a fool to stay in a non-fulfilling relationship. 'Habit, I guess,' I'd sigh. 'It's easier to stay together than to break up.'

'Remember when he refused to escort you to Buckingham Place to receive your OBE from the queen?' asked Judy, over a long-distance phone call. 'Have you forgotten that?'

Actually, I had forgotten. I possess the kind of memory that wipes out most distressing and bad events as I've always thought this makes for a more serene life. I certainly don't bear grudges, but it's also a somewhat ostrich head-in-the-sand mentality, not facing up to the truth. But I did recall that Robin had said that he would have been delighted to escort me

1998 – my son Sacha escorted me to receive my OBE from the Queen, then we celebrated at the Ivy with Katy and many friends.

The invitation to Katy's twenty-first birthday party.

if I had been receiving a *damehood*! A mere OBE wasn't important enough for him to have to be photographed with me. Consequently I took Sacha to the palace and was proud to do so. However, Robin seemed quite pleased when in 1998 *Tatler* magazine included us as a couple in their list of Britain's top 250 party guests.

I never asked Robin what he did during the daytime or most weekends when we weren't together, but in retrospect, I think he had a whole life I knew nothing about. He called himself an art dealer, had many connections in the art world and did purchase some excellent pictures and furniture for me, for which I heard he received a healthy commission.

Things really started to disintegrate when he refused to come with me on the two-month tour of *Love Letters* in April 2000. After my opening night in San Francisco, when I asked him why he hadn't at least sent me flowers, he told me that since it was just a piddling little unimportant tour it wasn't worth bothering to send flowers. I was quite hurt by this as so many of my friends had sent loving notes, cards and beautiful bouquets.

My friend, the cynical super-agent Sue Mengers, whom I had known since she was a secretary at the William Morris agency and who became Anthony Newley's agent during the late sixties and early seventies, had adored Robin ever since she stayed with us at Destino. He gave her a pedicure one day whilst advising her on art and antiques and they would often sit giggling and gossiping together. After we split they still saw each other. Every time I visited her, however, she nagged me about not giving Robin any money after we parted. When she died in 2011, she left Robin $100,000 and some antique French furniture.

I would have liked to remain on good terms with Robin, but that was not to be. He insisted to many mutual friends that I had 'dumped' him, horribly and unceremoniously, without a care for his feelings or well-being, which was absolutely untrue. I had cared for him a great deal, but by the same token I did not feel that I owed him anything in the way of a cash settlement – which is what he wanted – or that I should sell my villa in the south of France and give him half the

Sue Mengers, her husband Jean Claude Tramont and Stella Wilson sample the delights of Club 55 in St Tropez.

proceeds so that he could buy his own house. He told this to many people, including my press agent Jeffrey Lane and my manager Peter Charlesworth, who was appalled. 'How can you possibly ask her to do that? Joan's not rich. She's worked hard all her life and she has many dependants – why should she give you *anything*?' Apparently this angered Robin so much that he never spoke to Peter and Jeffrey, nor to many of my other friends, again.

He only continued to see various friends he had met through me, even though he instructed his own coterie of close friends not to have any more contact with me – and they obeyed! Robin started to refer to me as 'that ghastly woman' and when I contacted a couple of friends whom I had met through him, I was told in no uncertain terms that they couldn't possibly see me or remain friendly with me as that would upset Robin too much. Oh, really! But I still think of him fondly though I doubt he feels the same!

It has always puzzled me that a man feels he should have a monetary entitlement from a woman after the end of a relationship or, in fact, vice versa. It made me realize just how special Percy was in letting his ex-wife keep their apartment and all the furnishings and asking nothing for himself after they divorced. That to me is the definition of a true gentleman.

Chapter Five

HUSBANDS

Men – can't live with 'em, can't kill 'em – so an old saying goes. Well, I happen to disagree, particularly where marriage is concerned. I believe strongly in marriage (certainly where children are concerned) and if you're lucky to find the right partner, marriage is the glue that binds a couple together. If there are rows and rifts (as there always tend to be) being married is such a strong commitment that people usually think twice or thrice about quitting the marital bonds. There is overwhelming evidence today that marriage brings greater benefits to children. Of course, no one is going to live always happily ever after – there will always be arguments. There are many pitfalls in a marriage, particularly if you stupidly marry too young, as I did, and choose the wrong partner, as I also did!

OPPOSITE: *'A good man is hard to find – you always get the other kind.' – Mae West*

I've been married five times, so I guess I should know a thing or two about marriage. Although five is much more than average I feel I must discount two marriages. The first, at a time when 'nice girls don't' and if you did you had to get married or you would cause a major scandal for your parents. My own friends, however, were starting to accept the fact that living and sleeping together before marriage – and really getting to know and accept each other's faults, quirks and irritating habits – was preferable to shotgun weddings in which one married in haste and repented at leisure.

So to pacify my parents, I married on my nineteenth birthday and was totally unprepared for what married life would turn out to be like. I also knew very little about my new husband. Bloody hell, if I had known, I wouldn't have married him! So, that turned out to be a major mistake. Marriages two and three to Anthony Newley and Ron Kass were successful in that they brought me three wonderful children but the insurmountable difficulties I had to face – serial infidelity and substance abuse – made these unions fail. I also truly believe that the problems with Tony and Ron were not of my making, as you will see when you read about them. Marriage number four, as has been widely documented, was simply an act of lunacy.

When Ivana Trump asked if I would be one of her twenty-five bridesmaids at her last nuptials, I quipped 'Darling, I'm afraid I can't – I'm always the bride, never the bridesmaid.'

Maybe I was naive in that I expected things would get better in my marriages but unless you are totally sure of your partner's commitment to change their bad habits, I found to my cost that they don't.

Marriages need a strong bond to survive the problems they can encounter, particularly with the glare of the media and the instability of show business. I had admired the photographs of eighteen-year-old Elizabeth Taylor in 1950, a couple of years before my own first marriage, when she married hotel heir Nicky Hilton. How pure and virginal (and obviously madly in love!) she looked in her cinched satin gown. But it was not to last. Needless to say that although that union lasted less than a year, Elizabeth went on to have seven more!

My honeymoon in Cannes was less than idyllic – so were his budgie smugglers!

Comparing hairstyles with Sharon Tate at her glamorous wedding to Roman Polanski at the Playboy Club.

One of the most memorable weddings I attended was that of Roman Polanski and Sharon Tate given at the louche Playboy Club in London. It was at the height of sixties fabulousness so all the women wore micro-mini dresses and patterned tights, and sported enormous hair, while the men showcased a variety of moustaches, long sideburns and flowered shirts. But none of the women could hold a candle to the gorgeous bride. In a short white crochet dress with masses of flowers in her luxuriant blonde locks, she was the absolute picture of joy and happiness. Tragically, I was also at her funeral only a few years later, after the Manson gang viciously murdered the beautiful and pregnant Sharon in her Hollywood home. The funeral reception was held at producer Bob Evans's house where in bad taste, after lunch, some wit exclaimed, referring to the funeral of one of the other victims, 'Right, let's go off to the second feature now.'

My weddings were not always the joyous occasions they were meant to be, even though in photographs I look happy enough. Maxwell Reed and I married at Caxton Hall, a simple registry office in London. My wedding to Anthony Newley was in a registry office in Connecticut – no honeymoon, as he had to rush back to the theatre for a performance. As I've mentioned, when Tony, myself and our two children moved into a beautiful house at Summit Drive in Beverly Hills, I was told it was an unlucky house for married couples. 'Everyone who's lived there has divorced,' I was told, 'Barbara Rush and Warren Cowan, then Janet Leigh and Tony Curtis . . .' Tony Newley and I followed suit and were divorced shortly after, and when Sammy Davis, Jr moved in with May Britt a few years later, their marriage also hit the rocks.

My marriage to Ron Kass looked like a fairy tale in the photos. I am glowing and pregnant in a billowing white dress on the island of Jamaica and, with the Caribbean sun setting in the background, it looked idyllic. Sadly the marriage started to fade after that dangerous seven-year mark.

You can't judge a marriage by its photos. Humphrey Bogart and Lauren Bacall looked positively miserable in their wedding photo but theirs was one of the happiest marriages in Hollywood, ending only with his death. Priscilla Presley by contrast looks as if her groom Elvis is goosing her, judging by the mischievous look on his face, but again that marriage was to be short-lived.

One of the campest weddings I went to was that of Liza Minnelli to David Gest. Held at New York's massive Collegiate Church it was attended by an eclectic galaxy of disparate stars from Jane Russell and Mickey Rooney to David Hasselhoff, Donny Osmond, Elizabeth Taylor and Michael Jackson. The bride had twenty maids of honour who were allowed to wear whatever they liked, so the diversity of costume was highly amusing and most of them wore black! The groom had twenty assorted groomsmen of all ages, including my pal RJ Wagner, who shot me a wry grin walking down the aisle.

Percy and I sat in the pews with Arlene Dahl and her sixth husband, Marc Rosen. We waited restlessly a very long time for the ceremony to begin, wondering what the delay was and we subsequently heard what happened. Matron of honour Elizabeth Taylor had travelled to the venue in her bedroom slippers but in spite of the several 'gofers' she employed, she had forgotten her shoes! Then, alongside best man Michael Jackson and others of the wedding party, she sat on the stage and waited. (It was the only church in NY that has more of a stage than an altar, and the sacristy where the wedding party waited was called 'the green room'.) When Liza finally walked in and met David at the altar they seemed enchanted with each other.

My favorite picture of Percy and I on honeymoon in Malaysia.

David kept attempting to pucker up and kiss the bride well in advance of his cue, prompting the pastor to break them apart like dogs in heat. When he finally announced, 'you may now kiss the bride', David launched himself on Liza and sucked on her face like he was trying to vacuum her tonsils out. In spite of such a forceful and passionate declaration of lust, the marriage lasted barely a year.

Long-lasting marriages in Hollywood, especially between actors, are rare, but one of the happiest was Paul Newman's fifty-year-plus

Six years and still in love – celebrating at the Bel Air Hotel, 2009.

marriage to Joanne Woodward. I knew them well and they were the perfect Hollywood couple until his death. But I guess they weren't exactly Hollywood, as they lived in Connecticut – maybe that's the secret!

So much of my adult life has been in tumultuous and unhappy marriages and relationships; I've finally found peace, serenity and security with Percy. I feel incredibly lucky. So lucky, in fact, that in February 2013 we celebrated our eleventh wedding anniversary. Eleven years is almost a record by Hollywood standards – and I'm delighted to say we are as happy today as we were that blissful day in 2002 when we had the most glorious wedding ceremony and party at Claridge's. It was the fairy-tale wedding I had always wanted and never had a chance to have. The happiness in our faces in the wedding pictures is indicative of how happy we were, and I'm willing to bet that if you take a photo of us today you'll still see that same look on our faces (as long as he hasn't snored the night before!).

Having finally found my true soul mate and husband forever in Percy Gibson, I realize that although I've had more weddings than most, quantity doesn't necessarily mean quality.

Looking back it seems that Max, Tony, Ron and Peter put me down, criticized and insulted me far too often. Although none of my husbands, with the exception of Max, were ever physically violent towards me (because they all knew that I would never tolerate that), I believe that verbal violence can often be just as distressing and upsetting as words often linger longer than bruises.

Was it my own fault that I brought out such a perverse streak in these four very different men or was I just a lousy chooser?

I have never been the mousey, stand two paces behind, obedient 'little woman' type. Even with Maxwell Reed, as a teenager, I was feisty, opinionated and emancipated in an era when women were expected to cook, clean and wait on their spouses hand and foot and obey them implicitly.

Maxwell Reed was fourteen years older than me. He was also a film star and, as a schoolgirl, I had been one of his biggest fans.

'I shall marry him one day,' I had blithely informed my fourth-form classmates, admiring his photo stuck under my desktop. 'He's so handsome!'

'Handsome is as handsome does,' replied one wise thirteen-year-old, darkly.

Nevertheless, throwing caution and Mummie's advice to the wind, this eighteen-year-old virgin accepted a date from this thirty-two-year-old Lothario, he of the dyed black hair and heavily pencilled brows, and stupidly allowed herself to be deflowered on their first date!

Well, I didn't exactly allow it. Technically he raped me by giving me a strong 'Mickey Finn' disguised as a rum and coke. Since I had naively accepted Reed's offer to visit 'the Country Club', as he called his flat on the top floor of a dingy building in Hanover Square, I should have known better.

The 'sultry pinup girl' and the fading film star at the Chelsea Arts Ball New Years Eve Gala.

The act, if you can call it that, was awful and degrading. He ripped off my clothes when I was unconscious and I was violently sick afterwards. However, because I had 'done it', which nice young girls never did in the fifties, I attempted to wipe the incident from my mind and actually started dating him!

Oh, foolish child. At just eighteen I was as *au courant* in the ways of the world as eleven-year-olds are today. I blinded myself with what I thought was love, which was then requited by this fading film star who drove an enormous blue Buick, smoked American cigarettes and whose ambition was to go to Hollywood and conquer it. Fat chance! Max was already over the hill in England, but because my star was on the rise we soon became a hot couple in the British tabloids.

My parents were strict and there were so many rules to be obeyed and curfews to which to adhere. But I felt that I needed to live my life to the

Everyone was impressed with Max's stunning blue Buick – especially my baby brother Bill.

full, so it was only when I threatened to run away and live with Max if my parents wouldn't allow me to marry him that they reluctantly relented, although they were violently against the marriage. Stupidly, I was flattered to have been asked and bragged to my school friend Beryl, 'Told you I'd marry him!'

During this time, I was under contract to the J. Arthur Rank organization and working non-stop either in movies or in the stills gallery where Rank was attempting to cement my reputation as a sultry pin-up girl.

It was a mad working whirl of exciting activity. The tabloids screamed: 'Britain's best new actress since Jean Simmons!' and 'England's answer to Ava Gardner!' I sincerely believed Ava hadn't a thing to worry about.

I was becoming hot property but Max's star was melting faster than an iceberg in Africa. Surely a recipe for marital disaster.

The sex was awful! But since Mummie told me it would be and that women just had to put up with it, I gritted my teeth, thought of England and watched television, which luckily was at the bottom of the sofa.

As the wedding day drew near, I realized that I had made a dreadful mistake – I didn't really want to marry Max. I was too young and I was becoming very successful. I would have been satisfied just to see him three or four times a week, or live together, but my parents were adamant that could not happen. 'What will people think?' screeched my mother in horror. 'I'll never be able to show my face in the West End!' said Daddy.

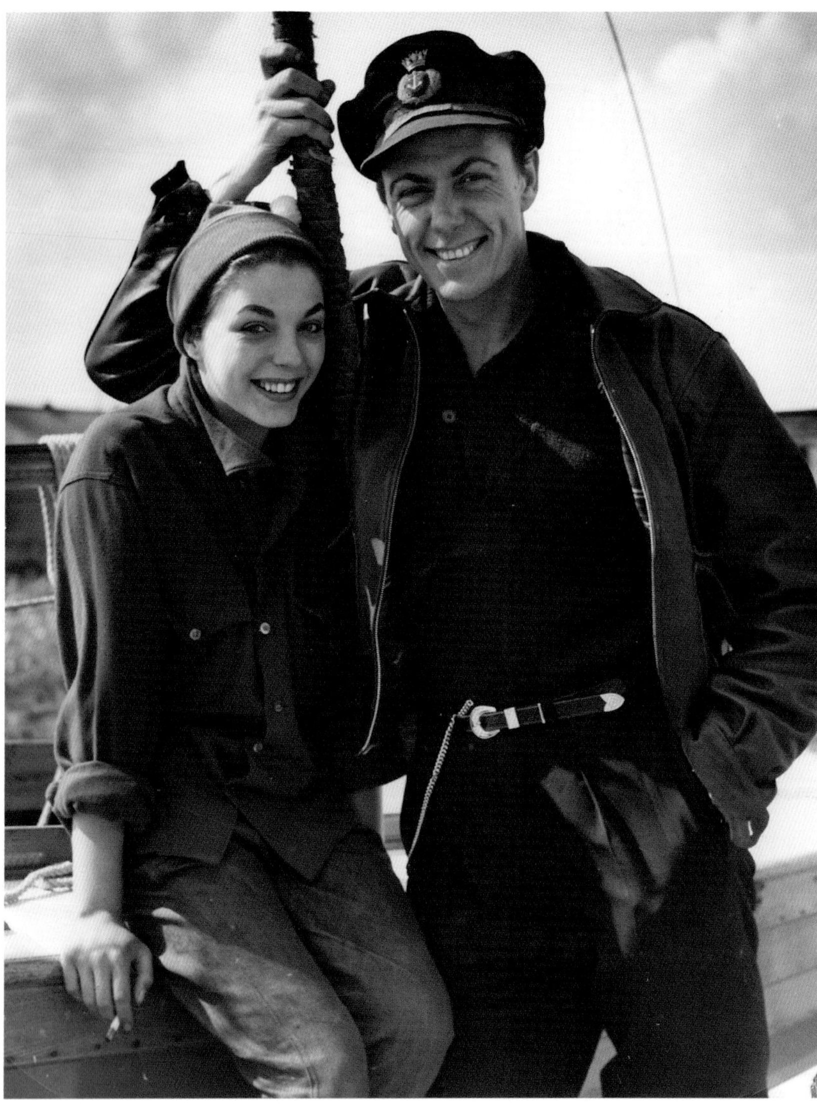

He had a boat! And a Captain's hat to go with it.

I should have run for the hills when I proudly read this review from a major critic of my performance in *I Believe in You* out loud to Max: 'Joan Collins makes a tremendous impression as the wayward girl. She has a dark, luscious beauty putting her in the Jane Russell class, but Joan already seems to be an actress of greater ability, and looks like the most impressive recruit to British films for many a moon.'

If looks could kill, I would have been dead. Ignoring Max's dark and furious stare, I blithely read out the next one from the *News of the World*: 'A dozen of my darkest red roses to Joan Collins . . . fire and spirit in her acting and that odd combination of allure and mystery that spells eventual world stardom.'

When I finished reading them, Max glowered at me furiously then barked, 'Better milk it for all you can, kid, because by the time you're twenty-three your looks will be gone and you'll be forgotten.' He then sulked for two days, refusing to talk to me.

But as I have always had an ostrich mentality, sticking my head in the sand when I didn't want to face reality, I ignored these signs. So we married in a registry office and my parents gave us a lavish reception at Ciro's nightclub with half of London's show-business set attending.

Almost immediately after the wedding the rot really set in. He became insanely jealous. If a man even glanced at me in the street he would threaten to 'cut up that pretty little face so no one will ever look at you again' and I knew he knew the unsavory men he hung out with could do this.

Although I gave interviews chirping that I was a modern hard-working woman and hence wouldn't do housework, Max insisted on being fed and watered properly. So after an arduous twelve-hour day of filming, I would slave over a hot stove to fix him a full English dinner. Chops, spuds and peas were my specialty but if he didn't like the way I did them, he'd chuck the plate across the room, screaming insults.

Strangely, I'd seen my father do this to Mummie a couple of times so I wasn't that surprised.

Housework was not my métier and I deeply resented the fact that I was being put into the 'little woman' category while I was still a teenager and at the same time as I was being referred to constantly in glowing terms as 'Britain's Best Bet for Stardom.'

I quickly became deeply disillusioned with my marriage to Maxwell Reed. In the eighteen months we were together I made nine films and performed in five plays, some of which were thankfully on tour or on location so I was thrilled to get away from him. Reed was so contrary about everything that when I wanted a kitten as a pet, he bought me a spider monkey instead!

This rascally animal lived in a cage attached to the ceiling over the bottom of the bathtub (which I had to clean). I was not particularly fond of the little demon which, when let out of its cage, would perform acrobatics around the living room, swinging from curtains and chairs and cackling like a mad parakeet.

'A dozen of my darkest red roses to Joan Collins . . . fire and spirit in her acting and that odd combination of allure and mystery that spells eventual world stardom.'

Max was always trying to get me into the kitchen – he never succeeded!

I finally insisted we get rid of it when my parents came to visit and Spider, perched on the arm of a chair, proceeded to pleasure himself in front of my dear mother, who almost had a fit of rage!

That was Spider's last stand, as it were, and almost the last act of the ridiculous marriage.

Shortly afterwards, when Max and I were at Les Ambassadeurs nightclub, a swarthy Middle Eastern gentleman ogled me. When I went to the ladies room, he offered Max £10,000 if he would let me go to bed with him! To my horror Max wanted to close the deal with this Arab sheikh. 'And he'll even let me watch,' he hissed as the sheikh grinned at me lasciviously. 'And with the ten grand he pays us we can go to Hollywood, baby, buy a new car, hit the big time!'

Bursting into tears, I ran from the club into the night and back to my parents' pad in Harley Street, where they happily welcomed me, even if I heard 'I told you so' several times a day. Max and I separated and shortly after I went off to Rome to film *Land of the Pharaohs.*

Infuriatingly, he too bagged a role in some epic also shooting in Rome. One day, whilst sunbathing on the beach at Fregene, outside the eternal city, he loomed over me wearing some ridiculous white shorts and demanded I return all the jewellery and money he'd given me. I was not earning very much (£50 a week at Rank and somewhat more for *Pharaohs*) but he demanded I give him everything in my savings account 'otherwise the boys will get you'. I'd met these 'boys' – terrifying men with names like Jack Spot and Reggie Kray – so I knew the score there. I was so scared I sent the few trinkets I possessed to his hotel: a couple of rings (yes, he even wanted the wedding ring back), a charm bracelet and necklace – basically all the jewellery I had.

Luckily, fate stepped in by way of a Hollywood contract but I had to wait three years for a divorce. At least I was safely in America, I thought. But one day, whilst I was in a bubble bath shooting a scene for *The Opposite Sex*, a process server rushed on to the set and slapped me with a subpoena to appear in court in Santa Monica. These papers informed me that I must give Maxwell Reed the money he 'deserved'. My lawyer advised that, since

I was now earning the princely sum of $1,250 a week, which would rise to $5,000 a week in five years, 'You should pay up or Reed could drag the case on for years and eventually be granted more, because he said he discovered you.'

'That's a complete lie!' I said furiously. But I was also frightened. The threats of carving up my face made me have nightmare sweats, and I knew that his tough-guy acquaintances would probably enjoy doing it, too.

So I had to go to court. The divorce cost me $10,000, which, since I didn't have it, I had to borrow from the studio. I had to pay for his and my own legal fees and give him all the money in my bank account – about $1,500. I know this doesn't sound like much today but, in 1956, it was a fortune. The judge cross-examined me curiously as to why I, a very young woman, had to pay a thirty-five-year-old man all this money. I couldn't answer this – the judge was right, of course. I was desperate to get rid of Max so the judge reluctantly granted me the divorce.

So, with sister Jackie, I left the court, aged twenty-three: poorer, wiser and with a growing distrust of men.

And that was divorce number one!

Safely in Hollywood I thought, but process servers were lurking on the set to subpoena me for a divorce.

After divorcing Maxwell Reed, I was totally against the idea of marriage, although I had been offered some interesting propositions!

Then suddenly around the age of twenty-seven, I started to become broody. I found myself peering into prams, making 'goo goo' faces at babies and smiling idiotically at infants in their mother's arms.

Yes, I was ready for motherhood and unconsciously I was looking for a father figure for my unborn children. I soon found him in the unlikely shape of Anthony Newley.

Tony, or the Young Master as he liked to be called, was starring in the West End in the box-office smash *Stop the World – I Want to Get Off*, a semi-autobiographical musical for which he had rightly received superb reviews as he sang, danced, acted and mimed brilliantly. It was a veritable tour de force.

Tony and I loved dancing and gave constant parties at our house on Summit Drive.

Our romance took off fast as I was fascinated by his talent, quirky humour and saucy Cockney charm. He was two years older and about three inches taller than I was, with piercing navy-blue eyes, a shock of thick black hair and a wiry physique. He was as funny as hell with an outrageous, self-deprecating wit underneath which raged deep insecurity and a basic fear of women – but I didn't know that yet.

Newley had been a child actor, having made a big impact at fourteen as the Artful Dodger in David Lean's masterpiece, *Oliver Twist.* At the time I was a dedicated scrapbook-maker and had admired 'Young Master Newley' so I had stuck pictures of him into my vast movie-star scrapbook.

He then starred in the movie *Vice Versa* and soon became something of a teen idol in British films. Before *Stop the World – I Want to Get Off*, he also had an extremely successful pop singing career in the UK and was a rival of Tommy Steele.

Tony had been married previously and was still paying alimony to an ex-wife. He continued to do so years after we were divorced, another thing that probably added to his innate bitterness towards women. He admitted this in another autobiographical movie made in 1968, *Can Heironymus Merkin Ever Forget Mercy Humppe and Find True Happiness?*

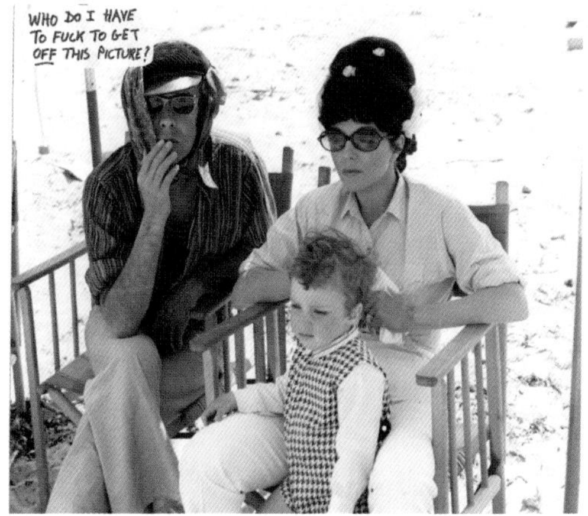

I captioned these pictures from 'Hieronymous' out of boredom and pretending not to notice Tony's flirtations.

During one little ditty he vocalized lewdly, 'Men are forever opening and stabbing the divine wound.' Tony's mother, Grace, was sweet and birdlike and clucked around him like a mother hen. She had given birth to him illegitimately in the 1930s when an out-of-wedlock child was an unforgivable scandal. Grace had told him often that she had tried to abort him, so understandably he had a total love/hate relationship with her, which tormented him throughout his adult life.

Although Tony soon professed abundant love for me, he also, by his own admission, had never been able to be faithful to one woman. How foolish of me not to have seen the warning signs here. He confided this to me during our stormy courtship, which took us from London to Los Angeles to New York and to Paris, where we were more often than not with our two best friends, the happily married Leslie Bricusse and his gorgeous actress wife, Yvonne Romain.

Leslie and Tony (or Brickman and Newberg as they christened themselves in homage to their idol and favourite director, Ingmar

Bergman) were the hottest young musical team in Britain and the year after Tony and I met they conquered that Everest of theatre: Broadway.

During one of Tony and my major spats, the Bricusses and I took off for a short break to Jamaica. Little did we realize how close we had come to never seeing civilization again as that was the time of the infamous Cuban Missile Crisis when newly elected President John F. Kennedy closed all the ports and airspace to the USA. But that was of little concern to me as I sulked on the beach wondering (accurately, as it turned out) with whom my Cockney lover was sleeping. My assumption was correct as some forty-five years later a woman purporting to be Tony's daughter attempted to contact my own daughter, Tara. As it turned out, since there was only three months difference in their dates of birth, my suspicions on that sunny day in Jamaica were correct. Another son, who also contacted my children recently, was apparently born shortly before Tony and I met. It seems he had quite a few children both in and out of wedlock, as he had two more after we divorced.

During our last argument in New York, he again admitted he didn't think he could be faithful and as I knew he was also having an affair with a young blonde in *Stop the World – I Want to Get Off*, I broke up with him. I started dating the handsome young actor Terence Stamp, a fact that soon hit the Manhattan tabloids.

As Mathew Mugg in Dr Doolittle Tony was at the top of his game whilst I was happy being a mother and playing house.

Tony was suddenly driven to extreme jealousy by what he considered his property dating a younger, more handsome guy. He started bombarding me with messages and flowers, even stalking me at various clubs and restaurants, but I stubbornly refused to meet him. Then one blustery November afternoon in Central Park, the day before I was leaving for London, Tony made a grand gesture. He apologized for his recalcitrance by 'popping the question'. He got down on one knee and proposed, and within a week we were playing Happy Young Marrieds in a lavish apartment on Sixty-third Street.

Now, I'm not stupid, but in terms of taking on board the subtext of what men are saying, I again exhibited the famous Collins Ostrich Syndrome. Tony admitted he didn't think he could be faithful but he also said 'I'll try, Flower, I'll really try.'

However, I got what I wanted: two beautiful babies within two years and although I was aware of Tony's still wandering eye, I was too happy being a wife, a homemaker and a mother to let it impinge on my consciousness.

I was even unfazed when I discovered a pert blonde perched on Tony's lap backstage, when I unexpectedly popped in to visit him during the 1965 Broadway run of *The Roar of Greasepaint – The Smell of the Crowd.* I was eight months pregnant with Sacha at the time so my hormones told me not to rock the boat.

At Jackie's wedding to Oscar Lerman. Little Tara was a flower girl.

PHOTO: HARRY BENSON

But once an actress, always an actress. When Tara was nearly one year old, I accepted my first movie role in two years. It was opposite Vittorio Gassman, one of Italy's top actors, and although I wasn't that keen to go to Italy, Tony persuaded me, saying it would be 'good for me' and I could take Tara and his mother!

BELOW: *The red hankie was one of Tony's signature looks.* BOTTOM: *He really loved his kids.*

I'm sure it was good for him too. He had been the toast of Broadway, he had a hit record; he was attractive and famous and he had a way with women that few could refuse. The saying 'when the cat's away' has much truth to it.

He and Leslie had been been working on *The Roar of the Greasepaint* while I was still in Italy. However, it was a failure so Tony went to London and stayed with Daddy and my teenaged brother, Bill, in our flat in Harley House. When I returned to London, the discothèque scene was in full swing and my father informed me that he'd heard Tony had been down to Dolly's and other saloons in the West End with 'scrubbers'. 'People are saying, "there he goes again"', said Daddy. He also told me that Tony often didn't come in until three or four in the morning and that 'girls were calling all the time'.

But when I confronted Tony with this, he said that these girls meant nothing to him and still vowed undying love.

At the end of 1965, just after Sacha was born, we moved to LA where Tony began a new career as a bona fide American movie star thanks to *Dr Dolittle*. We started seeing wonderful friends and giving great parties when we moved to our new house on Summit Drive in Beverly Hills.

But although he was now starring in movies like *Sweet November*, Tony became more and more reclusive. When he wasn't filming, he often hid in his lavish study, barely surfacing for meals and occasionally looking through me with disinterested eyes. The humour and fun were saved for parties and our friends Sammy Cahn, the Bricusses, Peter Sellers and Barbra Streisand.

Since our children had begun kindergarten and I had virtually given up my career, I decided to become madly social. I started attending dinners, parties and movie premieres with a variety of gay young men and living it up at discotheques where I would dance away the night, and my doubts about Tony.

OPPOSITE: *Our second baby, Alexander Newley was born at Mount Sinai hospital in New York.*

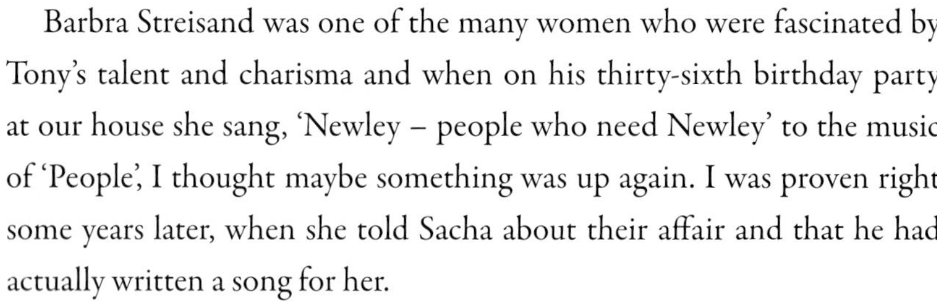

Barbra Streisand was one of the many women who were fascinated by Tony's talent and charisma and when on his thirty-sixth birthday party at our house she sang, 'Newley – people who need Newley' to the music of 'People', I thought maybe something was up again. I was proven right some years later, when she told Sacha about their affair and that he had actually written a song for her.

Then came the crunch. In Malta in 1968 Tony wrote, directed and starred in the notorious film, *Can Heironymus Merkin Ever Forget Mercy Humppe and Find True Happiness?* I played his long-suffering wife, tastefully named Polyester Poontang, in this epic, who watches resignedly as a host of women – some pretty and some pretty ugly – shared his bed.

Malta, 1968. Just before the end of my marriage. Looks like I can see the writing on the wall. I'm dressed as Polyester Poontang – a pretty tasteless name!

Naturally, I was not without sin here, as unable to curb Tony's womanizing, which was becoming more and more blatant, I had stepped out with a few guys myself. I became so much of a fixture at the Daisy Discotheque that Tony invested in a new disco called The Factory, 'so I know where Joan is at night,' he joked.

I realized that our marriage was really over when Universal gave me a private viewing of *Heironymus Merkin* and my eyes were opened properly for the first time in years; I saw my husband, in full technicolour almost naked, making love with and kissing a parade of women, none of whom meant anything to him. Even though we were married, he still couldn't fully commit and I finally saw that Tony really only cared for Tony.

So I took the children and went back to London.

And that was divorce number two!

I was thirty-five and definitely not wanting to get hitched again when I met Ronald S. Kass. With two failures under my belt, I sincerely believed I was not good marriage material, but I liked Ron and he certainly liked me. Very shortly after we met, introduced by the trendy tailor Doug Hayward in his shop in Mayfair's Mount Street, the tall, handsome American asked me to marry him. Since my divorce from Tony was not yet final and as Ron was still married to Anita, with three young sons under six, I felt that he was jumping the gun to say the least. But Ron was nothing if not insistent and we had much in common. I really enjoyed his company and he was one of the few people who matched my physical energy. He was able to stay up and dance and talk all night, then jump on a jet to Geneva or New York the next day. He was an Aries, the first sign of the zodiac, also known as the child sign, and he epitomized the best of the sign's characteristics. Aries the Ram is a fire sign which is extremely compatible with my air sign, Gemini: restless, impulsive and slightly hedonistic – ready for anything.

Ron was a terrific organizer, a get-up-and-go guy. At the time he was head of the Apple Corporation, The Beatles production company, and he was a graduate of UCLA Business School. He always knew what he wanted; and as the seventies dawned what he wanted was Joan Collins.

Ron Kass with Paul McCartney when he was running Apple records in London.

Ron was extremely ambitious and seemed to combine leadership with compassion. Running Apple was an extremely prestigious job. He had a huge office in The Beatles building at No. 3 Saville Row and regularly hung out with John, Ringo and Paul.

While I was still legally married to Tony, Ron and I saw each other on and off for a year, and he bombarded me with love, attention and proposals of marriage. I was torn. I had loved and lost Tony to a horde of other women and I was extremely scared of committing to Ron and having another failed marriage. But he was unrelenting in his pursuit and his protestations of total dedication and love for ever. A year passed and I still hadn't made up my mind to sign the final divorce papers because I knew how much it would hurt Tara and Sacha, who wanted to see their parents back together again.

Then one morning in LA, while Ron was on a trip to Rio, I awoke after a very realistic dream. I dreamed he was having an affair with a beautiful twenty-six-year-old South American girl. I hastily made the long-distance call to tell him about the dream and I couldn't believe it when he admitted he'd been seeing the girl I had imagined in my dream!

'But she means nothing,' he pleaded. 'It's you I want but you won't commit to me.'

After that call I thought seriously about my future. I was in my late thirties, ancient by movie-star standards, and even though I was getting some work in guest slots in television and was being called Queen of the Horror Flicks, I knew my days as a leading lady were numbered. I had two young children to clothe, feed, house and educate, and Tony was only giving me $1,250 a month to do all this and I received no alimony at all. It was not enough for the life they had become accustomed to.

OPPOSITE: *With my darling baby girl Katyana Kennedy Kass in my Sheldon Avenue bedroom, decorated in my favourite toile de jouy fabric, 1972.*

So what if I'd had two failed marriages? Elizabeth Taylor had managed three by my age. I'd take the plunge – I would marry this charming man who seemed to be the answer to a girl's dream. Soon after we married, my darling Katyana was born and the good times began. Katy was born in June 1972. Like me she was a Gemini and we always were and still are extremely close. The years between 1972 and 1975 were some of the happiest of my life.

When The Beatles broke up, Ron went on to become president of Warner Bros records in the UK and then turned to producing movies. We had a beautiful, large family house in Sheldon Avenue, Highgate, and I was the happiest of housewives and a doting mother.

Then the shit hit the fan: suddenly Mr Denis Healey, then Chancellor of the Exchequer, announced major tax increases for the rich.

Well, we weren't rich but we were certainly scared. The prospect of 80 per cent tax when we had six children between us to support was daunting to say the least. Very much against my will, Ron insisted we sell the house in Highgate, pack up all the kids and move back to the hills of Beverly again.

Ron was now partnered with Edgar Bronfman, the mega-rich head of Seagrams, the giant Canadian liquor company. Edgar wanted to be in the film business and he wanted Ron with him, so they formed a company called Sagittarius Films. Edgar even became Katy's godfather.

But alas, Edgar Bronfman turned out not to be the knight in shining armour Ron thought he was.

The day after we threw a fabulous twenty-first birthday for his son Efer, as we called Edgar Jr, Edgar Bronfman fired Ron.

What girl could resist this?!

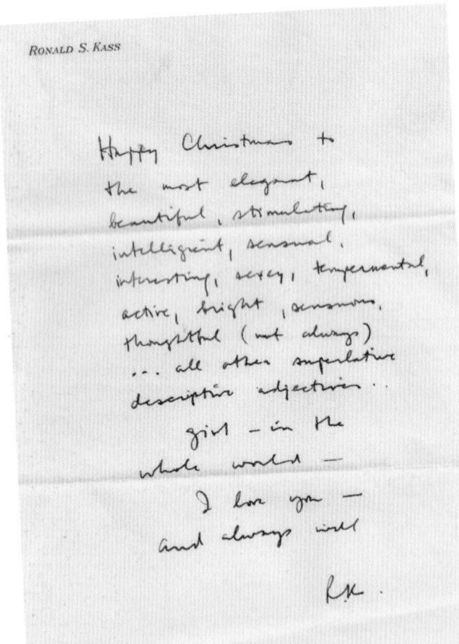

RONALD S. KASS

Happy Christmas to
the most elegant,
beautiful, stimulating,
intelligent, sensual,
interesting, sexy, temperamental,
active, bright, sensuous,
thoughtful (not always)
... all other superlative
descriptive adjectives.
girl – in the
whole world –
I love you –
and always will

R.K.

Oh happy day – I hoped. Marriage #3 to Ron Kass, Jamaica, 1972.

I had pulled out all the stops to organize the party, so the star-studded guest list was mostly my Hollywood friends – Kirk Douglas, Billy Wilder, Dione Warwick, George Segal, David Janssen and many more luminaries helped blow out the twenty-one candles, even though most of them had never met Junior.

Losing his job was such a huge blow to Ron that his ego suffered massively. He had adored Edgar, not to mention his lifestyle – private jets, villas in Acapulco, five-star hotels in the south of France. He became terribly upset and uncommunicative and, as he was out of work, the burden fell upon me to support six children and ourselves.

That is when I believe that Ron started taking drugs. He was hanging out with a rather louche bunch, many of whom worked behind the scenes in the music business. We then began a nomadic existence to support our lifestyle. We had to keep selling our houses in order to live on the profits. We sold Chalette Drive with the tennis court and huge swimming pool and bought Carolyn Way with its smaller pool and a little pond with goldfish. Then we had to sell that to buy an even cheaper house on Bowmont Drive. No tennis court, a tiny pool and a little backyard.

We still went back and forth to London where Ron had kept his charming rented house on South Street in Mayfair. In fact, we kept up a great 'front'. We spent money. I don't know *how* we did or where we got it, but we did it.

In spite of his shock over the demise of his collaboration with Bronfman, Ron threw himself into producing.

After *The Optimists* with Peter Sellers, in which our baby daughter, Katy, had a tiny role, he produced *Melody* in conjunction with David Puttnam. Then he obtained the rights to the Noël Coward play *Fallen Angels* and produced it for Anglia TV with Susannah York and me in the lead roles.

For my fortieth birthday – everyone had to go in 1920s costume.

But by 1978 Ron and I were rowing a lot – usually about money. He felt I didn't pay enough attention to him and that I was more interested in my children, my friends and my career. Well, quite frankly, at that time they *were* more interesting. Ron had changed from being a fun-loving and energetic man to an angry, gloomy person. And the drugs were taking their toll on his personality, his looks and our bank account.

The night before the axe fell. Edgar Bronfman, his wife Georgiana (who's since married Nigel Havers), the Kass-Newley clan, Edgar Jr and his girlfriend.

Licking the bowl of my chocolate mousse, with my brood in the kitchen of Sheldon Avenue.

Ron had started getting up from the table when we were at restaurants with friends. He would sit morosely for twenty minutes then leave the table. He would then return ten minutes later and join the conversation with great animation.

I didn't realize for some time that these bouts of Jekyll and Hyde behaviour were because he had started to use cocaine – but I started to suspect after I discovered a cache.

When I finally confronted him, we had a furious, name-calling row. He denied absolutely that he was using and told me I was paranoid to even think it and that the cocaine had been planted by someone 'out to get him'.

Things really came to a head in the late seventies when he co-produced *The Stud* and *The Bitch* with Jackie's husband, Oscar Lerman. He wanted me to appear almost naked in some scenes in *The Stud*, which I didn't want to do.

We argued and argued and had vicious rows. He ignored all the kids except Katy, and he started taking more and more cocaine, while still insisting that he was clean.

By the time our beloved eight-year-old Katy had a terrible car accident and lay in intensive care in a coma for six weeks, our marriage was on the rocks. Constant, jealous fights and arguments about money had eroded what love I had felt for him. Ron was quite profligate. He thought nothing of spending hundreds of pounds having expensive stationery printed with his company's name when I was scrimping on buying new shoes for the kids. Then I shut him out physically which, of course, infuriated him more.

Whilst Katy was recovering at home on South Street with an army of nannies, physiotherapists and healers around her, I went back to the West End in *The Last of Mrs Cheyney*, which Ron produced with Duncan Weldon because we desperately needed the money.

ABOVE: *I made a series of extremely popular commercials for Cinzano with Leonard Rossiter. One of the least known was this of the skating disaster. Katy came to watch.*

The play was quite successful, but when I asked the company manager one weekend for a small advance, he sheepishly informed me that all my salary had to go to Ron. 'That's what he insisted on,' he said.

Then one afternoon my brother Bill found a ton of unpaid bills in a drawer in Ron's desk plus dozens of bank statements revealing that we were in debt with a joint overdraft of £155,000! I was absolutely devastated as I hadn't bought anything but food and medicine for months! I confronted my bank manager, Stuart Wells of Coutts, who showed me my signature on the overdraft document.

'But that's a forgery.' I said. 'It's not my writing at all.'

'I'm sorry, Joan,' said Stuart ruefully, 'but he brought these papers in a year ago and swore you'd signed them.'

I tried to confront Ron but he was now living in a kind of vacuum, only coming alive around Katy, whose recovery was our main concern. He finally admitted that he had graduated to taking heroin but insisted he was going to an acupuncturist to get cured.

I was still performing eight times a week in *Mrs Cheney* and as sole breadwinner I begged Ron to go to LA to sell or at least rent our Bowmont house and deal with the dozens of creditors who had surfaced there. He refused with various lame excuses so as soon as the play closed I flew to LA to face the music. Once there I found our car had been impounded along with our TV and some appliances. There were more piles of unpaid bills and people were calling all the time to be paid for things they had done, including our cleaning lady and the gardener. It was a nightmare.

BELOW: *My precious Katy.*

Bowmont Drive, 1979. Putting on a brave face in spite of the baliffs banging down the door.

Ron's 'live-now, pay-later' attitude was ruining us. I had trusted him and he betrayed my trust. Many of my friends had asked me if Ron was taking drugs but I had always said no. I was saving face and hoping to save my marriage but I knew that would only happen if Ron quit the drugs and got a proper job. We went to counsellors, marriage specialists and psychiatrists to no avail.

By the time *Dynasty* came to save my life and my career at the beginning of 1982, ours was a marriage in name only. It was a shell, a sham – a pretence that we kept up just for the sake of Katy's welfare – and so we spent two years living in the same dark flat in Century City. I had managed to rent out Bowmont. Our bad marriage dragged on.

Still out of work, Ron was 'deteriorating', as one of our many counsellors and doctors told me. He was still lying about his drug taking and had developed an obsessive love/hate relationship with me. He constantly wrote me notes filled with vitriol or love and even had me followed by a detective, convinced that I was having affairs. Not much chance with *Dynasty* taking up most of my days and the rest of the time devoted to an essentially fatherless Katy.

Although there was huge interest in me due to *Dynasty*, my personal and financial life was in ruins. Coutts sued me for the £150,000 debt Ron had run up by forging my signature.

I couldn't risk Ron compromising my life again, and Katy's future, so I finally insisted on a legal separation and moved back into Bowmont Drive, which had by now become vacant again. The judge said I had to give Ron $5,000 a month temporary spousal support, plus I had to pay the rent on his LA apartment. Once again, I was forking out for a man!

With the eyes of the world on the popular character of Alexis, Ron then sold 'intimate' secrets of 'Life with Alexis', as he now liked to call me, to a British Sunday rag. I was completely appalled by the so-called revelations and only glad that ten-year-old Katy was too young to see them. His act was tawdry and sleazy in the extreme and it finally made me see the light.

ABOVE: *Katy well on the road to recovery.*

I was extremely sad that such an intelligent and ambitious man had ruined his life, and almost ruined mine, by taking drugs. At first it had been marijuana – 'Not habit forming,' he'd said – then cocaine and finally a filthy substance called heroin. My heart bleeds for anyone who has a

BELOW: *With my girls receiving a Variety Club award, 1999.*

Smiling through yet another breakup.

partner who is addicted to these substances, as unless they are aware of their addiction and resolve to give up, there is little hope for them.

My third marriage had failed and it was time to end it. So, that was divorce number three!

If I thought I'd had troubles with my previous three husbands they paled in comparison to 'The Swede', a mixture of obdurate dullard and calculating sociopath.

As is the case with many men of this ilk, he cleverly concealed that side of himself when we first met. Peter Holm was charm and good looks incarnate as he sat beside the swimming pool at my friends' Jeffrey and Madeleine Curtis's house in Datchet, Berkshire, gently strumming a guitar with a guileless smile on his suntanned face.

I guess I'd always been a sucker for a good-looking guy, which he certainly was: tall with blond hair and blue eyes – all the attributes for which the Swedish race are known. Think a male version of Britt Ekland. But beauty is only skin deep, as my dear old grandma used to say, and boy was she right in this case.

A whirlwind courtship began almost immediately as Peter Holm followed me back to Hollywood a few weeks after we met. I was riding high in the popularity charts with my role in *Dynasty*. There were magazine shoots practically every weekend, endless interviews, trips to exotic places and gifts galore from top designers. I was flavour of the month but fortunately, having been 'at this rodeo' before, I was down-to-earth enough to know it couldn't last. The adulation might have gone to some actresses' heads but it didn't to mine. I was still smarting from the final, unhappy years with Ron and trying to deal with my financial affairs, which were still in an absolute turmoil.

Although I was earning good money – about $40,000 an episode – nothing stayed in the bank. I was still trying to get out from under the debts Ron had run up, I had three children to support, including eleven-year-old Katy who was still recovering from her accident.

When Peter came to stay with me at my Bowmont Drive house he soon became aware of my financial problems. I had business managers, lawyers, accountants, an ex-husband to support, a live-in couple, a press agent, a secretary and a secretary for the secretary! Money was haemorrhaging out as fast as it came in and I was totally overwhelmed. Never being savvy with financial matters, I was good at earning it, great at spending it, but hopeless in between.

Peter then made a clever move. He started to advise me in business matters. He was extremely tough and hard in dealing with people – I think his idol was Donald Trump – and within a matter of months he had started to clear the decks of many of my unnecessary hangers-on.

He was the smoothest of smooth con men: charming, self-effacing and seeming to be highly knowledgeable about financial matters. Having been a pop star in Sweden for about ten minutes, he regaled me with anecdotes about how he too had been ripped off by his advisers. 'I don't vant to see this happening to you, sveetie,' he would say over and over again.

As I was working twelve hours a day with weekends given over to Katy, finding and fitting new outfits for *Dynasty* and doing publicity, his constant (but subtle) badgering finally worked. Eventually I told him that he seemed confident and able enough to handle my business affairs. All of a sudden I was earning much more money. I made a perfume commercial for a scent called Scoundrel for Revlon, I had a line of hats, a line of lingerie, a line of eyewear, I wrote several books and, in my hiatus from *Dynasty*, appeared in movies of the week and guest slots.

Las Vegas, 1986. Fourth time unlucky.

'The Swede' soon proposed but I had absolutely no intention of ever marrying again. Peter had no rapport at all with twelve-year-old Katy; in fact, he barely spoke to her. He was jealous and combative with twenty-two-year-old Robert Kass, who was also living with me, to such an extent that one day he threw him out of the house and told him to never return.

Tara and Sacha were now both living mostly in London so they hardly saw Peter but when they did there was little communication, and it was the same with my friends. None of them liked him. He made no effort at conversation because he had no interest in anything except himself, his car, his computer and, as I eventually found out when the rose-tinted spectacles fell from my eyes, my money.

In the early halcyon days of romance, his constant demands for marriage were both irritating and flattering. Later, he nagged me incessantly, and threatened to leave me if we didn't tie the knot. When I reiterated I wouldn't marry him he often sulked and would sometimes disappear for days too. 'You treat me like a dog, sveetie – look at all the money I've made for you in the last year.'

That was true or at least it seemed to be true. Several times a week he insisted I sit and absorb the figures on his computer, which spat out the balance sheets of all the money I had accumulated 'because of me, sveetie – you couldn't have done it without me'. It certainly looked impressive. This was first time I had earned big money in my life and it kept on growing. 'It's all because of me, sveetie,' Peter kept repeating, 'and if I'm not here you'll just go back to your old ways and those parasites who just take, take, take from you.'

He'd also fired my agents, the prestigious William Morris agency – a very bad mistake as I discovered later. 'You're so famous, sveetie – you don't need any of those parasites. If people want you they'll come to *me*.' How utterly stupid I was.

The Swede and I on the town at an event attended by Prince Charles and Princess Diana.

He ultimately wore me down. After Peter had negotiated a hefty salary for me as both producer and star in the mini-series *Sins* – although as this was the time of my apogee I doubt a monkey could have done worse – I finally threw caution to the wind. We married in a secret ceremony in Las Vegas in 1985, but only after I extracted a prenuptial agreement. With my best friend Judy Bryer was my reluctant maid of honour, her husband Max gave me away and Eddie Sanderson took the pictures. When Peter and I went to London ten days after our wedding he refused to let the paparazzi take a photo of us together at the airport and stalked ahead of me, snarling, 'She's the star, take her.'

Working harder than ever with *Dynasty*, *Sins* and all my other projects to promote, and trying to spend as much time as I could with Katy, I didn't give much thought to what Mr Holm was doing during the day at home in Bowmont Drive. I suspected (and finally discovered my suspicions were correct) that he had been bringing girls back to my house. When I

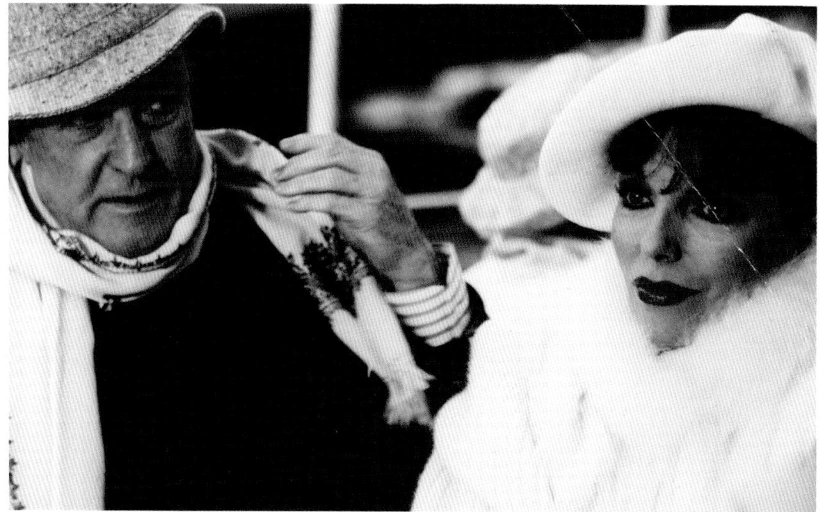

During a trip down the Seine on Sins, *Gene Kelly and I both wore wigs. A gust of wind almost blew them into the water so Wardrobe found us a couple of hats to keep the wigs from blowing off!*

wondered out loud if some of the outfits in my wardrobe had been moved or even worn, he simply scoffed, calling me paranoid. While Alexis's husband Dex was screwing her daughter on the set, 'The Swede' was at his little home office screwing everyone in a skirt!

And Peter soon had a bigger office. With the success of *Sins*, which we filmed in the south of France, he insisted we buy a grand, gorgeous, massive house off Coldwater Canyon, back on Cabrillo Drive. I thought it was far too big but Peter insisted that as I was such a big star now I should live like one.

And so I did. The house, which was previously owned by my friend Laurence Harvey, was a massive movie-star palace. My dressing room was the size of a large boutique and I had my own gym, a jacuzzi, a guesthouse and a bar facing an aquarium filled with tropical fish.

Peter Holm installed a state-of-the-art office, which only he was allowed to enter and had a special triple mechanism lock made for it. All my files and records were kept there and if I wanted to see the state of my finances, I had to ask permission. Peter's rules became ridiculous. No one was allowed to use a certain phone in the house, which was only for him. And whenever we had fights and I would get upset, he would laugh and sneer, sarcastically saying, 'If only people could see the great Alexis now. What a pathetic cry baby!'

Most people who met Peter now disliked him on sight. His arrogance, brusqueness and pig-headedness made him totally anti-social. I realized how much of a sociopath he was when he screamed at our maid one day

L.A., 1987. Judy Bryer and I celebrating the end of my marriage to the Swede.

The British cartoonists had a field day with our messy divorce.

and fired her immediately because he felt she hadn't cleaned the kitchen well enough.

I now took to staying late at the studio and having lots of headaches at night. Katy, now recovered and old enough to go to boarding school, wanted to go back to London and be closer to Tara and Sacha anyway, and I knew she'd be better off not being around this man. He had turned into a terrifying fiend – angry, sulky and incredibly rude – and it was scary.

In exchange for making me good business deals and investing well, I had agreed to pay him 20 per cent of what I earned; these were my highest earning years, and only after eight months of marriage I realized Peter had made himself close to a million dollars.

Then one day, in a classic movie scenario, I came home from work early and discovered him in our bed with another woman!

When I exploded and demanded how he could do this to me, he laughed and said I was just acting. When I said I wanted to end our marriage and get an immediate annulment, he flew into an obsessive rage. 'I love you so much I won't live without you,' he spouted. What a lie. I was finding out that he lied about everything. How sad that so many of my husbands could lie so convincingly.

I started withholding his commission cheques and he told our accountant, 'If she won't give me back those cheques I'll file for divorce and I'll get every penny I can from her. I'll get more than anyone ever has.

I'll go to the *Enquirer* and tell them stories. I don't give a shit – everyone will believe me and then I'll sue the ass off the Joan/Alexis.' I felt helpless and trapped. I was working fourteen-hour days. I was famous but I was a wreck.

One day my friend Dyan Cannon said, when I confided in her, 'Shine a light into the darkest corner of your relationship and see what you find.' When I finally did look, I realized how I'd allowed Peter to worm his way in and totally control my life. It was my own fault since I had allowed him to get away with it.

When the pre-divorce proceedings started Peter spent hours a day reading law journals. He told my friend Mallory Jones, 'I'd rather end up ruined and in the mud as long as I can drag her down with me. And I intend to do that if it takes me every last breath and every last penny.'

I realized our marriage had just been sham to him. I had been his meal ticket. How could I have been so hoodwinked, so utterly stupid? Of course, the fact he never asked for a penny during the first year of our relationship, and kept telling me to check up on him, allowed me to trust him and he was then extremely charming, affectionate and amusing to be with (or at least with me).

HOW PETER & HIS PASSION FLOWER CHEATED ON JOAN COLLINS

—and how he schemed to rip off her $millions

Collins Granted Divorce From Holm

Chronicle Wire Services

Los Angeles

A judge granted "Dynasty" star Joan Collins a divorce from Swedish businessman Peter Holm yesterday, and the sultry actress jubilantly exclaimed, "I don't want any more husbands."

"I don't need a husband. I need a wife," Collins, 54, joked after Superior Court Judge Kenneth Black dissolved her fourth marriage because of "irreconcilable differences."

Asked for her views on Holm, Collins declared: "I think he is a bit of a loser.

"I feel nothing but relief, I am very happy, and now I want to get on with my life," said Collins, who was wearing a long white, broad-shouldered jacket over a miniskirt.

During the brief hearing, Black asked Collins whether there were still irreconcilable differences between herself and Holm. "Yes," Collins replied.

"Will a delay save your marriage?" Black asked.

"No," she said.

"A dissolution is granted," Black declared, and then left the bench.

The British actress sued Holm for a divorce last December, 13 months after they married, citing irreconcilable differences and alleged fraud.

Collins' attorney, Marvin Mitchelson, predicted Holm will be denied the $80,000 a month he has requested in spousal support.

Holm, 40, was not present at the hearing. But his lawyer, Stephen Drucker, said his client may still win retroactive temporary spousal support at a hearing October 7.

Holm will also try to claim 20 percent of Collins' $5 million earnings during the 13-month marriage, Drucker said. Mitchelson claims Holm has already received the more than $1 million due him.

Collins went through her first divorce in 1956 when she shed her first husband, actor Maxwell Reed. She married singer-composer Anthony Newley in 1963 and the couple had two children before divorcing in 1972.

Collins' third marriage in 1972 to music producer Ron Kass produced a daughter before it ended in divorce.

So did the tabloids…

The divorce proceedings in 1987 took five days and were so filled with drama they made *Dynasty* look like *Little House on the Prairie.* Peter's long-term mistress, the one I had caught him in bed with and who was ridiculously nicknamed Passion Flower, took to the stand and histrionically fainted, which made all the papers, the nightly news and *People* magazine. Peter was desperate to prove the prenuptual agreement was invalid so that according to California law he had the right to half of everything.

The court case dragged bitterly on until finally the judge said our prenuptial agreement was valid, granted me the divorce on irreconcilable differences and allowed 'The Swede' only $80,000 in compensation. 'He's already taken enough off you' he intoned drily. Regardless, I still felt I got off cheaply.

And that was divorce number four!

I first set eyes on Percy Gibson in April 2000 in New York City.

I was doing a book signing at Rizzoli's, the high-end bookstore, preparatory to going to San Francisco to start a short tour of the two-hander play, *Love Letters*. Although I was only fifteen minutes late for the 6 p.m. start of the signing, I was disappointed to learn that Paul Newman and Joanne Woodward, two of my oldest friends, had popped in at six on the dot and I had just missed them. Since the Newmans were not only show-business royalty, but also adorably nice, I was sad to have missed them.

After half an hour of signing, Jeffrey Lane, my press agent, said there were two young men from the *Love Letters* company who wanted to meet me. In the corner, next to the psychology section, stood two good-looking guys in their thirties. I greeted Max Torres, the stage manager, and then shook hands with Percy Gibson. He was tall, dark-eyed, handsome and well-dressed, with good shoes and shirt but sporting a rather unfortunate mustard-coloured jacket! I thought he was American, and I also thought that he would be better looking if he let his dark hair grow a trifle longer as he had almost a crew cut, never my favourite look. But he was extremely attractive and had a wonderfully endearing smile.

'You look awfully young,' I remarked to Max, who looked rather like Matt Damon.

'How about me?' asked Percy.

'Oh, you'll do,' I smiled.

'Good,' he smiled back endearingly. 'How are you liking your hotel?'

'It's the *pits*,' I said. 'The bedroom's the size of a dartboard, there's no closet space and no room service either. I can't even order coffee in the morning.'

My favourite picture of Percy.

'I'm so sorry,' Percy seemed genuinely concerned, 'I'd been told you were happy there . . .'

'We'd better get back to the signing,' interrupted my press agent, grabbing my arm hastily and whisking me back to a queue of eager book-buyers.

'Bye guys, I'll see you in San Francisco,' I said.

The Phillips Club, where I was staying, was indeed totally unsuitable for what I was doing – promotion and publicity for *Love Letters* and my book. This involved several media events every day, so I needed many changes of photogenic outfits and, since there

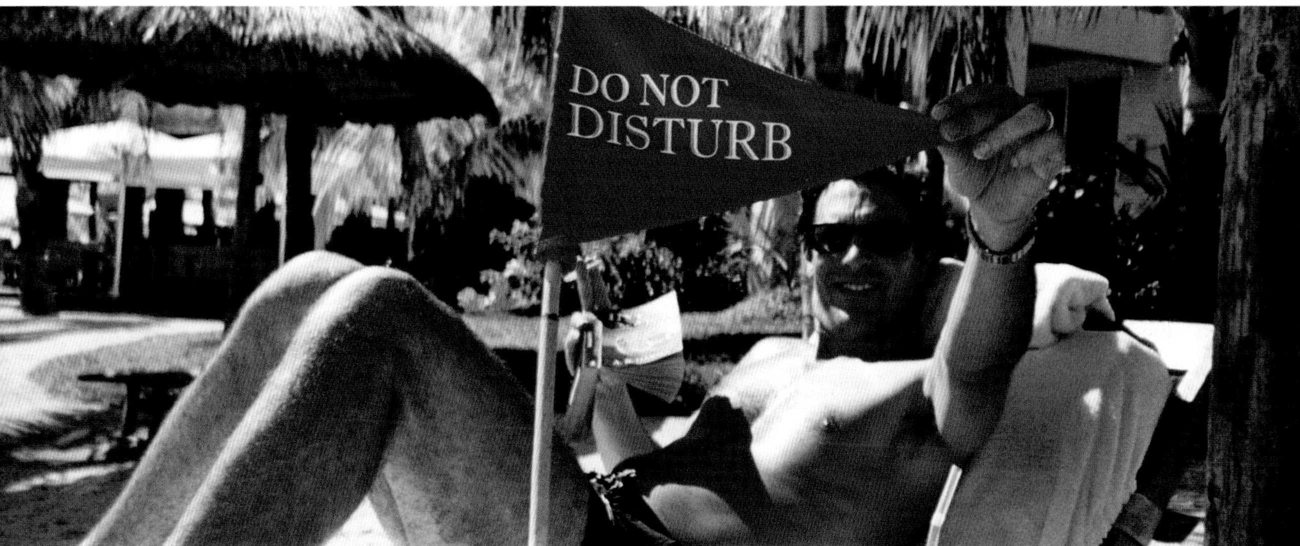

On our honeymoon in Malaysia, 2002.

was no room to swing the proverbial cat at the Phillips let alone see yourself in a full-length mirror, I was understandably frustrated.

'Of course, Diahann would never have stood for this sort of accommodation,' teased Jeffrey, somewhat undiplomatically, the next morning as we were crossing the George Washington Bridge to yet another TV interview. Diahann Carroll was one of his clients and my friend from *Dynasty* days. We had great fun being the politically incorrect 'black bitch' and 'white bitch', slapping each other's faces and screaming insults to each other, to the amusement of the crew.

'She's very insistent on only being treated like a star,' he continued.

'Why didn't you tell the producer's people – that Percy guy we met – that I wasn't happy in the suite?'

'I did, but they said there was nothing they could do about it now.'

'Never mind.' I leaned against the cool leather of the limo and gazed down at the tumbling iridescent river. 'I'll be in San Francisco in a couple of days. I hope the accommodation is better there.'

Katy and I were met at San Francisco airport by Percy (still wearing the mustard jacket!) and Charles Duggan, the producer of *Love Letters* – a great friend who had also produced my US tour of *Private Lives*. We chatted happily in the car and I gently admonished Charles about the fact that he wouldn't let me change my hotel in New York.

'That's not true,' said Percy. 'I called your press agent several times to see if you were happy there, and each time he said you were fine.'

The first time we 'stepped out' together at the GLAAD Awards in New York in 2000. Does he look tense or what?

He looked quite concerned, and Charles piped up, 'I heard him telling that to Jeffrey on the phone.'

'Well, never mind.' I smiled at Percy, whose concern and sincerity were touching.

'We hope you'll like this one.' He smiled back beguilingly.

December, 2001. Outside my London flat the day we announced our engagement.

The hotel was fine – simple, spacious and close to the theatre. Contrary to some people's opinions, I don't go for the overdone and over-decorated deluxe suites and prefer more homey surroundings, especially since Katy was my companion on this tour. So the two-bedroom suite with a little kitchenette to make coffee and breakfast was perfectly okay. The kitchen had been stocked with groceries, cookies and wine, and my favourite Casablanca lilies were on the table, as were the English newspapers, which Percy had found out I liked to read every morning.

'He is so considerate,' I remarked to Katy, as we unpacked. 'And cute, too!' she giggled.

The two-week stint with George Hamilton as my co-star at the Marines Memorial Theatre in San Francisco sped by. George is one of the funniest and most amusingly self-deprecating of actors. Backstage at the interval, Percy, Max, Katy and I would be in fits of laughter as George regaled us with his endless supply of anecdotes and jokes, and more seriously his exceptional knowledge of all things medical. How he kept his tan during those cold April month I'll never know, but keep it he did.

Love Letters is a light, two-handed play in which the actors are seated next to each other at a table, reading their love letters from one another from the time they were teenagers until the death of my character, Melissa. There were some sweet laughs, but audiences usually went to the touring show just because they had been told that it's amusing and because many famous names had performed in it all over the US – Charlton Heston and his wife Lydia, Robert Wagner and Jill St John, Larry Hagman and Linda Gray, Jessica Tandy and Hume Cronyn, and Uncle Tom Cobley and all had played often to packed houses. The actors liked it because they didn't have to learn lines and there were minimum rehearsals (one day for us). It was an easy gig and a quick way to pick up a few bucks.

On our first matinee, George, Percy and I were sitting backstage at the interval lamenting the lack of audience laughter.

'You know why they're not laughing,' I said, gloomily, 'because this play's *not* fucking funny!'

Percy laughed uproariously at this and later told me that he thought that I was very funny and quite adorable. (The feeling was becoming mutual.) As the tour continued, it became clear that we were very compatible and Katy absolutely adored him.

During the run in San Francisco, George was dating the novelist Danielle Steel, who lived there, so Katy, Max, Percy and I usually went out to dinner together after the show. As often happens on theatrical tours, we all bonded together like a family and exchanged many confidences.

Percy Michael Jorge Gibson was born in Lima, Peru, to a Peruvian father who was fifty-five at the time (and whose great grandfather was Scottish – hence the surname) and a Scottish mother, Bridget Monahan, a schoolteacher who was forty-two. Theirs was a tempestuous yet loving relationship, for Bridget was feisty and opinionated and Jorge was the typical South American macho man – the boss and the breadwinner with a temper and a touch of chauvinism thrown in. In this respect he would not have been unlike my own father, a strict, hot-tempered, Jewish chauvinist born in 1902, just a few years before Jorge Gibson.

We love being in the South of France. We're each other's best friend, accomplice and we always make each other laugh.

So Percy and I had much in common, for our fathers were of the same strict intransigent generation. There were more than thirty years between Percy and me, but that didn't matter one whit as the camaraderie between us flourished on tour.

After two weeks, George left the company and in San Diego Stacy Keach joined us to play the male lead. As is common on tours, heavy press duty was required upon arrival at each town. Often, I had to rise at dawn to prepare for early morning talk shows. The first morning in San Diego, bleary-eyed and with badly applied makeup, I stumbled into the lobby to meet Stacy with the local press agent.

There, to my surprise and delight, sat Percy, who had not only long ago ditched the mustard jacket for a cool-looking navy blazer but was offering us two containers of steaming Starbucks latte. 'It was too early for room service, so I got you a latte. I know you like it with four sugars.'

'You didn't have to do that,' I said, thrilled by his thoughtfulness. 'You don't have to be here.'

'I know, but I just want to make you happy,' he smiled.

I felt a great wave of warmth for this handsome young man who was so completely dedicated to his job and to making his stars feel good; quite unlike most company managers I had known.

'He's the best company manager I've ever worked with,' said Stacy. 'Percy always goes above and beyond the call of duty and that's rare in our business.'

At one of these press events, I realized I'd run out of eyeliner. 'I'll get you some,' offered Percy. When he returned I opened the package to find a mascara wand.

Percy in his LA office.

'Isn't that it?' he asked, a bit confused.

'No,' I smiled, 'I guess you're not gay.'

'Afraid not,' he smiled back.

And that, as Claude Rains said to Humphrey Bogart in *Casablanca*, was the beginning of a beautiful friendship.

Percy had been legally separated for a year after an eight-year marriage. In his generosity he had let his ex-wife have their New York apartment and furniture. He had then taken a sabbatical to look after his mother in Glasgow. She had been taken ill and he had seen that she was settled in a home for Alzheimer's patients before returning to New York. He had been working in theatre since college after he left Peru, and was a very well-respected company manager who had worked on many New York shows.

Although Percy was not seriously involved with anyone at that time, I was in a relationship with the art dealer, Robin Hurlstone, which was frankly going nowhere. As our tour continued in Houston, Phoenix and Austin, Percy and I became so close that I started

In our New York bedroom – there's that green toile de jouy again!

calling him my 'Latin from Manhattan'. In Austin, Texas, we dined one night with our producer, Charles Duggan, Stacy and some other friends, and Michael Caine joined us for coffee. He was shooting the movie *Miss Congeniality* with Sandra Bullock and was in fine, funny fettle. Percy, Charles and I were limp and exhausted with laughter as Michael, in his inimitable deadpan way, told us anecdote after anecdote. Afterwards Michael said, 'That Percy is a really nice young man.' And I was realizing that, more and more, he was becoming more than just nice.

After the tour ended a series of coincidences occurred – it seemed that every time I was in any city, Percy was also there. When I was in London he was en route to visit his ailing mother in Glasgow; when I went to New York to film a commercial he was in rehearsals with Jean Stapleton for *Eleanor*. I wanted to see some theatre, so we went to see *Kiss Me, Kate* together, one of the most romantic stage musicals, at the Martin Beck Theatre, directed by Michael Blakemore. When the Broadway stars Marin Mazzie and Brian Stokes Mitchell each sang 'So in Love', Percy's and my eyes met and I felt the sort of butterfly frisson in my stomach I hadn't felt for years. He looked into my eyes and I looked into his and we just knew that there was something more to our relationship than just friendship.

Yet because he was so much younger than I was, I knew I shouldn't consider those thoughts. I knew Percy found me attractive, as many a long night on tour we had talked and philosophized about life and our feelings. As a South American Latin male he had none of the hang-ups that North American and British men have about age. 'If a woman is beautiful, it doesn't matter if she's sixteen or sixty,' he told me. Well, I was firmly in the second category and he was only thirty-four but by now I liked him enormously and was extremely attracted to him.

In August 2000 I started rehearsing a musical movie musical in LA, *These Old Broads*, with Elizabeth Taylor, Shirley MacLaine and Debbie Reynolds. It was huge fun but hard work as I had to learn several musical numbers with Debbie and Shirley, who were both professional hoofers, which I was not.

And who should be in LA at that time, company managing *Eleanor* at the Canon Theatre, but Percy. He visited me on the *These Old Broads* set, and we often had lunch or dinner together and went to a couple of parties. My single girlfriends thought he was very sexy and quite adorable.

Wedding bliss – fifth time lucky! With Tara, Sacha and Miel.

'Does he have a brother?' several of them asked.

'Unfortunately not; they broke the mould when they made him,' I would reply, laughing. Actually, I wanted to keep him to myself because I knew the truth: I was falling hard for Percy Michael Jorge Gibson.

In January 2001 I was still renting an apartment at the Sierra Towers, a ritzy building on Sunset Boulevard, and desperately trying to finish my fourth novel, *Star Quality*. Since I had not yet entered the twenty-first century in terms of computers (I couldn't even type and still am one-fingered when I text or email), all my manuscripts were written in longhand, so had to be typed and printed. The woman who usually did this for me in LA was not available and I was frantically trying to find someone who could decipher my hieroglyphics when Percy suggested that he could easily do it. Every day he came to the apartment at ten o'clock and while I wrote he transferred everything to my computer.

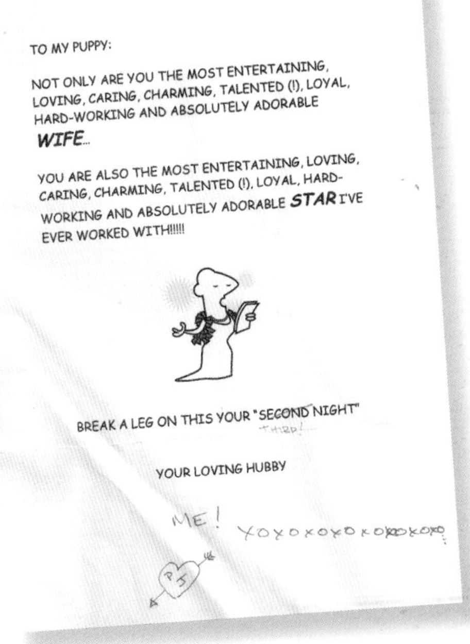

TO MY PUPPY:

NOT ONLY ARE YOU THE MOST ENTERTAINING, LOVING, CARING, CHARMING, TALENTED (!), LOYAL, HARD-WORKING AND ABSOLUTELY ADORABLE **WIFE**...

YOU ARE ALSO THE MOST ENTERTAINING, LOVING, CARING, CHARMING, TALENTED (!), LOYAL, HARD-WORKING AND ABSOLUTELY ADORABLE **STAR** I'VE EVER WORKED WITH!!!!!

BREAK A LEG ON THIS YOUR "~~SECOND~~ THIRD! NIGHT"

YOUR LOVING HUBBY

ME! XOXOXOXOXOXOXOXO

P J

Percy loves sending me funny love notes.

I had appeared in an episode of *Will and Grace* a couple of years back and they wanted me to do another one but they wouldn't send me the script, although the start date was imminent. Eventually the script arrived two nights before the first table read and it was dire. I'd wanted to do *Will and Grace* because it was a terrific show and I'd enjoyed the last one but to play a woman who insists on having an operation to get her shoulders extended by eight inches was frankly ludicrous. 'I can't do this,' I wailed to my agent, Alan Nevins. 'They want me to play a woman who gets a shoulder transplant, for God's sake. It's utterly ridiculous, but I want to do the show. Do you think they'll rewrite it?'

Alan spent a morning of fevered talks with the *Will and Grace* producers but they flatly refused. The gist of the conversations with Alan was, 'Who does Joan Collins think she is? She's not doing *Dynasty* anymore and we're a hit show. We're hot and she's not. Tell her we won't rewrite and she's gotta do it the way it is.' When Alan told me on the phone I became extremely upset and broke down in tears. Mercifully Percy was there with a tender shoulder to cry on. Before we knew it we were in each other's arms and what we had both been thinking about for the past seven months finally happened. It was the moment I always felt would occur one day and it was just wonderful.

So now I was having a fully fledged passionate affair with Percy, who was quite honestly sweeping me off my feet. It was giddy, it was fantastic, it was all the romantic fairy tales that young girls dream about, but I was *not* a young girl. I was a woman in her sixties in love with a man in his thirties. We tried to keep it a secret, but a few of my friends started to suspect as we both had that heady glow that comes from being in love. He was the best lover I had ever had and I knew that the kind of passion we had for each other was terribly special – truly once in a lifetime.

Having fun at Destino. My two girls adore Percy and he them.

By now Robin Hurlstone was eager to visit me in LA, even though his mother was still not well, but I kept putting him off. I had the perfect excuse in my looming deadline for *Star Quality*, so I told him I

I love buying Percy flamboyant shirts ever since a journalist once observed he looked 'effortlessly masculine' in them!

was writing morning, noon and night and that Percy was putting it all on the computer for me. But Robin decided to come anyway. I was in a frightful bind. Should I tell him before he flew to LA? Should I wait until he arrived? Should I not tell him at all and continue the deception? He solved it anyway. He and Charles Duggan flew out to surprise me. They had only told me the day before that they were coming, so I was in a state of high anxiety.

The night they arrived Nolan Miller had a screening of an early print of *These Old Broads* for twenty of our friends at his LA apartment. Robin and Charles came, as did Percy. It was an interesting evening, to say the least, particularly when the two first met and sized each other up and I sensed that male feeling of two stags at bay. I was completely agitated as I tried to concentrate on the movie sitting between Gore Vidal and George Schlatter.

The next afternoon Charles came to my apartment for drinks and I bustled about fixing them for him and Robin, being cheerful and chattering away. I mentioned several times how well the book was going and how helpful and wonderful Percy had been, when suddenly Robin fixed me with a beady, accusing eye.

'This Percy fellow, you seem to talk about him a lot. Have you got a crush on him?'

'A crush? Don't be silly,' I cried but I literally felt my face flame. I don't think I had blushed since I was a teenager, but blush I did and it was a hot crimson-faced one.

'My God, you're blushing! Look, Charles, she's blushing, it must be true, then.'

Charles, who had, of course, been with Percy and me many times on tour must not have been that surprised as he had remarked on our friendship several times. 'She sure is,' he said, laughing. 'Maybe it's just the wine.'

Later that night, after Charles had left, I confessed everything to Robin. It was one of the most difficult things I have ever had to do. For someone who hates confrontation and hates even more hurting people close to me, it was intensely traumatic.

The following afternoon I left for New York, as I had to do press for *These Old Broads*. Robin stayed behind in Los Angeles, in my apartment. Producer and sports promoter Jerry Perenchio had offered me a ride on his beautifully equipped private plane that had been remodelled and decorated to seat just thirty passengers in total luxury. Although Jerry wasn't going to New York there was a group of his American football associates on board. When I boarded, the flight attendant escorted me to a palatial stateroom with a double bed and huge TV. 'Mr Perenchio wanted you to be comfortable,' she said, smiling.

With the producer of Love Letters, *Charles Duggan, who suspected the relationship between Percy and me.*

I relaxed with a Bellini and rang Judy Bryer, my closest friend, to tell her the events of the previous night. It had been extremely distressing to confront Robin with the news that I had become seriously involved with Percy, but I have always tried to be honest with people and tell the truth. I could never do what a famous actor-friend of mine had done when he wanted to end his long-term relationship: he told his agent to tell her 'It's over'. Much as I loathed hurting people it was clear to me that the Hurlstone relationship had been frozen in a not very mutually rewarding rut for several years and that Percy and I had fallen madly in love. I didn't know what the future held, but I felt so strongly about him that nothing else mattered.

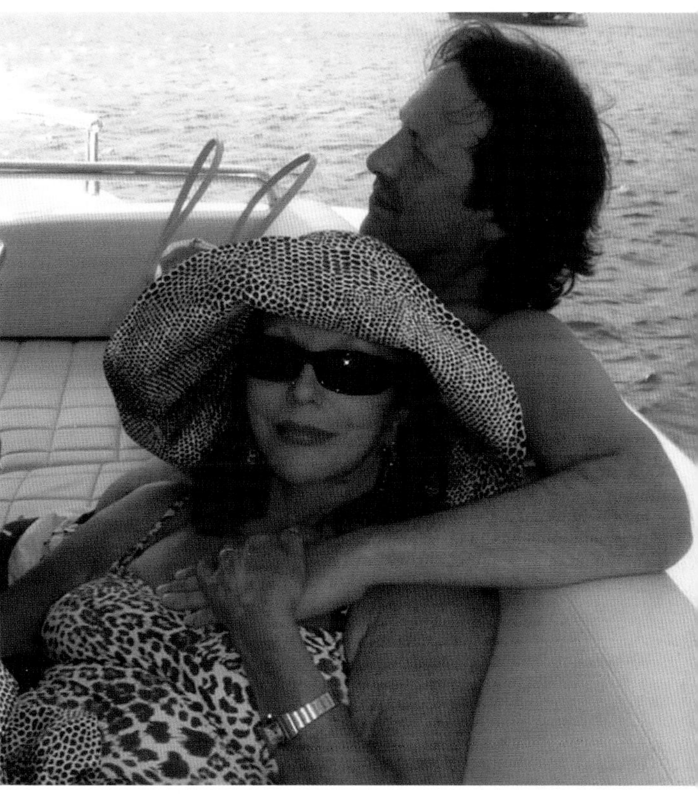

As the plane took off and I saw the shoreline of Santa Monica far below us, I noticed a stream of yellow fluid coming out of the plane's fuselage. 'The plane looks like it's sprung a leak,' I joked to Judy. Then there was a knock on the cabin door and an agitated attendant stammered, 'We're sorry, Miss Collins, but we've developed engine problems and we have to dump fuel over the ocean and go back to base.' I was so horrified that, coupled with my emotional state of mind, I burst into terrified tears.

I kissed a lot of frogs, but I found my prince!

Back at the terminal we were told that the plane couldn't function and we were to be put on a smaller plane as Mr Perenchio was 'very upset, and doesn't want to ruin your trip'. I spoke to Jerry, who was absolutely mortified. 'We've never had any problems with this plane in the ten years I've owned it. I guess I'll just have to buy another one,' he joked. And even though I was upset, he made me laugh. I've always loved how the truly rich live, especially when they appreciate it.

Jerry's stand-by plane to New York was quite small and as I sat between his football friends, I couldn't stop crying; I had hated hurting Robin and I felt I was being unfair to Percy with my vacillating and refusing to commit. The football pals asked me if I was okay, and, drying my eyes with my second box of Kleenex, I assured them it was just a bad case of hay fever.

A week later I met with Robin again in my London flat to reiterate that I wanted to end our relationship. He did not take it well, becoming upset and insulting about Percy and me. I decided to go to Forest Mere, a health farm, and retreat for the weekend to make the final decision about what to do. After three days of staring zombie-like at the ceiling and thinking back over my years with Robin and what kind of future I had with a man who

We renewed our vows at the Bel Air Hotel after seven wonderful years.

not only couldn't stand most of my friends, my family and my children, but who made me feel insecure, I made the decision. Robin Hurlstone packed his toothbrush (which is all he ever kept at my flat), and shortly afterwards Percy Gibson and I left to begin our new life in New York City.

Our gorgeous wedding at Claridges was one of the highlights of my life. I had never felt happier or more secure with any man before. When the band played our favourite song, 'The Way You Look Tonight', and Percy and I took to the dancefloor, I looked into his eyes and said 'I finally got it right'.

After being happily married to Percy for over eleven years now, I realize what true love really is; the happiness, contentment and mutual respect we have for each other has been totally fulfilling. Percy is brilliant with people and helps me all the time with everything in my life. We are each other's best friend and accomplice.

He has become the glue that binds our extended family together. Tara and her children simply adore him, as does Ava Grace, Sacha's daughter, and he will spend hours on holiday playing with them in the pool, helping with homework or refereeing disputes. Not only is he completely dedicated to looking after me but he cares so much about Katy, and is always available to solve the myriad problems that technology has brought into our lives. My sister loves him as do my brother Bill and his wife Hazel. In fact, Percy is that very rare person – a truly *good* man.

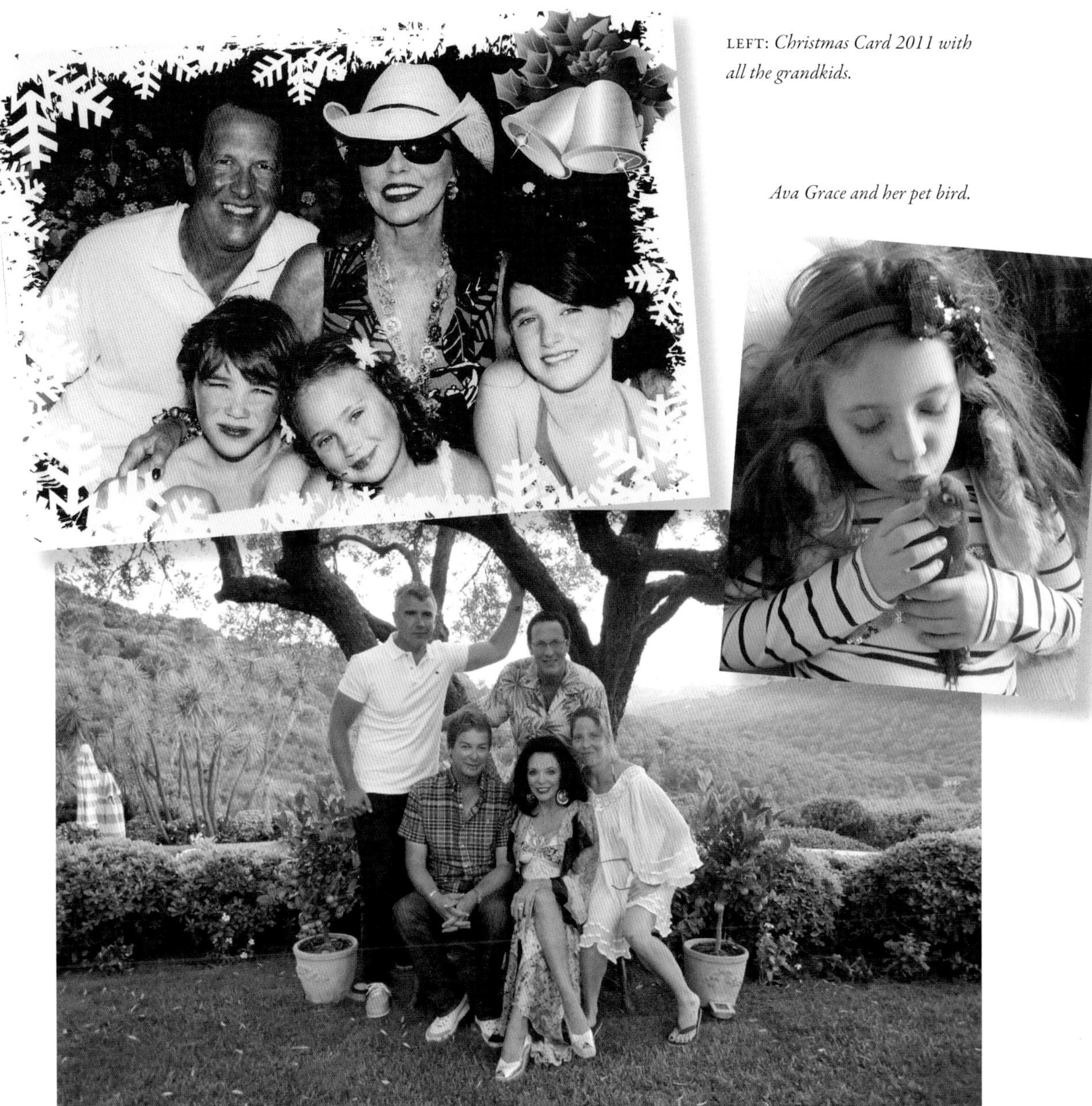

LEFT: *Christmas Card 2011 with all the grandkids.*

Ava Grace and her pet bird.

At Destino, summer 2012, with Ivan Massow, Julian Clary and Katy under our olive tree.

I know a lot of people envy the joy and contentment we have together. We can spend twenty-four hours a day together and he is unutterably considerate and caring to me always. We have our rows, of course, but they are part of a true relationship. He had an excellent relationship with his mother so is always respectful and gallant towards women. I know he loves me for who I am and not the 'Joan Collins' some people think I am.

And when people say to me 'What about the age difference?', I blithely reply, 'Well, if he dies, he dies!'

Chapter Six

FRIENDS

The following are some of my closest friends, who I believe would rush to me in the middle of the night in an emergency. I've been extremely lucky most of my life to have many friends of both sexes. In my schooldays I was uprooted so much that I never developed lasting childhood mates so now my oldest friendships are those I formed during my early days in Hollywood.

Judy Quine

Judy Balaban Kanter Franciosa Quine was the privileged daughter of Barney Balaban, the austere president of Paramount Pictures. She was considered Hollywood royalty as her much respected father was somewhat of an innovator in the film industry. When I met her in the mid-fifties, Judy was married to Jay Kanter, the youngest and most go-getting agent in Hollywood, whose major client was Marlon Brando along with many others.

OPPOSITE: *Elizabeth Taylor, Shirley Maclaine and Debbie Reynolds in 2000. We were the best of 'frenemies' in* These Old Broads.

They were both extremely popular and their house on Rodeo Drive in Beverly Hills was a mecca for all the young stars and movers and shakers of the day. Judy had gorgeous, flaming red hair, two adorable little girls, an enviable social life and great taste. Although slightly older than me, she already had a 'salon' and I studied her closely and emulated her exceptional hostessing skills. She quickly became my best friend and I was able to discuss everything with her from boyfriends to career moves and she always gave great advice. When I was invited to the Cannes Film Festival, I decided

Katy is very close to Judy Quine.

that my wardrobe would consist of all-white outfits because, 'I look beautiful in white,' I cockily informed her. When Judy's peals of laughter finally ceased she teased me unmercifully about my vanity and she still calls me and even emails me 'Beautiful In White'. Being a single girl in Hollywood, I spent quite a few Christmases and Thanksgivings in LA with the Kanters at their warm and welcoming house.

After divorcing Jay, she married Anthony Franciosa, the volatile Italian American actor, with whom she had another daughter, and then Richard Quine, a writer and actor who died some years ago. She still lives in Beverly Hills, and is involved as a political activist and consultant. She was one of Grace Kelly's bridesmaids and wrote *The Bridesmaids* about that glamorous, historical event. She is currently writing for *Vanity Fair* and recently wrote 'Gore's Girls' about Gore Vidal's lady friends, of which I was one.

Judy Bryer

My other Judy friend is Judy Bryer, née Seal. I met Judy in London in 1968 when she became Tony Newley's secretary and assistant. She then came on location to Malta while we worked on Tony's strange autobiographical movie, *Can Heironymus Merkin Ever Forget Mercy Humppe and Find True Happiness?*

Both being Geminis from England, Judy and I quickly bonded. For two years she had been dating an attractive and much in demand confirmed bachelor Maximilian Bryer, a TV director who was fifteen years older, but he was loathe to commit. 'I have a sure-fire way to get him to commit to you,' I told her. So off we went on a series of exciting weekend jaunts to Rome, Paris and Venice in which I made sure she sent plenty of pretty postcards to Max detailing the fabulous time she was having with me and 'the various princes, counts and handsome Italian playboys' we were seeing.

It wasn't long before Max, realizing the prize he would forfeit if he lost Judith Seal, proposed over a long-distance telephone call and the happy couple married in September 1968 – I was matron of honour and Tara and Sacha were flower girl and page respectively.

They've now been happily married for over forty years and Percy and I recently celebrated Max's ninety-first birthday with them in Las Vegas, where they now live.

Judy became my personal assistant during the eighties and nineties and then sometimes acted as my stand-in on *Dynasty*. She is kind, wise and has a fabulous memory.

Even though she lives in Vegas we still speak at least once a week and remain extremely close. She was the first person to whom I confided my romance with Percy, of whom she said, 'What a nice young man,' when she first saw us together on tour in Houston, Texas. She wholeheartedly approved of our marriage and our relationship. This was a great relief because when I had informed her I was marrying Peter Holm she had screamed, 'No – you can't. You must be mad – he's awful!' She was driving at the time and almost crashed into a lamp post.

Judy is a caring godmother to Katy, and I am godmother to her daughter Victoria. Through thick and thin Judy has remained my best friend and I hope she always will be.

Judy Bryer with George Hamilton when we were performing Love Letters.

Jeffrey Lane

In 1968, while on location for *The Executioner*, a movie I was making with George Peppard, I was sitting outside a stately Gloucestershire mansion playing with three-year-old Sacha when a diminutive, exquisitely groomed young man came over and introduced himself as Jeffrey Lane, Columbia's head of publicity. I thought he was awfully young to have such an important job but he was exceedingly good at it, as I discovered during the movie and for the many years after when we worked together.

That night at a party at producer Charles Shneer's house, Jeffrey Lane and I sat in the corner all evening giggling like schoolgirls – and we've been giggling ever since. Wise and witty, Jeffrey is a great escort and raconteur, and I've attended many events with him as my date and laughed our way through more dinners than I can count.

During my ill-judged relationship with Peter Holm, Jeffrey was staying with me in the West Indies. When Peter decided to announce our engagement without consulting me, Jeffrey almost hit the roof. 'Major mistake,' Jeffrey hissed. 'We're now going to have every paparazzo in the Western world descending upon us.'

Jeffrey and me with a tiny fake Oscar.

But Jeffrey and I plotted to make the best of it, however, now that 'The Swede' had let the cat out of the bag. Jeffrey organized a photoshoot to manage the damage but 'The Swede' refused to pose for it in spite of Jeffrey's reasoning and eventual pleading, so Peter and I had one of our biggest fights. He stalked off back to the hotel and I stalked off in the opposite direction, after chucking my engagement ring into the surf.

Jeffrey, in white shorts, long white socks and a small baseball cap perched on his hairless skull scurried crablike into the sand to try to retrieve it, muttering furiously about 'the stupid Swede' and what a stupid mistake I was making. In the distance, the herd of paps were descending on me like a horde of buffalo as Jeffrey became more and more crimson-faced (it was extremely hot and he doesn't do sun).

I collapsed into hysterical laughter at the sight of Jeffrey standing outside 'The Swede's' window as he attempted to cajole Peter who still refused to pose for even one photograph. What kind of fool was I to marry him?

Jeffrey and I have had many adventures since then. We see each other often in LA as he is one of life's great enhancers – great company and hysterically funny.

Jan and Johnny Gold

Johnny Gold was one of the most popular characters of the Swinging London club scene. After running Dolly's, one of the first fabulous discos of the sixties, he went from strength to strength. After Dolly's came the fabled Tramp, for which he partnered with sister Jackie's husband, Oscar Lerman.

Tramp was the 'must go to' disco of the seventies, eighties and nineties. If anything was happening in London, Tramp was where it was happening. Everyone went – the Stones, the Beatles, Rod, Elton, Roger Moore, Michael Caine, Peter Sellers – it was a who's who of showbiz and affable Johnny Gold was the ringmaster who made the circus sparkle.

Celebrities galore congregated every night not just to dance to the great disco sounds and devour the super sausage and mash suppers but to watch other celebrities (which celebrities love to so) and most especially to hang out with Johnny.

Jan and Johnny Gold at her birthday in Saint-Paul-de-Vence. INSET: *One of Johnny's Christmas cards.*

Funny, gregarious and warm, Johnny Gold never forgets a face and he has never lost his cool, even when fights occasionally broke out at his club.

At his eightieth birthday in 2012, stars and celebrities flew in from all over the world to celebrate and to toast him.

He was, and still is, the confidant to many famous faces so when he wrote his tell-almost-all autobiography he tactfully omitted some of the more incriminating tales of the often outrageous and naughty antics during those louche nights at Tramp. I can't count the number of evenings I spent in Johnny's company with his lovely wife Jan, my sister Jackie and her husband Oscar.

Lovely Jan has also been a friend for many years, ever since she was a top model. She is one of the warmest and kindest of human beings and also one of the most devoted grandmas I've ever known – little Liam is a lucky boy.

Sue and Dick St Johns

In the 1990s, when publishers Random House insisted on suing me for $2 million, I was locked into the biggest fight of my life. A horrible court case and a vicious counsel, Robert Callagy, had started to turn me into a quivering mass of jelly. Callagy used rough intimidation techniques on me, throwing down my manuscript with a supercilious sneer or firing belligerent questions that were impossible to answer. He was a total bully and so intimidating that I was doing badly on the stand and it looked like I could lose my case.

However, the night before my second appearance in court to face Callagy, Dick St Johns, who was also a lawyer, rang me: 'Don't let him rattle you. If he tries to confuse you, say you don't remember. You're not a supercomputer – be strong, be assertive, just be . . . be . . . why don't you become Alexis?'

Sue, Percy and I chillaxing at her flat after one of her fabulous feasts.

'What a good idea,' I chirped.

So the next day, dressed in my most powerful power suit, I sat and gave Callagy the 'full Alexis': basilisk stares, cool shrugs and an icily amused demeanour. It worked! I won the case and much of that was because of Dick St Johns sage advice.

Sadly, Dick has since died but his wife Sue is still a great friend. An avid theatregoer, she doesn't miss an opening in London, and she's out on the town every night in yet another elegant outfit. She's a good gossip and we make each other laugh a lot – and if our group includes Christopher Biggins, which it did last summer in the south of France, it's non-stop jollity.

Arlene Dahl and Marc Rosen

I first glimpsed Arlene Dahl in the fifties walking across the Fox lot surrounded by an entourage of hairdressers, makeup artists and a man holding a huge umbrella to protect her ravishing white skin and red hair. Several decades later we met in New York and her skin was still like porcelain.

Like me, Arlene is well travelled down the matrimonial road. In fact, she has travelled it more than me, because Marc is her sixth husband. Extremely feminine and elegant, Arlene Dahl was considered to be one of the most beautiful women in the world during her heyday, and she is still lovely and full of life. She has written many wise books on beauty and health, and writes columns on astrology, on which she is an expert.

With Arlene and Mark in our Manhattan apartment.

When Percy and I met initially, Arlene did our charts and told us that we were exceedingly compatible in every way, which turned out to be true! Arlene and Marc have been married for nearly thirty years and they too are extremely compatible.

Marc Rosen is warm and extremely simpatico. He is a friend and advisor to my son Sacha, and is almost avuncular in his interest in and care for our family. He designs exquisite perfume bottles, among his other business ventures, and is a witty raconteur. So much so, in fact, that we've closed the New York restaurant Swifty's more times than I can remember.

Nikki Haskell

Nikki is the original 'Miss Perpetual Motion'. A fellow Gemini, she is able to multitask and yet not really concentrate on any one task for too long. Nevertheless she is a good businesswoman almost by instinct. She also loves socializing and is never happier than when networking at a party. She knows where it's all happening, either in New York or LA, and will jump on a plane to party to either city as other people jump on a bus.

I met Nikki in the 1960s when Bob Hope and I were judging a 'Twist' competition in Hollywood. We awarded the prize to Nikki, and she and I have been friends practically ever since. Known as the diet queen of Hollywood, she has a successful line of products for weight loss. This same weight-loss line got her into a lot of financial trouble recently, and she had

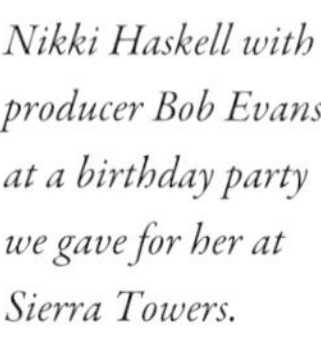

Nikki Haskell with producer Bob Evans at a birthday party we gave for her at Sierra Towers.

to declare bankruptcy. But like the eternal optimist she is, she managed to dig herself out of it and is now back in business.

Christopher Biggins

Biggins and I both love our grub, and he cleans up really well too.

Christopher Biggins probably has more friends than Nigella Lawson has had hot dinners but he is without doubt one of the greatest life-enhancers. His loud, totally infectious laugh is what first brought him into my life. I was trying to concentrate on Bobby Short performing at the Carlyle Cabaret Club in New York in the early eighties. At a nearby table Biggins was holding court and his hearty giggles kept on interrupting Bobby's act. I tried shushing him, which finally worked and he came over and apologized. We lunched together a few days later, hit it off and have been a fixture in each other's lives ever since. He is without doubt one of the most hysterically funny people I know. His humour is caustic, witty and outrageous, and one cannot be around him for long without being doubled over with laughter.

When he stays with us at Destino, we are in hysterics much of the time. A true bon viveur, he is also incredibly generous with his time and commitment to many charities. He probably performs or MCs gratis at

least 200 times a year. If ever someone deserved an honour – a CBE or an OBE – it is Biggins and it is shocking that he has not been awarded one.

In 1993 I persuaded Steven Berkoff to give Biggins a role in *Decadence.* In the scene in which he sits with me at a bawdy table of dissipated toffs, he and the late wonderful Edward Duke, also a great friend, had everyone in so many fits of laughter that Berkoff threatened to kick us off the set.

Biggins loves people so he thought he had died and gone to heaven when he stayed with me at my house in Beverly Hills and I showed him the town.

At George Burns's ninetieth birthday party at Barbara and Marvin Davis's mansion, practically every star from the golden era of show business was present from Carol Channing to Michael Jackson. Biggins wasn't shy about introducing himself to all of them, although when he met Frank Sinatra he became totally tongue-tied for the first time ever!

Barbara Davis

Barbara Davis is the widow of the redoubtable Marvin who took over the 20th Century Fox lot and converted it into high-rise apartments and offices. Barbara is now the 'hostess-with-the-mostest' in LA and is out on the town every single night. She's also a very funny woman who reminds me of Gracie Allen in her delivery, as it is deliberately disingenuous although she is whip-smart. She also doesn't have a mean bone in her body.

She started the fabulous Carousel Ball in Denver (to fund research into a cure diabetes) in the eighties and I've been attending ever since. When they relocated to Beverly Hills, the bi-yearly October Balls continued even more lavishly with amazing guests of honour such as Denzel Washington, Halle Berry, Barbra Streisand and George Clooney.

Barbara is the 'go-to' lady, especially if you have any health problems at all. She's seemingly *au courant* with every doctor, specialist and surgeon in the US, not to mention totally knowledgeable about all the hospitals. She and Marvin founded the Marvin and Barbara Davis Research Building at Mount Sinai hospital in LA and she's a tireless philanthropist.

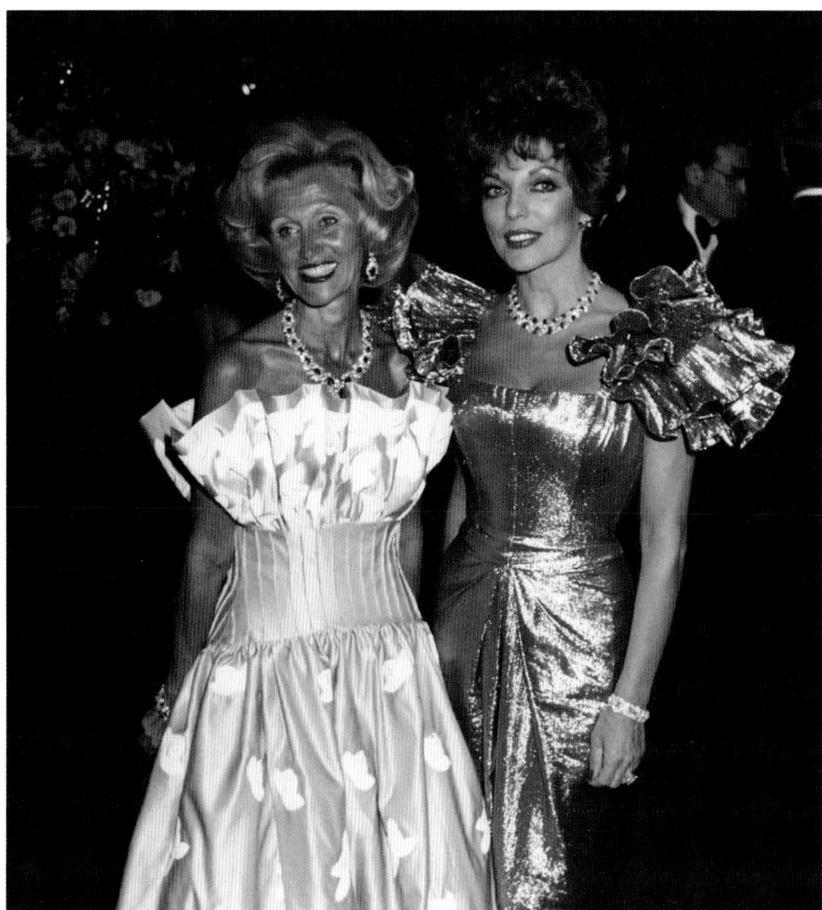

LEFT: *With Barbara Davis at one of her glamorous Carousel Balls in Denver during the Eighties.*

The Bricusses

I met Evie and Leslie Bricusse backstage at the Royal Film Performance in 1962. I was with Warren Beatty and we both thought Evie (whose actress name was Yvonne Romain) was gorgeous: she looked like a young Gina Lollobrigida. Soon after, when Tony Newley and Leslie were basking in the success of *Stop the World – I Want to Get Off*, we teamed up as a fabulous foursome and have been the closest of close friends ever since.

Leslie has the Midas touch with his music and has written dozens of hits including all the songs from *Stop the World* and *The Roar of Greasepaint* with Tony, as well as 'Candy Man', 'Goldfinger' and my particular favourite, 'Pure Imagination'.

He's won two Oscars and several Ivor Novello awards but I think he will agree that one of his greatest achievements is his marriage to Evie

ABOVE: *Evie and Leslie Bricusse.*

for nearly five decades. They've been there for me through thick and thin, as I've cried and laughed on their shoulders during four marriages and three divorces. Leslie is a great giver of counsel on many other matters, too.

The Bricusses are extremely popular and have many friends in London, LA and the south of France. We are never far away from each other as I also have homes in those places. I started to write my first autobiography, *Past Imperfect*, at the beautiful Bricusse hacienda in Acapulco and Leslie gave me plenty of input, and the title! He has an amazing memory for dates and knows when everyone's birthday is, which I sometimes begrudge. Their son Adam was my first godson, and he and Sacha grew up together so they are great friends. We are all still like family.

Tessa Kennedy

Tessa Kennedy is a brilliant interior designer who has designed magnificent interiors for the homes and boats of many famous people. She's also originated many of the exquisite rooms at Claridge's and the Ritz in London.

She is also a godmother to Katy. When Katy was in intensive care for six weeks at age eight, Tessa was there with her daughter Milica practically every day. She has helped me through a lot of dreadful times with her support and prayers.

Tessa has five grown children and many grandchildren, whom she adores. She's a fierce and formidable poker player and one of our core group of players, as well as being a hot-shot Scrabble aficionado. Tessa jumps on a plane to LA, India or some exotic place with the same insouciance that most people take a train to Brighton; she *never* gets jet lag and only needs five hours of sleep a night!

Alison and Martin Davis

Two other great poker players are Alison and Martin Davis. They are so skilled that they play in world poker tournaments and often win! Alison Papworth was a beautiful actress and a Bond girl in *For Your Eyes Only* as well as in *Octopussy*. Most notoriously she sat on Mel Brooks lap in *History of the World*, as he squawked delightedly, 'It's good to be king!' She is also a fabulous, in-demand interior designer.

Martin is a property developer and fervent supporter of the charity of which I am patron, the Shooting Star CHASE children's hospices. He is deeply concerned about children all over the world and gives generously of his time. He calls me Lady Eaton and I call him Lord Chelsea – because he moves homes so often.

BELOW: *Martin and Alison Davis, Julian Clary and Ian Mackley, Alan Nevins and Tessa Kennedy and us at Destino after a tough poker game.*

Baron Enrico and Baroness Alessandra di Portanova

Ricky and Sandra di Portanova reigned as the uncrowned and undisputed King and Queen of Acapulco all through the eighties and nineties. Their incredible Villa Arabesque was one of the most fantastic homes I've ever stayed in. Glamorous Sandra was American and one of the wittiest women I knew. When Ricky was deciding whether or not to invest in a new private airplane she quipped, 'Darling, you can't afford a G2 and me too!'

'Nothing succeeds like excess' was one of Sandra's favourite sayings.

They threw parties practically every night that were legendary, as was her amazing collection of exotic and extraordinary table decorations. I stayed with the Portanovas in Acapulco and their home base in Houston at least thirty times, and I practically never saw the same table settings twice. Gold vases, silver candlesticks, shells, coral, flowers, fruit, glittering ornaments and precious stones – she collected everything and used them all in stylish and inventive tableaux that were a feast for the eyes as well as for the palate. She called them her tablescapes.

Incredibly popular, her villa was always full of the rich, the famous and the infamous, from Henry Kissinger and Plácido Domingo to Tom Hanks, Sylvester Stallone and George Hamilton.

I first saw the Portanovas lunching at Harry's Bar in London in the late seventies. It was April and a young, titled woman came to their table to try and book them for lunch or dinner 'anytime'. 'Darling, we're not free until October,' said Sandra dismissively. I was most amused and shortly afterwards we became great friends.

Partying with Ursula Andress and Jerry Hall.

Although Sophia Loren and I were not close friends we both adored Nolan Miller and often run into each other at parties.

Sandra was tireless both in her charity work, particularly for the poor children of Acapulco, and throwing spectacular parties and entertaining brilliantly, always wearing a flamboyant and low-cut couture gown. When any of my girlfriends or I went to stay in Arabesque we always packed our cases to the gills with glamorous gowns and beautiful kaftans for pool lounging. Everyone was always dressed to the nines. In true eighties style Sandra wore an amazing collection of what she called 'beach jewellery' and she kept the diamonds and the emeralds for night-time.

Despite his title and name, Ricky was British and he spoke and looked like a 1930s movie star. He constantly smoked enormous cigars, drank quite a bit and was madly in love with Sandra and she with him. They were larger than life but sadly their lives were not long enough.

Sandra died in 2000 and Ricky passed away two weeks later, they say of a broken heart. I, and so many of their friends, will always miss them and their amazing lifestyle and *joie de vivre*. Acapulco was never the same again.

Stella Wilson

Stella Wilson came into my life one frosty London morning. She was the London press agent for public relations agency Rogers & Cowan and was supposed to arrive at my flat at noon and take me to ITV for an interview. Instead she rang the bell at 11.45 and I, alone in the flat since I don't have staff, déshabillé in a towel and half made-up, was quite put out. 'Don't you know it's just as rude to arrive at someone's home too early as it is too late?' I snapped. We both immediately saw the funny side of my diva act and broke out laughing. We've been laughing ever since and Stella became not only my press agent for many years but one of my closest girlfriends.

Stella caught the bouquet on my wedding day at Claridges, 2002.

Petite, charming and funny, Stella and I have travelled the world together, not to mention crisscrossing the UK for my book launches. She is always the calm in the eye of the storm, managing the media with authority and sweetness. She retired ten years ago to a delightful house in the middle of France (L'Isle sur la Sorgue) just two hours away from mine, so we see each other often.

A few years ago I heard a strange bleating sound in my garden in the south of France. When Stella and I parted some foliage it revealed a tiny kitten, practically newborn. 'Oh, how sweet,' cooed Stella.

'I'll get rid of it,' snarled the gardener, picking up the poor creature by the scruff of the neck.

'Nooo!' Stella and I yelled. Then she scooped it up and held it tightly while we waited to see if the mama cat would appear to claim her infant. After a night's vigil, we finally put the kitten in an old straw bag and I placed an ancient stuffed camel toy next to it.

Alana Stewart and I have been friends for years . . . and been through many husbands together!

'Don't you think we better feed it?' asked Percy. So after consulting the internet we filled an eyedropper with milk, which the kitten drank from ravenously. The following day we took the kitten to lunch at Club 55, still in the straw bag, where it caused much amusement and 'oohs and oo la la's' from the sophisticated clientele. After lunch we took it to the vet, who informed us the little mite was female and gave her a shot. Stella decided to take her home and call her Lola, after the showgirl in Barry Manilow's song. She absolutely adores Lola who is now a big, healthy grey cat and last year brought her back to visit. We were terrified she would try to escape so we kept her in a downstairs bedroom where my grandchildren fussed over her. I must admit the cat had charm, not to mention longevity!

Betsy Bloomingdale

I met Betsy Bloomingdale when I first came to LA as a young starlet and was stunned by her style and elegance. Betsy is the undisputed Queen of Los Angeles society. She has been on the world's best-dressed lists many times and her dinner parties are legendary.

She is the best friend of Nancy, widow of President Ronald Reagan, and they were part of the 'Reagan Kitchen Cabinet', with Betsy referred to as 'The First Friend'.

Betsy is extremely generous with her time and efforts with many charities and she still lives in a glamorous fifties Palladium-style mansion where she gives stunningly elegant dinner parties with Hollywood and New York's elite and where we are often invited. No jeans and T-shirts for these events. Everyone at Betsy's table dresses immaculately.

She is a brilliant hostess and her book *Entertaining with Betsy Bloomingdale*, is full of great wisdom.

Betsy possesses a great deal of mischievous fun and loves a gentle gossip when lunching with the girls, where she's always elegantly turned out. I once asked her for one of the secrets to her great vitality and *joie de vivre*. She said, 'Mrs Astor told me – I get rid of some of my boring friends every year. I just decide not to see them. I get younger ones. In this town, you can get stuck in the same circle with the same people. I'm lucky in that I have wonderful children who have wonderful husbands so I spend a lot of time with them.'

'What good advice,' I said. 'I think I'll do that too.' So I have! I dislike the expression 'class' but Betsy Bloomingdale possesses it in spades.

Theo and Louise Fennell

If I had to name the most popular couple I know, it would definitely be Theo and Louise. *Everyone* adores them because they are so amusing to be with, generous to a fault and incredibly caring. I've never heard anyone say a bad word about them, nor have I heard them say a bad word about anyone either.

Theo is a brilliantly inventive jeweller. His elegant emporium in Chelsea is full of the most original and spectacular jewellery and objects of every description. He is extremely witty and his *bon mots* are hysterical, and when he does his comedy dancing routine we all fall about laughing. We often do duets together at parties – one of our favourites being 'I Cain't Say No' from *Oklahoma!*

A very popular couple – not to mention handsome too. The Fennells in the South of France, 2011.

The Fennells are both tall, blond, handsome and exceedingly hard working. Several times a year, Louise puts on great clothes sales of many of the top designer labels. Not only did she write her bestselling book *Dead Rich* in 2012, but she was immediately contracted to write the sequel, *The Fame Game*. A true Renaissance woman, they have two beautiful, tall, blonde daughters – Emerald and Coco. The latter is another of my godchildren, who designs a sweet line of summery dresses for sale online. Louise is the sort of friend who, if you called in the middle of the night and needed anything, would be there in a flash. Extremely empathetic and funny as hell, the Fennells are true life-enhancers.

Jack Rich loves all my grandkids – one-year-old Ava Grace doesn't look too thrilled though.

Jack Rich

Darling Jack is Percy's and my mutual best American friend. We met in New York at the beginning of our relationship and we liked each other immediately. The blond, handsome ex-dancer is still a whiz on the dance floors or the beaches and boîtes of Saint-Tropez, where he has visited us practically every year.

The grandkids adore him as he teaches them the latest dance-craze steps and he is much in demand as an extra single man in New York. He is part of our family and when we are in New York we include him in everything we do. He loves to gossip and knows everything that's happening in fashion and on Broadway. He produces, stages and choreographs fabulous fashion show events and has promised little Ava Grace that he will have her in one of his shows.

He also has a wicked sense of humour and, when pushed, gives the wittiest hatchet jobs in town!

Alan Nevins

Alan Nevins is one of the most get-up-and-go agents I have ever known and, believe me, I've known too many. Extremely tall, dark and handsome, we met when he was the young assistant to the superagent Irving 'Swifty' Lazar. Swifty, the legendary agent who brokered the 'Frost–Nixon' deal and who had represented me from my very first autobiography, was known for exceptionally brilliant business ploys and supreme agenting skills.

Through Swifty, Alan learned the ropes of how to make the best deals for authors and eventually became a first-class wheeler-dealer in the cut-throat book business. He then became a manager for actors and directors. He's the only agent I've ever known who replies to an email within minutes. A regular visitor to Destino, he's a huge asset to any dinner party and he's also a hell of a poker player!

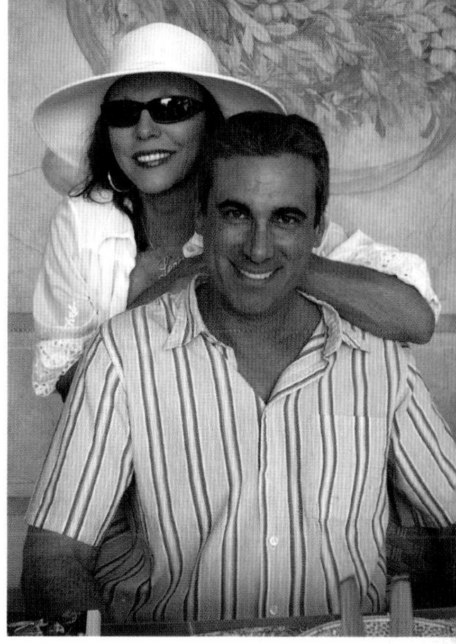

Super-agent Alan Nevins with client at Destino, 2012

The Delevingnes

Charles and Pandora Delevingne are one of the golden couples of London society. I met six foot two inch, good-looking Charles in the seventies when he came to the front door of my house in South Street, dressed like a true dandy in a three-piece suit and bowler hat. He was a property developer then, as he still is, and an extremely successful one.

I first saw slender, blonde Pandora at a costume party at Nicky Haslam's country house in 1980. Still a teenager she was dressed as a nymph and bounded about the party with great verve.

Charles Delevingne wih my goddaughter Cara age eight at Club 55 in St Tropez.

Their three beautiful daughters have inherited their parents' looks and are extremely popular; Poppy and Cara have become top models. Cara is another one of my godchildren and much in demand everywhere as a model for her bubbly personality and photogenic beauty.

The Delevingne's and I have travelled practically all over the world together. They love travelling and holidays even more than I do and we always have masses of fun and tons of laughs wherever we are. Charles often sits next to me at dinner parties and he always helps me to clear my plate as he has a more than healthy appetite. They have legions of friends, including royals, but are deliciously down-to-earth and much loved.

The Delevingne clan with Pandora's father Jocelyn Stevens and Lynn Wyatt in the South of France.

Ivan Massow

Ivan with us and Jack Rich at Destino.

Ivan always says if it wasn't for me, he would be dead by now. Originally a friend of Sacha, we became very close a few years ago when he persuaded Percy and me to take leading roles in a somewhat weird semi-documentary he was producing and directing called *Banksy's Coming to Dinner*. During filming, which only took one day, Ivan – not surprisingly – became quite manic. In the following months as we saw each other a great deal whilst he edited the film, I started to worry about his mental and physical health. He was admittedly drinking huge amounts and possibly doing other things which are not helpful for one's health. After spending two days at Destino, I observed that between him and his friend, they had consumed a case of wine plus several bottles of vodka. I sat down with Ivan and pulling no punches told him in no uncertain terms he was an idiot to wreck himself by his dissolute lifestyle. To my surprise and delight, Ivan checked himself into rehab the following month and hasn't touched a drop for over four years. 'It's all thanks to you,' he says.

Ivan is a genius at business – a top-notch entrepreneur who was a self-made millionaire before the age of twenty-five. He is a forthright gay rights campaigner and activist, extremely active in UK politics and a chairman of the Institute of Contemporary Arts. He also set up Britain's first financial firm for gay clients.

He is also brilliant at buying and selling houses for profit. He decorates them with many portraits of himself – several of them by my son, Sacha. In 2007 Ivan went to live in Barcelona with his dog for three years. Everything finally turned out well and we are now involved in several projects together.

He has enormous energy and is always full of new and exciting ideas; he's stimulating and fun to be with, and extremely generous. We will always be great friends – even if he can't keep still!

St Tropez

CLOCKWISE: *Captain Sully, the brave pilot who saved the plane that crashed into the Hudson River, at the Vanity Fair Party; Damien Hirst dressed as a nun for an Elton John party; Michael Jackson and Elizabeth Taylor at the Albert Hall; Max and Judy Bryer, and Celine Dion and her husband René Angelli in Las Vegas; Tony and I doing Noël Coward's* Red Peppers; *President and Nancy Reagan at the White House; Andy Warhol; With Prince Albert of Monaco and his wife Charlene, Monte Carlo 2012; Elton John; Tracey Emin and Percy at Club 55; Tara and Sacha making beautiful music together*

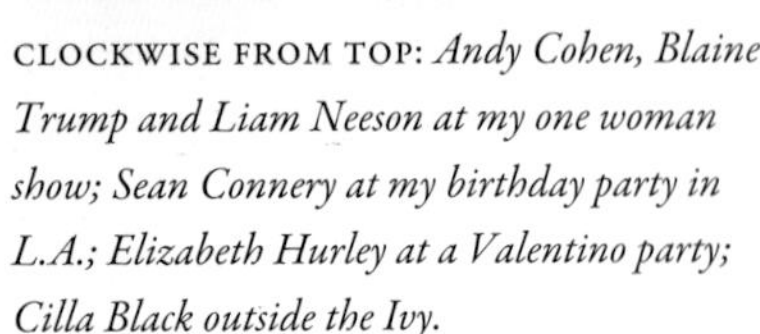

CLOCKWISE FROM TOP: *Andy Cohen, Blaine Trump and Liam Neeson at my one woman show; Sean Connery at my birthday party in L.A.; Elizabeth Hurley at a Valentino party; Cilla Black outside the Ivy.*

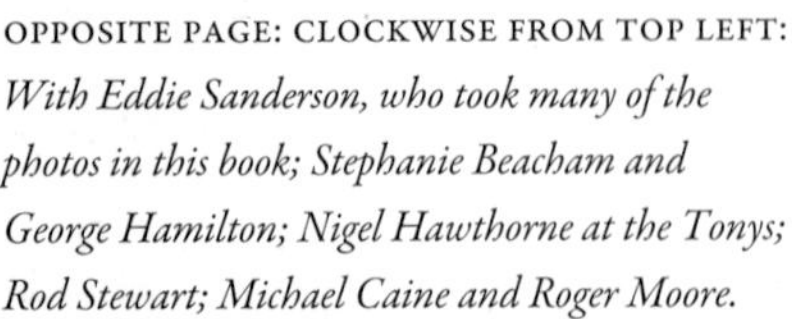

OPPOSITE PAGE: CLOCKWISE FROM TOP LEFT: *With Eddie Sanderson, who took many of the photos in this book; Stephanie Beacham and George Hamilton; Nigel Hawthorne at the Tonys; Rod Stewart; Michael Caine and Roger Moore.*

JOAN COLLINS
PRIME TIME
Variety Club
Variety Club
Greatest Children's Charity in the World

Joyce and Simon Reuben

I've known Simon Reuben for many years as he has been my brother Bill's best friend since they were young. Bill, Jackie and I spent a lot of time in the late seventies and eighties at Tramp nightclub, which was owned by Jackie's husband Oscar Lerman. Simon would often be there observing the action, smiling and, like Bill, being a very low-key guy. And when Katy was in hospital he was a regular and caring visitor

Joyce and Simon Reuben enjoy a good laugh in London.

Since then, he and his brother David have built an empire based on property and the internet and are now regulars in the Top 10 of the *Sunday Times* 'Rich List'.

Joyce and Simon are extremely charitable and give a great deal of money and time to good causes including The Reuben Foundation Children's Cancer Centre at Great Ormond Street hospital.

Simon is not only a brilliant businessman but also an expert on movie memorabilia. He can tell you not only who starred in some obscure thirties film but also the directors and the supporting cast. I've tried hard to stump him but haven't succeeded yet.

Dividing their time between London and their glamorous house in Saint-Tropez, every year they give one of the best parties on the Côte d'Azur. We spend many lunches together in Saint-Tropez at Club 55 and Percy has to fight Simon to try and get the bill occasionally, as Simon's generosity knows no bounds.

Joyce is the kindest, most engaging and most generous of friends. Nothing is too much trouble for her – she is beautiful, slim, elegant and modest, and everyone who meets Joyce adores her. I've never seen her in the same outfit twice!

She is a great conversationalist and supports many charities, and loves the theatre and movies. She adores Paul Newman and, being the Patron of the British Film Institute, she organized an evening to show *Rally 'Round the Flag, Boys*, a film that Paul and I made in 1958. I gave a speech about him afterwards and then Joyce gave a dinner for a hundred people. It was a magical, memorable night of the kind the Reubens so easily manage to give.

Nolan Miller

Nolan was like my other brother. His death in 2012 left me shattered. He was the most solicitous, kind and wonderful friend, not to mention a fabulous designer.

I first met Nolan in the wardrobe department at 20th Century Fox when I was cast in *Dynasty*. Exceedingly tall, elegantly dressed and extremely handsome, Nolan was the epitome of old-world charm. He was a true gentleman in an age when that creature rarely exists anymore. He had already been a top fashion designer for movies and television and had dressed, amongst others, Joan Crawford, Lana Turner and Barbara Stanwyck. He particularly adored Barbara Stanwyck, who was one of his closest friends and he admired her tremendously. He had a wealth of outrageously funny anecdotes about all the other actresses he had clothed but Barbara Stanwyck was special.

His story of how Phyllis Diller had stripped off in front of him and the entire wardrobe department had me in stitches. During the eighties he designed dresses for *Love Boat*, *Fantasy Island* and *Charlie's Angels*, but he admitted that making couture gowns for Linda Evans, Diahann Carroll and me on *Dynasty* was his favourite. By the time *Dynasty* ended the wardrobe budget was in excess of $30,000 per week. When limited edition Krystle and Alexis dolls were released, Nolan even designed the flamboyant frocks the dolls were wearing.

With Darling Nolan Miller in his house in Los Angeles.

We became great pals during *Dynasty* and became even closer after the show ended in 1989. I continued visiting his atelier on Robertson Boulevard, as no other couturier could produce such exquisite and flattering gowns. I still treasure some of my beautiful dresses with the Nolan Miller label in them.

When, in the nineties, most actresses favourite mode of dress became jeans and a T-shirt, Nolan announced that he had become a 'dinosaur' and 'couldn't stand that look', so he started to design a collection of glamorous outfits for QVC, Saks Fifth Avenue and other department stores.

'Squeeze in dear'. Better stop eating those buns.

When we were preparing for the TV movie *These Old Broads*, in which I played the girlfriend of a Mafioso boss, Nolan was staying with me at my villa in Saint-Tropez. He and I would shop at the flashy boutiques their searching for flamboyant finery for my character. We always used to spend hours discussing my elegant costumes for *Dynasty*, which was a true collaboration, so for *These Old Broads* we reprised our alliance to make me look like an over-the-top gangster's moll.

It was during Christmas 2006, when he was staying with myself, Percy and a group of friends in a house we'd rented in Acapulco, that we heard him coughing all night and I told him he should see a doctor. Tragically it was a foretaste of the serious illness that finally took his life six years later. In 2012, his friends Selim and Mary Zilkha and I gave a wonderful memorial for him. Many stars came and the speeches were full of admiration and sadness at his death. Everyone who ever met him liked him and he was truly 'nice'.

Nolan never said a bad word against anyone, even though there were those who tried to destroy him. With his acerbic wit, charm and easy-going personality he was able to surmount the viciousness.

But it is as the best, most loyal and incredible friend that I shall always remember Nolan and I still miss him.

Jackie Collins

My chapter on friends wouldn't really be complete unless I included my sister Jackie. She and I understand and empathize with each other more than practically any other of my friends and her loyalty is unbounded.

When I was a fledgling actress and she was still a schoolgirl, she painstakingly collected, cut and pasted all my press clippings into a scrapbook and with great care would write the date and publication of each one.

Jackie's burgeoning writing talent began when she was only nine or ten years old. She wrote exciting short stories, which I used to illustrate, drawing and painting her characters from my imagination.

She was always a forthright supporter of me and my life. Although there was a period in our lives, during the Peter Holm marriage and then

With my lovely brother Bill and sister Jackie. She has the best cheekbones in the family.

the Robin Hurlstone relationship, when perhaps we became more distant, we shortly thereafter reunited and became closer than ever.

She is one of the most generous, if not the most generous, person I know. Her munificence at Christmas is without par and no one can keep up with the lavish gifts she heaps upon her family and friends.

We share so many of the same memories and can confide in each other without fear. We gossip and giggle when we are together and we love to go see the latest movies together at weekend morning showings at our favorite Los Angeles shopping center.

Beautiful and caring, Jackie has forged a spectacular writing career, each book a massive bestseller, and she ain't slowing down! She is completely disciplined in her writing but somehow also manages to watch practically every major TV show on the air, and the various TVs and DVRs across her house are constantly 'on record'.

Although she is my sister I consider her a true and wonderful friend, whose advice I didn't always listen to at my peril ('How can you possibly marry Pete Holm – are you mad?' and 'Robin is the worst snob I ever met. How dare he correct my pronunciation?')

Thankfully she adores Percy so she and I are back together and having the best of times going out or just spending an afternoon home, enjoying her delicious cooking and watching TV!

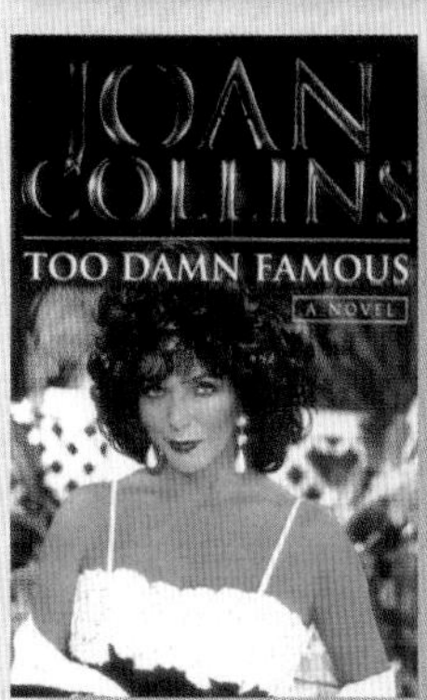

October 9, 1988

THE NEW YORK TIMES BOOK REVIEW

Best Sellers

Fiction

This Week		Last Week	Weeks On List
1	THE CARDINAL OF THE KREMLIN, by Tom Clancy. (Putnam, $19.95.) The C.I.A.'s Jack Ryan races to the rescue of America's highest-ranking secret agent in the Soviet Union.	1	10
2	BREATHING LESSONS, by Anne Tyler. (Knopf, $18.95.) The many facets of a 28-year marriage are revealed during a drive to a friend's funeral.	2	3
3	TILL WE MEET AGAIN, by Judith Krantz. (Crown, $19.95.) The exploits of a woman and her two daughters from pre-World War I Paris to present-day Los Angeles.	3	9
4	ALASKA, by James A. Michener. (Random House, $22.50.) The history of the 49th state told in fictional form.	4	15
5	SPOCK'S WORLD, by Diane Duane. (Pocket, $16.95.) An emergency meeting of the planet Vulcan's ruling council exposes its secret history and that of the Enterprise's Commander Spock.	5	5
6	THE SILENCE OF THE LAMBS, by Thomas Harris. (St. Martin's, $18.95.) A young woman F.B.I. trainee pursues a serial killer.	6	5
7	THE SHELL SEEKERS, by Rosamunde Pilcher. (St. Martin's, $19.95.) A woman and a painting tie together three generations of an English family.	10	34
8	THE BONFIRE OF THE VANITIES, by Tom Wolfe. (Farrar, Straus & Giroux, $19.95.) A bond trader caught in the jungles of New York.	8	49
9	KOKO, by Peter Straub. (Dutton, $19.95.) Three Vietnam veterans on the trail of a friend who may be responsible for a series of murders.	13	2
10	LOVE IN THE TIME OF CHOLERA, by Gabriel García Márquez. (Knopf, $18.95.) A Colombian poet's perdurable love for a woman is tested by life's changing conditions.	11	25
11	PRIME TIME, by Joan Collins. (Linden/Simon & Schuster, $19.95.) Five actresses compete for a glamorous role in Hollywood.		1
12	TRACKS, by Louise Erdrich. (Holt, $18.95.) The mysterious life of Fleur Pillager, a Chippewa woman with the powers of a shaman.		1
13*	THE AVIATORS, by W. E. B. Griffin. (Putnam, $18.95.) A volume in the "Brotherhood of War" series set in Vietnam.	15	4
14	DEMON LORD OF KARANDA, by David Eddings. (Del Rey/Ballantine, $18.95.) The battle for control of a continent continues in the fantasy saga "The Malloreon."	14	7
15	DOCTORS, by Erich Segal. (Bantam, $19.95.) The life stories of five members of Harvard Medical School's class of 1962.	7	11

Nonfiction

This Week		Last Week	Weeks On List
1	A BRIEF HISTORY OF TIME, by Stephen W. Hawking. (Bantam, $18.95.) A scientist's review of efforts to create a unified theory of the universe.	1	25
2	THE LIVES OF JOHN LENNON, by Albert Goldman. (Morrow, $22.95.) The rock-and-roll star as legend and as human being.	2	5
3	THE BOZ, by Brian Bosworth with Rick Reilly. (Doubleday, $17.95.) The life and controversial opinions of the Seattle Seahawks football player.	3	6
4	THE RAGMAN'S SON, by Kirk Douglas. (Simon & Schuster, $21.95.) The actor recalls his life as poor immigrant's son, waiter, steel mill worker, haberdashery salesman, film star, father and man.	4	7
5	LANDSLIDE, by Jane Mayer and Doyle McManus. (Houghton Mifflin, $21.95.) Two Washington reporters on "the unmaking of the President, 1984-1988."		1
6	THE DUCHESS OF WINDSOR, by Charles Higham. (McGraw-Hill, $17.95.) The life of the woman from Baltimore who married King Edward VIII.	5	12
7	TRANSFORMATION, by Whitley Strieber. (Beech Tree/Morrow, $18.95.) The author of "Communion" tells of more confrontations with "intelligent nonhumans."	7	6
8	GENERATION OF SWINE, by Hunter S. Thompson. (Summit, $18.95.) Commentary on the current decade.	6	13
9	PRESS ON! by Chuck Yeager and Charles Leerhsen. (Bantam, $17.95.) The legendary pilot on flying, the outdoors and his West Virginia roots.	8	2
10	THEY WENT THAT-A-WAY . . ., by Malcolm Forbes with Jeff Bloch. (Simon & Schuster, $18.95.) How the famous (and the infamous) met their end.	10	2
11	TRUMP, by Donald J. Trump with Tony Schwartz. (Random House, $19.95.) The career and business style of the New York entrepreneur.	9	43
12	SENATORIAL PRIVILEGE, by Leo Damore. (Regnery Gateway, $19.95.) A reporter's reassessment of the 1969 accident on Chappaquiddick Island.	12	9
13	TALKING STRAIGHT, by Lee Iacocca with Sonny Kleinfield. (Bantam, $21.95.) More experiences and opinions of the Chrysler chairman.	11	17
14*	THRIVING ON CHAOS, by Tom Peters. (Knopf, $19.95.) Ways for companies to survive in today's and tomorrow's turbulent world.	13	47
15	THE RISE AND FALL OF THE GREAT POWERS, by Paul Kennedy. (Random House, $24.95.) How economic and military forces affected the fortunes of great nations in the past 500 years.		34

Chapter Seven

ROYALS

The Queen

I first became aware of the then Princess Elizabeth when I was a young evacuee in Ilfracombe. In my parents' sudden, mad rush from London to escape the Blitz, unnecessary things like toys were left behind. I made do by playing with conkers and skipping on an old frayed rope but it was all rather boring until the woman next door produced a treasure and gave me an old cutting-out book from the 1937 coronation of King George VI.

Inside were two wonderfully pretty cardboard figures of the two young princesses, Elizabeth and Margaret Rose, aged about eleven and eight. How lovely the cut-outs were in their dainty, modest undies, and how much fun it was to press them out from the book and carefully try on the adorable and stylish outfits. I wiled away the hours dressing them up in their little kilts and pale jumpers and cardigans or lacy party frocks and having imaginary conversations with them. By the time the Doodlebugs stopped raining on London and we were taken back home again, the little princesses and their paper outfits were in total tatters.

OPPOSITE: *Glamming up royally, eighteenth Century style for* Sins.

A few years later, in 1947, my fascination with Princess Elizabeth resumed during the exciting preparations for her wedding to Prince Philip, or 'Phil the Greek' as my father rudely referred to him. I, however, thought that Prince Philip was as handsome as any movie star (eat your heart out, Montgomery Clift) as I cut and pasted pictures from newspapers and magazines of Philip and Elizabeth into a special scrapbook I kept just for them.

At a command performance in about 1968 with Tommy Steele and Richard Chamberlain.

The pre-wedding preparations were so outstandingly glamorous in an England still suffering from post-war austerity and rationing that I, my fellow schoolmates and, indeed, the whole country were gripped by complete fascination of the splendour, the like of which we had never experienced.

Princess Elizabeth looked radiant in her engagement pictures, glowing with happiness, and we all wanted to be just like her when we grew up – marry a handsome prince and live happily ever after.

The wedding day was another fairy tale. It was especially moving when it was reported that the princess had saved up all her clothing coupons to buy the fabric for her magnificent gown.

I watched her coronation from the window of a friend's house. One unforgettable moment was seeing a large carriage pass by containing a very large woman and a very small man. Noël Coward reportedly was asked, 'Who's that woman?'

'The queen of Tonga,' he replied.

'And who is the man sitting beside her?'

'Her lunch,' retorted Noël in his typically droll manner.

In the 1950s, Princess Elizabeth and Princess Margaret Rose became the pin-up girls of the media, setting the example for the future Princess Diana and Catherine, duchess of Cambridge. Everything they did became tabloid fodder and Elizabeth and Philip were the golden couple of that time.

What can one say about our queen that hasn't been said a million times? Everyone is aware of her numerous good points: her incredible energy, dedication, commitment and dignity; even under scrutiny she seems to have no bad points whatsoever. That is more than can be said for some of the reigning monarchs who recently helped her celebrate a lavish Jubilee lunch at Buckingham Palace. With the graciousness and a charm for which she is also famous, Queen Elizabeth bestowed a friendly handshake and a benign smile on a couple of monarchs whose abuse of human rights and democracy is notorious.

Some were shocked that our queen, a model of propriety and good manners, should have to entertain such obvious villains but sadly she had little say about that particular guest list. She must always remain democratic towards whomever she meets and greets, and maintains the tradition of the 'stiff upper lip' at all times, a quality for which she is most admired and loved.

I was lucky enough to meet the queen on a recent birthday of mine and she was, as she always has been towards me, extremely friendly, giving me a firm handshake and a lovely smile as I gave one of the worst curtsies I've ever done.

This was a wonderful birthday gift, as I have always been a devoted monarchist. I've met the queen several times. The first was in 1962 at a Royal Command Performance at the Leicester Square Theatre, when my date was a then unknown actor by the name of Warren Beatty.

In the following years I attended several other royal premieres. When I met the queen mother in 1983, she enquired if I was taking a break from *Dynasty*. I told her I was on hiatus, then tentatively asked her if she hated me in the show, to which she replied with a smile, 'Oh, no, my dear, we ALL love you!' I envisioned the female members of 'the firm', including the queen, spending every Wednesday night huddled in front of the TV having cups of tea and watching the antics of Krystle and Alexis with glee.

Few people know what taste the queen has in popular culture. When she attends the Royal Variety Performances, she looks suitably engaged. She even laughs at some of the better comedians and doesn't frown at some of the ghastly ones. She was surely riveted by 'Pudsey', the performing dog, and perhaps thinks about what new tricks to teach her corgis.

The Premiere Bar

At one of the Variety Performances I shared a dressing room with, amongst others, the salty-tongued Lauren Bacall. She was wearing a plain black pant suit and I was done up in a beaded full-length gown with a matching feather-trimmed cape. When I was called onstage to present, Bacall said, 'Eighty-six the feathers Joan Collins'

OPPOSITE: *The Queen Mother admits she's a* Dynasty *fan as George Peppard looks on approvingly.*

'What?' I spluttered. 'Why?'

'Over the top honey,' she said. 'Too much for the queen.'

Since I knew the queen was tiaraed and diamond necklaced and brooched to the nines, I chose to ignore Miss Bacall. The following day all the papers featured my feathers and me meeting the queen and Miss Bacall was just a blurry figure in the background!

I was presented to the queen and the duke of Edinburgh again at the Royal Albert Hall in 1982 for a charity concert for one of the queen's favourite charities – the Royal Society for the Protection of Birds. I was quite nervous. A series of events had conspired to make me tense, but it didn't show in the now-iconic picture by Richard Young. In the photo, my

Charity concert at the Albert Hall, 1982. Katy is suitably impressed.

LWT

nine-year-old daughter Katy had just presented a bouquet to the queen and was looking at her lovingly as I curtsied demurely and the queen and the duke smiled.

I had just spoken the lyrics to John Lennon's 'Imagine' accompanied by the entire Royal Philharmonic Orchestra (as one does!). This in itself was numbingly scary in front of not only the royals but 5,000 other elite members of the audience, plus I had also been the mistress of ceremonies. On top of that, as I entered through the stage door earlier, I had been accosted and served with a writ for not paying for a hire car that Ron Kass had leased three years previously (which had actually been returned long ago). It was terribly embarrassing, particularly as several photographers snapped away as I tried to enter the Albert Hall.

1998, with Anthony Newley at the Ivy, during my party to receive my OBE. We were friends by then.

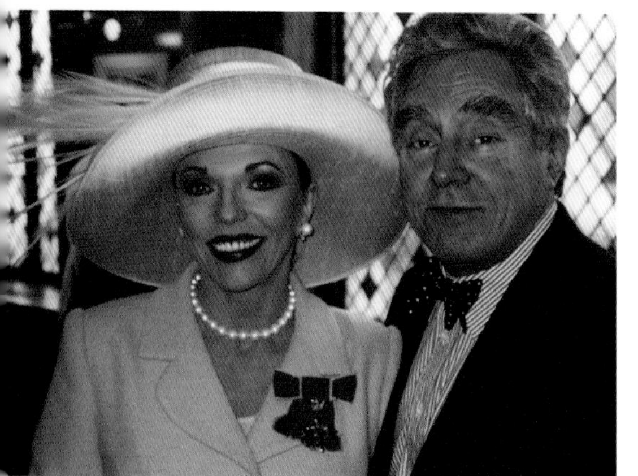

The queen, of course, knew nothing about the writ as I curtsied, my knees trembling. I was wearing the 'Dynasty Diamonds', a parure of rubies and diamonds that were totally fake. I wondered if Her Majesty could tell the difference between those and the magnificent diamond necklace that she was wearing – I bet she did. The following day when the picture was printed, the headlines were horrifying: 'Royal star Joan gets Writ'; 'A Writ on Joan's Big Night'. I sincerely hoped the queen hadn't seen them.

A more relaxed occasion for me was when she bestowed upon me an OBE in 1997. She greeted me with such a warm smile that I felt as though we were rather good acquaintances.

At a lunch in Windsor Castle in 1998, an extremely animated monarch talked with Michael Caine, Shirley Bassey and me, fascinating us with stories about some of the interesting artwork hanging on the hallowed walls. She was full of enthusiasm and seemed younger than a woman then in her seventies.

OPPOSITE: *I am presented with an OBE in 1998. Of course I was thrilled! I love the Queen.*

A hundred years ago if a woman lived to be in her late eighties, she would be feeble, bedridden and arthritic. Our queen is in such robust health and has such vibrant energy that people take for granted the gruelling 400-or-so engagements schedule she completes each year. As for that trip down the Thames in the pouring rain on her Diamond Jubilee in 2012 – if you allowed your grandmother to stand in the rain and freezing

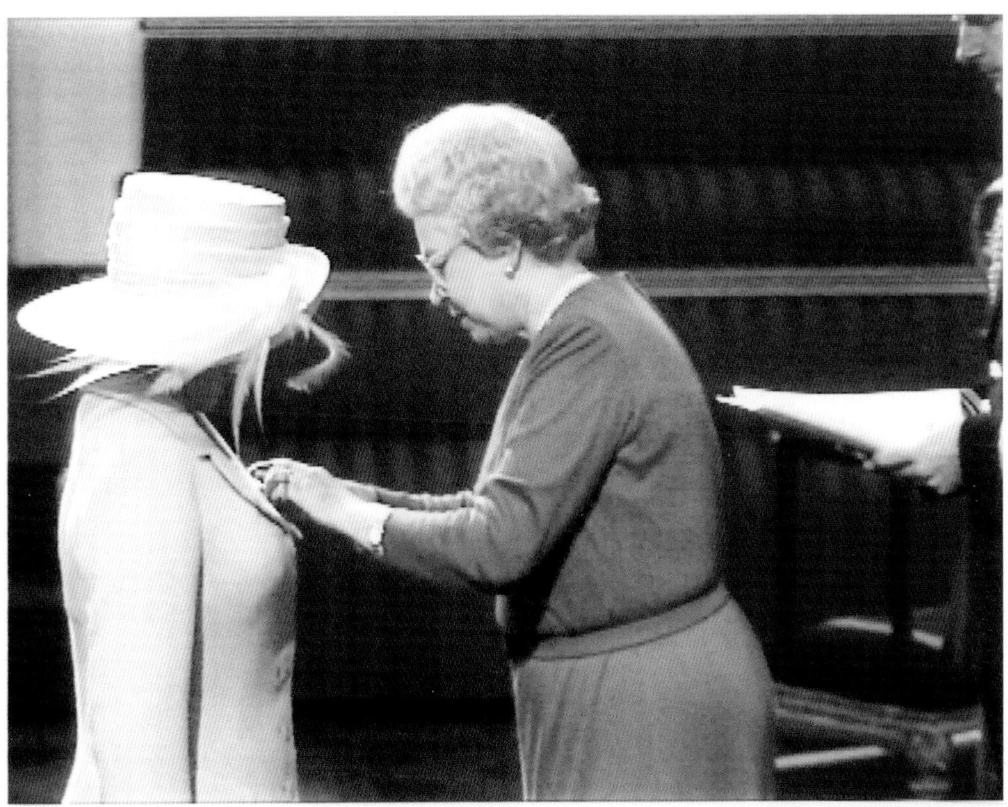

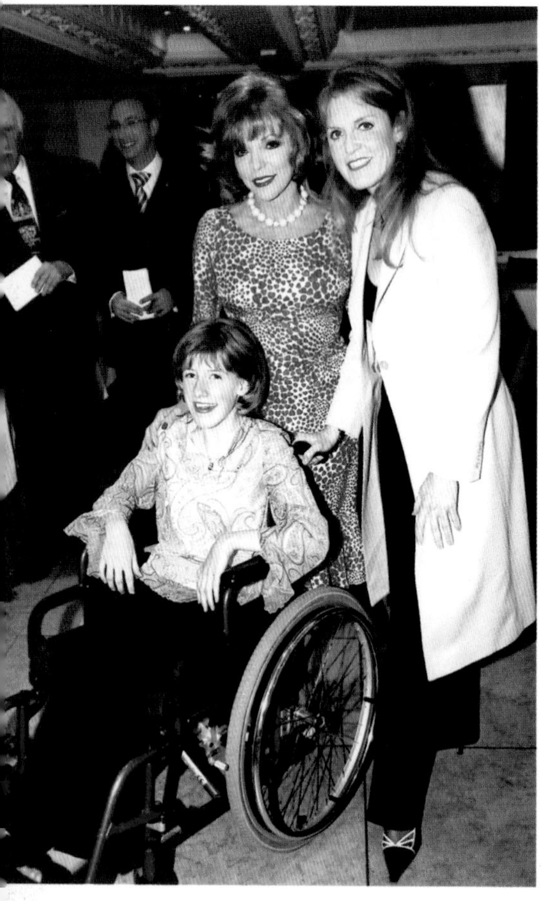

cold you would probably be arrested for abuse!

The queen's role entails a great deal of hand shaking, and much of it none too gentle as I can vouch. I observed some hand-shakers close up at the Royal Academy. I thought that she must have extremely strong fingers to survive some of those bone-crushers. Don't tell me shaking hands with over 4,000 people a year, standing still for hours on end without showing a flicker of discomfort and attending over 400 functions without revealing the faintest hint of ennui is not an outstanding achievement in itself.

The queen always looks immaculate and deports herself impeccably. Not for her lipstick on the teeth, a heel caught in a hem or a dress that blows up in the wind, which happens to most mere mortals and even actresses. She neither fidgets nor looks bored, she never yawns or sneezes and there is never ever a hair out of place beneath the stylish hat. I often wonder what hairspray she uses to guarantee that those well-coiffed curls don't move.

The Duchess of York always supports charitable causes. At Shooting Star Chase, of which I am a patron.

I would also be interested to know if the queen uses foundation. Her skin is admirably free of any freckles or sun damage at all, even though her face often has to be exposed to the full glare of the sun (she cannot even wear sunglasses to protect her eyes as the public must be able to see her) and, in fact, to the elements in all weathers.

A question that often surprises me is 'Why are you still working? Wouldn't you like to just lie around and put your feet up?' The very idea! I'm sure no one would dare address such a fatuous remark to the queen, who is in totally robust health. She's the one of whom people should be demanding, 'What's your secret, Ma'am?'

Our royal family is the envy of the world, and America, in particular, laps up anything to do with our monarchy: their memorabilia collectors are zealous; the royal wedding of William and Catherine was almost a public holiday with endless coverage throughout the day; and the film *The Queen* even received an Oscar! The monarchies of Norway, Sweden, Spain, Jordan, not to mention some of the US presidents, are no doubt

Bill Wiggins and me greeted by the Duchess of York as the Delevingnes look on.

more than slightly envious of the pomp and ceremony and the effortless attention our queen attracts, and frankly they should be.

There is simply no one in the world like Elizabeth II but there is only one question I've been dying to ask her: 'Ma'am, what's in the handbag?'

Princess Margaret

When Princess Margaret was introduced to my then fiancé Warren Beatty at a Hollywood party in the early sixties, her eyes lit up. Having always had an eye for a handsome face, she and Warren were soon locked in animated conversation.

I had been introduced to Princess Margaret at a royal premiere the previous year and Warren had remarked on her beautiful blue eyes and vivacious personality.

I had a chance to sample the vivacious personality several times in the following years, most memorably when she came to see Keith Baxter and me in Noël Coward's *Private Lives* at the Aldwych Theatre in 1991. One night the company manager excitedly informed us before the performance that Princess Margaret was coming to the show with seven friends. 'Will she come backstage after?' I asked.

'Only if she likes the first act,' he replied. 'She may even leave if she doesn't like it – she has been known to.'

'Oh dear, we better give sparkling performances then,' I said.

After the first act, in which we all did our darnedest, the company manager informed us that Princess Margaret 'loved it' and would like to meet the whole company onstage after the show.

Prince Charles is always Prince Charming when we meet.

We stood stiffly onstage as Princess Margaret entered stage right, tiny and regal in a tight-waisted cocktail frock and mink stole. She was sipping a large drink in a small glass, which she gave to an equerry whenever she shook hands with one of the cast. In the other gloved hand she held a cigarette in a long, amber holder.

'I liked the performance enormously,' she chirped to me in her high-pitched voice. 'I read the play again this afternoon and this production is quite true to dear Noël's concept.'

I was most impressed by her diligence in not only reading the play but also understanding all the nuances. But then she threw me for a loop when she announced in her piercing tone, 'But the girl, Sybil, where's the girl? Her voice is far too high-pitched. You know, I can hardly understand a word.'

Talk about pot calling kettle. Young Sara Crowe was summoned to the royal presence and sternly admonished to lower her voice. Sara looked understandably flummoxed by this critique but since she had received excellent reviews (some better than mine!) she left her performance as it was.

I was collecting some interesting *objets* for my new flat in Eaton Place when my friend, the property developer Ned Ryan, brought over two gorgeous silver boxes.

'A very distinguished lady wants to sell them,' he said. 'Are you interested?'

Well, the price was right so I bought them both and displayed them to good effect in my drawing room. Later, when I was polishing one of them, a very large cigar box, I opened it to find inside a card with these words printed, 'To Princess Margaret and Lord Snowdon on the occasion of their visit.'

Wow, I thought, that certainly is a very distinguished lady and I left the box out prominently.

At my Christmas party a few months later Ned Ryan, who had been invited but couldn't come due to a previous engagement with Princess Margaret, rang at about 10.30 p.m. and said, 'I'm with Bryan and Nanette Forbes and Princess Margaret and they're all bored, so could we come over to your party?'

'Sure,' I said, 'come on over.'

When Princess Margaret arrived with her entourage she stood in the hallway chatting to Roger Moore and asked for a glass of Famous Grouse, which luckily I had – 'In a small glass please,' she commanded, 'as I have tiny hands.'

As the waiter scuttled away I realized that Roger was ushering Princess Margaret into the very room where her silver box shone like a beacon on

Princess Margaret seems enchanted with Warren at a command performance in 1962.

the coffee table. I tried to head her off at the pass while hissing to Ned sotto voce, 'Hide the damn box, for God's sake.' He didn't need to be told twice. If she had seen it he could have been sent to the Tower! Luckily Princess Margaret enjoyed my party and being lionized by some of the glitterati of show business, and she never saw the incriminating silver box.

I admired Princess Margaret for the way she lived her somewhat hedonistic life by her own rules. It must have been difficult being the younger sister of the queen but I think she had a ball nevertheless!

Princess Diana

She was undoubtedly the most fascinating young woman of her generation and I was not alone in my admiration of her style and charm. When she married her prince in 1981, Katy and I sat enthralled in front of the TV watching the beautiful twenty-year-old walk down the aisle in her flouncy, fabulous Emanuel gown.

A few years later, I met her at a charity ball where we were both wearing Bruce Oldfield. Diana was exquisite in a silver lamé gown with big shoulder pads, and I wore a white silk jersey also featuring the shoulder arrangement for which I was becoming quite well known. We chatted briefly while the paps papped and the tabloids the following day screeched, 'Dynasty Di meets Alexis.'

Soon afterwards, I started working with Nolan Miller, *Dynasty*'s fabulous designer, on copying some of Princess Diana's more outrageous outfits.

When she went to Russia she wore a fitted grey wool coat and an astrakhan muff, so when Alexis went to Moldavia she wore an almost identical outfit complete with muff, matching hat and knee-length suede boots.

The second time I met her was in Palm Beach at a charity benefit given by the philanthropist Armand Hammer. I had hit it big in *Dynasty* and she had been married to Prince Charles for about two years but it seemed that the honeymoon period was waning.

I stood in line to be presented to her and was surprised when Princess Diana whispered, 'How do you stand it? How do you stand the attention of the press and paparazzi all the time?'

ABOVE: *Dynasty Di meets Alexis. Both wearing Bruce Oldfield, 1985.*

ABOVE AND LEFT: *Princess Diana visits the cast after* Private Lives *at the Aldwych, 1992. Keith Baxter and Edward Duke are in the background.*

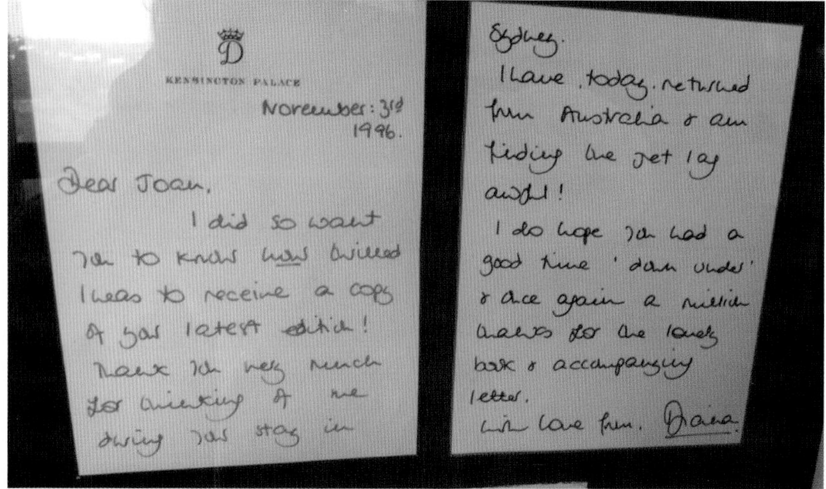

KENSINGTON PALACE

November: 3rd 1996.

Dear Joan,

I did so want you to know how thrilled I was to receive a copy of your latest edition! Thank you very much for thinking of me during your stay in Sydney.

I have, today, returned from Australia & am finding the jet lag awful!

I do hope you had a good time 'down under' & once again a million thanks for the lovely book & accompanying letter.

With love from, Diana

A letter of thanks from Princess Diana. She always hand wrote her thank – you letters – what excellent manners.

I was somewhat flummoxed but replied, 'Well, I guess you just have to try and ignore them as much as possible.'

'Not much chance of that,' she said gesturing towards the batch of international photographers in the bleachers whose long, intrusive lenses were trained on the beautiful young princess. 'They follow me everywhere. It's as if I'm in a goldfish bowl. Do they do that to you?'

'Thankfully not that much,' I answered, 'but I agree it must be very difficult for you.'

'It's horrid,' she shrugged, 'but, I suppose it's part of the job.'

When I moved down the line to meet Prince Charles he said his usual remark and one that is always used by his brother, Prince Andrew. 'What are *you* doing here?'

'I was invited, Sir,' I said curtsying gaily.

Later, Prince Charles sent an equerry over to my table to request a dance and under the eyes of a thousand snapping lenses we waltzed together whilst our future king talked animatedly in his beautifully modulated voice about philanthropy and how important it was.

Suddenly, to my astonishment, my then husband Peter Holm stalked over to Princess Diana and asked her to dance, which she did! A cartoon of the four of us appeared in a tabloid a few days later with the caption: ??

Diana was always a complete model of good manners. When she visited the theatre to see me in *Private Lives*, she was utterly charming and interested to hear about Noël Coward. When I sent her a copy of my beauty book she sent me a glowing handwritten letter of thanks in spite of the fact that she had just returned from a gruelling trip to Australia.

Our paths crossed several times during the years up until her death.

After her divorce, I heard that she and Dodi Fayed were in a relationship. I was quite surprised. I had known Dodi for years as he was a regular at Tramp, the nightclub co-owned by Johnny Gold and Oscar Lerman, Jackie's husband, where I used to often hang out.

He was a nice, rather quiet and polite young man. I had been on the same LA to London flight with him in May 1997 and had asked him while we chatted, 'Do you have a girlfriend in London?'

'No, I don't,' he said smiling 'I'm hoping to meet one, though.'

A couple of months later the world knew that he had indeed found a new girlfriend in Princess Diana.

If Diana thought she had been stalked by the paparazzi enough during her marriage to Charles, it was nothing compared to the furore her relationship with Dodi caused.

However, he was able to provide a certain amount of protection because of his great wealth. In July I was in Saint-Tropez on the fashion designer Valentino's boat when Giancarlo Giammetti, Valentino's business partner, spotted the Fayed yacht, *Kalizna*, moored nearby.

Bringing out his binoculars he scanned the ship and announced, 'I think I see Diana; I'll go and invite her for lunch or dinner.' Jumping on his water scooter he shot over to the boat.

But as he arrived, three burly sailors in white uniforms appeared on the deck holding what looked like Kalashnikov guns in Giancarlo's direction.

'I'd like to speak to the princess,' he shouted.

'Go away,' yelled a guard. 'They don't want to be disturbed.'

'But we're friends of Diana's,' he yelled.

The guns were raised ominously and a guard yelled, 'Leave now.' A crestfallen Giancarlo scooted back to the boat while we all craned our necks to catch a glimpse of the new young couple.

How tragic that it was less than one week later when I was woken at 6 a.m. in the south of France by my agent calling to tell me the awful news of Princess Diana's death.

My friend Stella Wilson and I sat in front of the TV for two days watching the dreadful events unfold as the short, sad saga of Princess Diana's life came to a close.

Cuervo Especial

Chapter Eight

DYNASTY

The call from my agent came as I was lying by the pool in my rented house in Marbella. It was August 1981 and I was on holiday with my family and some friends.

'They want you for *Dynasty*,' said Tom Korman excitedly.

'What's *Dynasty*? A Chinese restaurant?' I asked.

'It's a big TV series on ABC. Haven't you heard about it?'

'Not a word,' I said.

'Well, I'll send you some pages, but they need to know right away as they start shooting their second series in two weeks and they want you to play Alexis.'

'Hmm, that's a good name,' I said. 'How long is the gig?'

'They'll need you for about six weeks,' he said. 'I'll fax you some pages.'

When I read the scenes I thought them pretty interesting so I agreed to go to LA for the six weeks.

OPPOSITE: *Everything was excessive during* Dynasty, *even the drinking.*

That six weeks turned out to be nine years – nine of the most fruitful and fascinating years of my life, and it's hard to believe that it's over thirty years since it all began. In less than a year after I was cast in *Dynasty*, I went from being practically unknown in America to becoming one of the most popular actresses on television. My face was plastered in magazines and newspapers worldwide and my every move was chronicled and gossiped about.

I arrived in Hollywood on a gorgeous California day with the 'bitch of the year' part in my pocket. But, of course, I didn't know that yet. On my first day on set I had to wear the same costume that an unknown actress had

First day on set, on the stand being cross-examined by Brian Dennehy.

worn in the final episode of the first series, because even at the last minute, the producers hadn't cast the role, having offered it to, and been turned down by, Elizabeth Taylor and Sophia Loren, among others. They were having furious rows in the ABC boardroom about who should play Alexis.

Few of the ABC brass and producers wanted Joan Collins, although they changed their tune later. If they couldn't get Liz or Sophia, they were hot for Jessica Walter, and it was only because my old friend Aaron Spelling fought tooth and nail for me that they finally relented. So on that sunny November morning I donned a second-hand black and white suit, a big, white, wide-brimmed veiled hat and dark sunglasses, and walked into the courtroom where Blake Carrington was on trial for the murder of Ted Dinard, the lover of Blake and Alexis's gay son, Steven.

On my first scene on the stand, being cross-questioned by the prosecutor, played by the great actor Brian Dennehy, the entire *Dynasty* clan sat in the courtroom looking me up and down. I knew they were all commenting sotto voce to each other about my face, my figure, my acting and my attitude, so as I sat in the witness box, I was glad I had totally memorized the fifteen pages of dialogue.

OPPOSITE: *Aaron Spelling wanted opulence in* Dynasty *and he got it.*

I caught the eye of 'Blake' (John Forsythe) who gave me a grim smile. I wondered whether he was acting or if he hadn't enjoyed his breakfast, but I hoped the former as I was directing hate-filled looks his way, as Alexis despised Blake. Krystle Carrington (Linda Evans) smiled at me sweetly but then I recalled what her ex-husband, John Derek, had said about her: 'Every time I see Linda she smiles sweetly as if I were the only person in the world she wanted to see. Then one day I realized she smiled at everyone that way.'

My 'children', Steven (Al Corley) and Fallon (Pamela Sue Martin) stared at me ambiguously. The friendliest face of all in the spectator

'Put Alexis in gorgeous costumes all the time. The public loves her.'

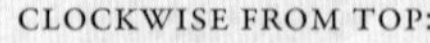

CLOCKWISE FROM TOP:
Alexis gives Blake the basilisk stare – he looks blank, Krystle looks sweet; Off set we were friendly; A battle in the boardroom.

LEFT: *September 23, 1984 – The Emmy Awards Presentation with Linda Evans and Diahann Carroll. The introduction is quoted as:*

DIAHANN: *'As the new girl they let me talk first.'*
LINDA: *'As the good girl they let me talk second.'*
JOAN: *'As the bad girl they let me talk whenever I want.'*

DAILY EXPRESS Tuesday February 14 1984

DAILY EXPRESS Tuesday February 14 1984

DAY TWO of the secrets of TV's hottest show—by JEAN ROOK

Sexiest thing in soap (BAR NONE)

YOU'RE wary of your first close-up encounter with Joan Collins in the 50-year-old flesh.

With no TV screen to shield her, the illusion could crumble, the money bags could show under the eyes. And all that Miss Collins is cracked up to be could crack up within six feet of you.

How Joan's revival put the bubbles back in Dynasty

At 8.30 a.m., in a break in the thickening plot of Dynasty, Miss Collins's hips swayed across to her make-up mirror. She must be the only woman of five foot four who can walk as tall as a palm tree caught in a high wind.

The face in the mirror was flawless. Miss Collins didn't need her reflection, or the applauding 70-strong crew of Dynasty to assure her she's still the fairest of them all.

At a time of day when most actresses are as black as their coffee, she was bubbling with enthusiasm and glowing like a 16-year-old at the dawn of her career.

"Did you see my pictures in Playboy and what did you think?" she said. (I thought I'd die of naked jealousy).

"Not bad, was I? At least they made up for those terrible newspaper snaps of me in my hair rollers. God, did you see that? I wasn't thrilled about it I can tell you.

"But more fool me for stepping out on my balcony in Gstaad. Twelve paparazzi with long lenses had shot me before the penny dropped, but they must have been out there all night.

SOARING

"At least it proved that although my hair may be thin, it's all my own. Of course I wear hair pieces and wigs for Dynasty but never off screen, and I'm certainly not bald."

In half a century, absolutely nothing has slipped off this woman whose portrayal of Alexis Carrington has uplifted Dynasty in its now soaring ratings.

Her figure is even more incredible than the £75,000 an episode they pay her. The woman is an hour glass in which the sands of time are permanently stuck. So how does she do it? Modestly she says: "All I take tremendous care of is my weight. If I put on five pounds I put on five years."

Before Alexis Carrington stuck her long cruel red finger in it, Dynasty was little more than apple pie in the sky. It was sweet enough gook, well sugared by Linda Evans as the sprinkle-brained blonde Krystle. But it had none of the sexual love bite of J.R. Ewing in Dallas.

Then enter Alexis. Within two torrid episodes, she uplifted Dynasty's sagging appeal like the boned bra Miss Collins looks as if she's wearing even when she's stark naked.

As Dynasty's creator Esther Shapiro put it: "Those women in Dallas all look and sound alike. They're passive sexual punchbags. Alexis could eat the lot of them alive."

But if the bloodiest-minded-ever Scarlet Woman has pumped passion and intrigue into a series soaring in popularity like its viewers' blood pressure, the blood transfusion has been mutual.

Dynasty has put new life into a one-time tired looking career which was only just saved by Miss Collins' parts in the films of her sister Jackie's novels, The Stud and The Bitch.

"I owe a lot to Alexis," Miss Collins told me between endless Dynasty takes.

But speaking of husband Ron Kass's attempt's to slaughter her reputation in print after their marriage failed, she added: "I'm not like her. I'm not vindictive. I don't believe in an eye for an eye and I'm not bitter.

PROUD

"I've got my children who make up for anything bad that could ever happen. I have a fabulous career—so long as it lasts. And I'm proud that I've made it against the odds.

"It isn't easy to crack Hollywood when you've been out of the business for a long time, you're over 40 and you're British."

Alexis's latest on screen lover (yet to be seen in Britain) is a 38-year-old six-foot-two super-stud called Dex Dexter, who in one steamy scene shares a double bath with her.

"We used £10 worth of soap bubbles instead of sheets to hide what was supposed to be going on."

More dangerous, mourn her friends and rejoice her enemies, is her latest off screen lover, 36-year-old six-foot-one blond Swedish businessman Peter Holm, whom some say is only in it for her money.

"I don't believe that; I'm sure Peter loves me, and it's never crossed my mind that I'll lose him because I've never lost a man yet.

"God, that sounds big-headed, it really does, but it's the truth," snapped Miss Collins like Alexis's predatory fingernails.

"I don't think of age in terms of numbers. It's a throwback to the Dark Ages when the only reason men and women got together was to have children.

"Michael Caine is my age and his wife is Peter's age and nobody makes a big deal about that.

"Nobody can be young forever, but age can make a woman better — look at antiques and vintage wine," said Miss Collins.

"They've been telling me since I was 36 that I am getting long in the tooth. That's why I'm so proud of those Playboy pictures.

"They've given a gre[...] of hope to women o[...] they've written to te[...] they've stuck me, nak[...] the doors of their frid[...] The ice cubes inside [...] be in full flood.

SUPER

But why, with all her, and so many confessions behind her, Joan Collins still suffer[...] one Achilees high heel [...] cannot bear—to the po[...] suing newspapers who [...] the expression without [...] sulting her—to be t[...] "Superbitch".

Miss Collins is super. [...] is a prize Crufts bitch. [...] suddenly draw in her [...] over a title which can [...] grab her the good pu[...] she's never shunned?

"The older kids didn'[...]

before honest [...]

[...] newspaper—until the children really got onto me about it.

"Sometimes it bothers me that I'm so stupid about it."

Joan Collins—an uplifting figure who has sent the Dynas[...]

TOMORROW: Blake, the King Lear jet

WHATTA DOLL: Former Dynasty vixen Joan Collins was never the shy type and neither is her new doll, all dolled up in red and black and feathers like a man-eating tootsie

"That sounds like a challenge and I adore a
DYNASTY

ABOVE: *The complimentary articles kept coming – oh it's a wonder I could get my hat on!*

RIGHT: *Playthings – some of the dolls that were created from my characters.*

During Dynasty *I was allowed to 'moonlight' and made several TV movies including this TV special with Morgan Fairchild called* Blondes versus Brunettes.

section was 'Jeff Colby' (John James), who gave me a secret wink and 'thumbs up'. John and I actually became the best of friends during the nine years of shooting and still keep in touch.

During Blake's trial for manslaughter, I had to testify that fifteen years ago he had fought with and possibly murdered my lover, Roger Grimes. I put plenty of sugar-coated venom into my speeches about Blake and I could see that the cast and crew seemed intrigued.

The following day, Nolan Miller, the designer of the fabulous *Dynasty* duds, told me that when he, Aaron and several suits from ABC watched the dailies, everyone gasped when I took off my sunglasses and raised the veil.

'Put a lot of hats on that gal,' Aaron instructed Nolan. 'She looks great in hats.'

Soon after Alexis entered Denver, *Dynasty*, which had been languishing in the ratings, began to climb inexorably to the top of them and the studio became flooded by fan mail for me. The edict from ABC was, 'Put Alexis in gorgeous costumes all the time. The public loves her.'

Alexis was a superbly meaty role, but I was still amazed at how fast the public took to her. They loved her one-liners and zingers to Krystle and Fallon. When Alexis first sees her daughter after fifteen years in exile, thanks to Blake, she purrs, 'I see you've had your teeth fixed, if not your tongue.' And when she rejects Dex after teasing him, she purrs before leaving, 'No one takes me to the cleaners and to bed on the same day, Mr Dexter.'

I realized that, although Alexis could be construed as somewhat clichéd, there was enough humour in her lines for me to build an interesting character, particularly if I could have input into her dialogue, which I often tailored to make more convincing, and into my wardrobe!

Up until then, most actresses on television dressed down in slacks, twinsets and blouses with pussycat bows. Even the *Charlie's Angels* girls wore quite simple clothes, albeit revealing, but since I had always loved fashion, working with Nolan on my outfits and helping to design them was a real joy.

It was huge fun hitting that 'dressing-up box', as we called the studio wardrobe department, to plot and plan what Alexis would wear for each episode – almost as much fun as seeing Alexis plot and plan the demise

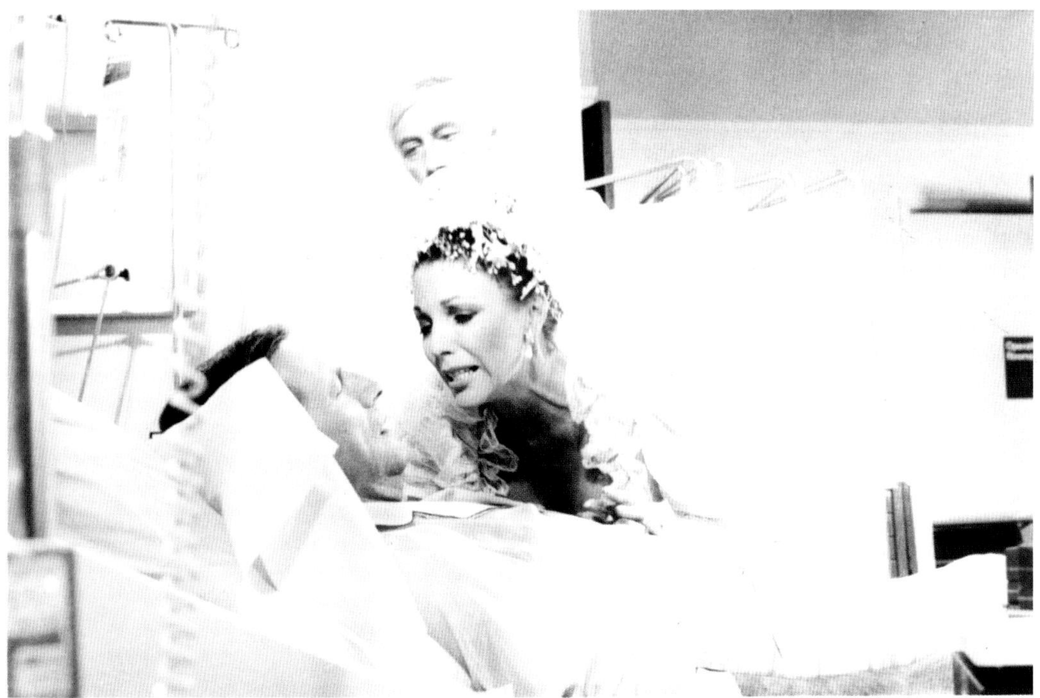

The notorious 'Cecil, don't you dare die on me' scene as Alexis marries him on his deathbed.

of Blake Carrington. Since we made twenty-eight episodes a year and I wore at least three or four outfits in each one, I must have worn at least a hundred costumes a year. After nine years it probably totalled over 1,000 outfits. Nolan and I worked closely, deciding what particular look would be suitable for the scene, and I think many viewers tuned in, amongst other reasons, because they appreciated the fashions.

I must admit that sometimes we did go over the top and I occasionally cringe when watching an old episode and seeing myself attired in some almost clownish outfit. One particular horror was in a scene with Blake and Sable. I'm in a massive, black, frizzy Diana Ross-type wig topped with a black embroidered fez hat. Under this I wore a long black slit-to-the-thigh skirt and a tight-waisted black and gold scarf slung jauntily over my shoulder, topped off with chunky gold jewellery and gloves – I looked ready for Halloween!

I was occasionally gifted with one or two of the outfits I wore on the series. Once, one of the producers' wives went ballistic when she saw a photo of Linda and me at a Hollywood party in our Alexis and Krystle gowns, but we had no choice other than to wear the costumes for these industry events. We had no time for our own personal shopping, our appearances promoted their show and an actress can only wear a dress once on the red carpet.

ABOVE: *Some of Nolan Miller's designs for Alexis.*

'I must have worn at least a hundred costumes a year.'

CLOCKWISE FROM TOP LEFT: *Nolan in his atelier; Out at the Carousel Ball with me; this gold lamé dress was another over-the-top number but the public loved 'em; the pink gown was worn for my 'daughter' Amanda's wedding during the notorious Moldavian Massacre.*

But in spite of a few mistakes, the Alexis look became an iconic symbol of the powerful eighties woman.

I'm often asked about the big shoulder pads we used to wear. Quite frankly I have always loved shoulder pads. They make our waists look smaller, our hips slimmer and they are more flattering than an Italian waiter. All the movie stars of the forties – Joan Crawford, Barbara Stanwyck, Lana Turner – wore padded jackets and nipped-in waists. It's a timeless and becoming look. Imagine a man's suit without shoulder pads – it would look like a dreary sack.

But us *Dynasty* gals needed to remain at our 'fighting weight' in order to wear these flamboyant creations, and it was a struggle to remain thin because the 'craft service' film catering table was always groaning with delicious, tempting goodies. All of the older actresses (Linda Evans, Diahann Carroll and me) had to be particularly disciplined, because the camera adds ten pounds. I would sometimes loiter by the craft service munching on a tasty celery stick and watching with envy the younger girls – Heather Locklear, Emma Samms and others – stuffing their faces and never gaining an ounce. Craft service didn't help us by stacking the tables high with pasta, hot dogs, soups, pizzas and all manner of snacks. The food was right in front of the entrance to the sound stage that housed all the interior sets so you couldn't miss it! From the moment we set foot on the sound stage at 7 a.m. or thereabouts until the last scene was filmed, usually between 7 and 8.30 p.m., there was non-stop food. The crew, who were quite hefty to begin with, usually gained at least a stone during the eight-month shooting season. I won't deny I usually embarked on a crash diet a week before we started shooting – I don't advocate it but needs must and so forth!

Soon the British public cottoned on, and headlines like 'Villainous JC set to take over from Villainous JR' started to appear. *Dallas* was already a big hit, and Larry Hagman was the number one villain on TV, but I was catching up! By the second year of *Dynasty*, we were the number one show not only in the US but in over seventy other countries too.

When the producers realized that the physical fights between Krystle and Alexis were pure viewing gold they tried to concoct at least one or two every season. But oh, how I detested those fight scenes! I've always disliked

LEFT: *That was real mud we were up to our necks in – vile!*

BELOW: *Krystle and I pose for a mock up fight.*

any physical violence, and Gene Kelly had sagely told me when I first came to Hollywood, 'Remember kiddo, you don't have to do anything rough or dangerous on set. They pay stunt-gals for that.' But Linda, who was quite a jock and about three inches taller than me, adored fight scenes and refused to use her double. In our first big fight scene in Alexis's apartment, as Linda and I faced up, Gene Kelly's words rang in my ears: 'You're putting some poor stunt-gal out of business!' So, after the dialogue, when it came time for Linda to throw me around, hit me and bash my head against the wall, I called upon my trusty double Sandy to be in the firing line. Ignoring Linda's scornful look, I sat sipping coffee next to the camera while the two of them went at it hammer and tongs. But I did let her throw me on to the bed and we hit each other with pillows. Boy, did the feathers fly – and oh, how the audiences loved it!

In 1983 *Dynasty* was nominated for an Emmy and I won the Golden Globe for Best Actress. When I accepted I crowed, 'I want to thank Sophia Loren for turning down the role and everyone from Aaron Spelling on

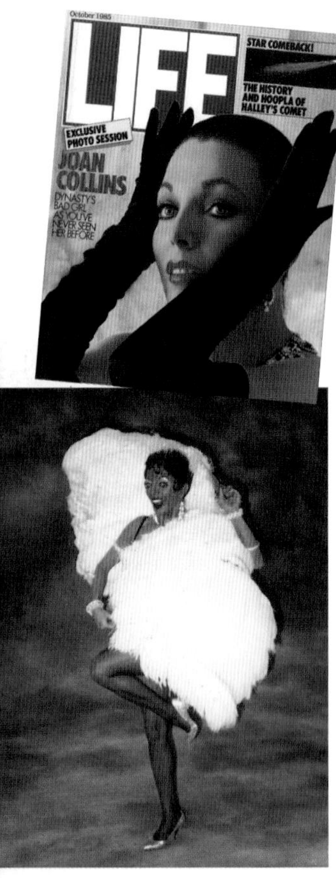

The Life *magazine cover and photo of me, as Josephine Baker from the layout.*

up!' I hope they understood my sense of humour. The following year I won the People's Choice Award, and went on to be nominated several more times for an Emmy and won other awards – some important, some not. As Billy Wilder said, 'Awards are like haemorrhoids – eventually every asshole gets one!'

I sometimes answered the phone onstage by chirping, '*Dynasty*-number-one-show!' I was on top of the world and with the success I became inundated with requests for interviews, photoshoots and magazine covers, all of which had to be worked around the fourteen-hour day, five-days-a-week shooting schedule. It was so tight that most of my weekends were taken up with them, not to mention the constant search for more outrageous, but chic, haute couture costumes, which most of the time looked fabulous.

And I only had to ask for something and I got it. When I told Jeffrey Lane that I'd like to do a *Life* magazine cover and layout of ten of the most iconic women in the world, lo and behold, my wish was granted. I spent two weekends in a row posing as Elizabeth I, Cleopatra, Josephine Baker, Catherine the Great, Marilyn Monroe and the Duchess of Windsor. In fact, I was featured on magazine covers over 300 times during *Dynasty*.

Aaron had insisted to Nolan that Alexis should always be more expensively and chicly attired than any of the other actresses, which most of them didn't mind. Then, when Diahann Carroll was cast as 'Dominique Deveraux', Blake's half-sister and 'television's first black bitch', as she referred to herself, the gloves came off in the overdressing department.

In the makeup room we used to joke about what we were going to wear. 'Darling, I'm in pearls and a mink hat today,' Diahann would remark. 'Really? I'm in diamonds and a sable coat!' I giggled. The competition to 'out do' each other sartorially did a great deal for the show as well. Even though our characters hated each other convincingly on screen, we were extremely good friends then and still are.

Unfortunately that was not the case between John Forsythe and myself. He was always rather aloof, although he was very warm towards my stand-in, Judy Bryer. He and Linda were also extremely close, and she relied on him totally. I was never invited to John or Linda's homes, or even out to dinner, although they attended a couple of soirées at my house. I found this rude at first, but Nolan suggested that the massive attention the Alexis character generated, propelling *Dynasty* to the top of the ratings, had perhaps caused a touch of the green-eyed monster, even though they were both making more money than I was.

Aaron told me that when I posed for *Playboy*, Mr Forsythe stormed into his office yelling, 'She's a disgrace to our show and bringing down the reputation of this series.'

ABOVE: *A tense night when the* Dynasty *cast went to the People's Choice Awards and the presenter handed the award to me – to John's chagrin.*

LEFT: *With my 'sister' Caress (Kate O'Mara) at a fancy dress ball at Alexis's mansion. I always called her Cassie!*

Things really came to a head in 1984 when *Dynasty* won the People's Choice Award for best ensemble cast. We were all seated together at a round table in the venue, dressed to the nines as usual. ABC's press representative had told us that if we won the glass statuette representing a pair of applauding hands, John would accept it. As soon as it was announced that we had won, the ten of us trooped up on to the stage and the starlet handing out the awards made a beeline for me and plonked it in my hands!

Dex 'The Stud' Dexter – Michael Nader, whose kisses often drew blood!

Somewhat surprised, I made a short thank-you speech and then handed it to John saying, 'Now I turn it over to our fearless leader.' He snatched it from me snarling, 'She's said enough!' and stalked offstage with all of us trooping obediently behind him. I was mortified. John hardly spoke to me for the rest of that season, and at the season finale when Blake tries to strangle Alexis, I called on my trusty body-double, Sandy, to be the recipient of his wrath, just in case!

However, very gradually, his attitude mellowed towards me so by 2005, when we filmed the *Dynasty* reunion, we hugged and kissed, fondly reminisced and were genuinely happy to see each other. I was very sad when he died in 2010 – he had, after all, been a huge part of my career and that really was the end of the *Dynasty* era.

Things really looked up for Alexis in 1983 when, after bonking Cecil Colby to death and becoming the richest woman in Denver, she meets handsome 'Dex Dexter' (Michael Nader). He was extremely good looking and charismatic, and soon became the resident *Dynasty* stud, but his kisses were so fierce I often ended up with a bloody lip! Our love scenes were hot and heavy and quite a few took place in a bubble bath or sauna. Alexis eventually dumped Dex when he had an affair with Amanda (Catherine Oxenberg), yet another long-lost daughter of Blake and Alexis. I loved working with Michael, and constantly badgered the producers to let us get back together, while they preferred us to be constantly feuding. We had great chemistry together and I ribbed him mercilessly when he wanted a rise and remarked that he found it 'hard to get by on just $40,000 an episode'!

Then in 1986, out of pure greed, the producers decided that since *Dynasty* was such a major hit they would produce a spin-off series and so *The Colbys* was born. John James as Jeff Colby was transplanted and they assembled a starry cast – Charlton Heston, Moses himself, was the patriarch, and Barbara Stanwyck, Stephanie Beacham and Maxwell Caulfield were some of the protagonists.

The producers were extremely anxious for me to guest star in *The Colbys* but I refused, believing that would confuse viewers even more. I wanted to remain loyal to the show that had done so much for me. Nevertheless John Forsythe and Linda Evans trekked over to do guest slots on *The Colbys*.

ABC decided to give *The Colbys* our 9 p.m. Wednesday night slot, which *Dynasty* fans had been religiously tuning into for years. But *The Colbys* was a hugely expensive show and not very good – a pale imitation. The disastrous result was massive confusion between the two shows which caused *Dynasty* to lose millions of viewers and its number one rating. *Dynasty*'s downward spiral was tragic, and the storylines became more and more fanciful to avert it – alien abductions, terrorist massacres in small Crimean countries and so on.

Tony and I reconciled towards the end of Dynasty*, much to the relief of the children.*

The writing was on the wall long before the footballer-sized shoulder pads went into cold storage. ('They'll be back!' I foretold accurately, and indeed massive shoulders continue to be the rage at the Paris couture shows.)

The ratings fell so rapidly that we were cancelled. Ironically, in that final year, after years of negotiating, *Dynasty*'s producers finally gave me salary parity with John Forsythe, although his contract stipulated that he had to get a few thousand a week more than any other actor. To my dismay, when I reported for work on this ninth season in 1989, I was told by our new producer and writer, Mr David Paulson, 'Sorry, Joan, we can't afford to pay you every week so you're only going to be in half the episodes.' Granted, I was making wheelbarrows of money by eighties standards. Nevertheless, John Forsythe appeared in every episode and therefore made twice what I made. It was galling. He wasn't on covers!

Immortalised in wax at Madame Tussauds. I wonder who they melted down to make me?

Heaven forefend that the fact I was a woman had anything to do with this. It was commonly believed in many businesses that women were disposable – 'But, *Dynasty* with less Alexis, surely that's network suicide,' a friend predicted. Sadly she was right. *Dynasty*'s ratings dropped dramatically each week as the producers brought in different actors and ridiculous scenarios to fill the gap. Sometimes angry fans would accost me, demanding to know why I hardly featured in their favourite show – as if it were my fault.

To say I was upset was putting it mildly. Linda Evans had already quit the show, so *Dynasty* now lost both of its leading ladies. Jack Coleman, who played the popular character of my gay son Steven from the third series onwards, also decided to leave along with Heather Locklear. The only original actors left from the first few series were John Forsythe, John James (who returned because *The Colbys* had failed) and Michael Nader. They brought in *The Colbys*' Stephanie Beacham as my hated and hateful cousin Sable but by then the series had lost its lustre. *Dynasty* was dying.

I was sad but also resigned, knowing that nothing lasts forever. *Dynasty* had been a hit – the biggest TV drama for almost a decade. It had brought me fame and fortune to a staggering degree, but I faced the fact that the decade that greed begot was limping towards its end. Besides, there's only so much 'I hate you, Blake, I hate you and I'll make you pay for this' that one actress can convincingly spit out before it gets boring to both the actress and the viewer.

The reunion of Dynasty. *Still in a big hat, but it was a disaster.*

Bye bye Dynasty – *last day of filming, March 1989.*

The final episode was ludicrous: Alexis discovers that Dex had fathered a baby with Sable ('How lovely, a change of life baby,' she sneered), Krystle is in a clinic in a coma, Blake is shot in the head, Fallon is trapped in a tunnel with her child, and Alexis and Dex fall through some banisters and tumble seemingly to their death. Freeze frame – they're left suspended in mid-air as 'The End' comes up on screen.

What a cop out! Our faithful viewers went ballistic, furious that there was no resolution or happy ending. So, by popular demand, three years later we made *Dynasty the Reunion*, which was presented to the public in 1992. Krystle has recovered from her coma and Alexis is as good as new. One character reports, 'She twisted her body in mid-air and fell on to Dex, who broke her fall but died in the process.' In the finale all the characters reunite and toast each other: a real happy, cheesy ending . . .

As the nineties dawned, the flashy outfits, outsize bling and supersize lifestyles that so many had attempted to emulate were no longer in vogue. They quickly became tacky and *démodé* as the world turned more casual and grungy. The eighties had been the 'me' decade – conspicuous greed, grab and graft had been the modus operandi, and nothing anyone did, however outrageous, seemed out of place or shocking.

It was the decade of Concorde, that gorgeous, sleek supersonic jet that whisked you between two continents in less than four hours. Breakfast in London, a quick lunch meeting in NY and back for dinner in Paris – high-flying businessmen revelled in this time travel, as did I. The bull market soared, the financial wizards and brokers came into their own, trading billions with the insouciance of Michael Douglas's wicked 'Gordon Gekko' in *Wall Street*, and sowing the seeds of the hedge fund phenomenon of the nineties and the apocalypse that ensued.

Mrs Thatcher and Mr Reagan epitomized the new prosperity in politics, and *Dynasty* epitomized it on TV. In the eighties 'the American Dream' came true for many, whilst the UK saw a renaissance of the British Dream, soon to turn into a nightmare.

It was one long spending spree, and not just for me. Everyone, it seemed, was doing a Viv Nicholson, the famous sixties pools-winner, and wanted to spend, spend, spend! The clothes budget on *Dynasty* was astronomical. Every leading actress wore between three and seven bespoke outfits each week and most of those gorgeously beaded and decorated evening gowns cost upwards of $7,000.

It was party season all year round in London, Los Angeles, Paris and the south of France. I was invited to fabulous events from Milan to Marrakesh, all expenses paid, of course. But relatively speaking things were much less expensive then. A ready-to-wear Chanel suit cost around $2,000, whilst today it can be as much as $20,000. And lunches and dinners at glamorous restaurants were only half of what they are now.

GRIFFIN'S EYE
EastEnders
U.S. SOAPS ON THE SKIDS
"Aw, c'mon Joan honey, I reckon we were real lucky to be offered this job."

The media used to love comparing Alexis with evil JR from Dallas.

Larry (JR) Hagman with Alexis at an awards ceremony in Germany where I received the Golden Kamera Award.

For example, just a few years after *Dynasty*, my $120,000 per episode and 'highest paid actress on television' salary was puny in comparison with what actors earned on television in the mid-nineties. The cast of *Friends* were reportedly paid $1 million each per episode and even now secondary characters on mildly rated shows can make $250,000–$300,000. $500,000 per episode is not unusual and allegedly Charlie Sheen's salary at the height of *Two and a Half Men* was $1.8 million per episode – fifteen times what I earned per episode in my highest season!

ABOVE: *With David Hasselhoff in* The Cartier Affair

We had great times in the eighties and partied like it was 1999, but 2000 came around all too soon and the world started to change radically. I learned way before *Dynasty* that good times don't last forever, but the flip side is that bad times don't either.

I have so many happy memories about *Dynasty* as well as some sad ones. I was upset when Ali MacGraw was fired in front of the cast and crew at the party to mark the conclusion the second series; it was extremely upsetting to watch Rock Hudson, once one of the handsomest and most bankable stars, wasting away from AIDS in season two; it was tragic to watch our fabulous ratings fading away as *Dynasty*'s plots became more and more far-fetched. But I wouldn't have missed it for the world and if they asked me to do it all over again, well of course I would, if only I could fit into the clothes.

Chapter Nine

FASHION

I've never been a stick insect or even a twiglet. When Twiggy ruled the fashion waves in the mid-sixties I was either pregnant or trying to get rid of the baby weight. The thinnest I ever became was when making a movie with an Italian crew in Mombasa, Africa. Since the food didn't agree with any of us we all ate lots of chocolates and sweets and the weight fell off. 'Ah, you look so *chic*!' beamed the Italian director as my waist and bust shrivelled and my costumes had to be taken in . . . but indeed I *did* look chic!

OPPOSITE:
Just a simple look for a Russian winter!

However, I don't recommend a chocolates and sweets diet and my mother would have turned over in her grave had she known. In fact, I don't really recommend any diet beyond common sense. It was my mother's upbringing and advice that taught me to follow a reasonably safe and healthy eating regime, and I no longer diet or attempt to have the body of a twenty-year-old, because I've seen the women who do and it's *not* attractive. It's called the '16/60' look: sixteen years old from the back, age sixty from the front, and I've always maintained that there is a very fine line between a daring, sexy older woman and mutton dressed as lamb.

What I do have is a passion for fashion. I've always adored the dressing-up box, as these photos throughout the decades, from the fifties until today, show . . .

In the early fifties, fashion for teenagers was non-existent. Girls still wore mini-versions of their mother's drab frocks or cardigan sets, and the word 'teenager' was seldom used. The term was a new phenomenon, somewhat disapproved of by a generation brought up with the credo that

Some of my fashion sketches from the fifties.

I designed this pink ballgown and wore it to the Oscars.

'As a teenager I hankered to be a fashion designer, sketching and painting designs.'

LEFT AND ABOVE: *I had a rather meagre wardrobe when I first hit Hollywood. For photo shoots actresses were always supposed to wear their own clothes. There was no such thing as a 'stylist' then, and you also did your own hair and makeup.*

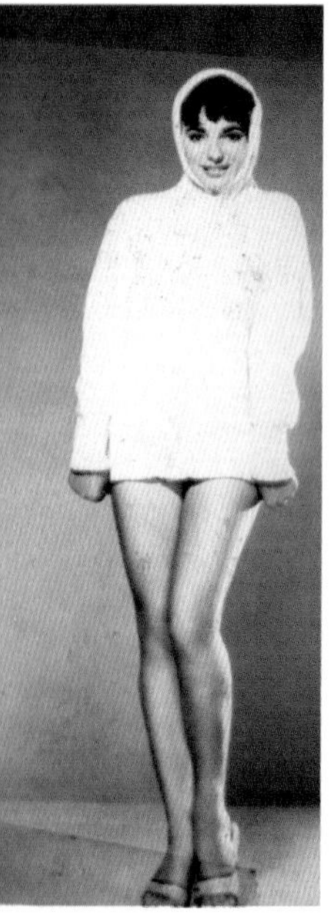

My own clothes were worn for all the various photo shoots. I can't believe how tiny my waist was.

'children should be seen and not heard'. As a teenager I hankered to be a fashion designer, sketching and painting designs, which sometimes my mother and aunts would actually have a dressmaker make up for them – imagine my elation!

I also adored Christian Dior's 'New Look' and persuaded my mother to buy me a big brown dirndl skirt with a tightly cinched waist and a tiny yellow fitted jacket on top from the 'Zara' of its day, C&A.

I went through my bohemian 'Juliette Gréco' period at sixteen – all black, turtleneck, tight pants and a wide belt – but when I went to Hollywood I had to up my game and become a fashionable girl about town. This meant that, at twenty-one, I had to dress like a woman in her forties, which was the style then. Joan Crawford once said, 'I feel I owe it to my public to always look good. When you're young you can get away with the careless, un-groomed look. But not to bother with grooming over the age of forty is a mistake.'

OPPOSITE: *How to wear an apron. A studio shoot in which I didn't wear my own clothes.*

I have never really liked jeans, probably because their ubiquitousness has become terribly boring. Do people really want to look just like everyone else? Besides, when I wear tight jeans, I find I'm constantly tugging at and rearranging them because they feel so uncomfortable. But loose-fitting jeans look horrible, and the 'chafe-factor' is the same with either one. It's a 'lose–lose' endeavour.

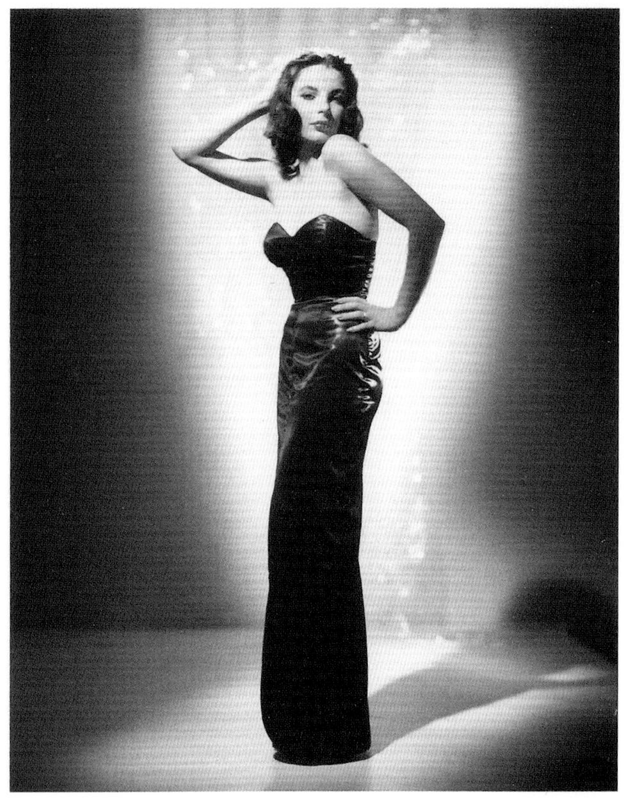

ABOVE LEFT: *Biggins and I having a ball at a ball.*

LEFT: *One of Nolan Miller's more elegant creations.*

ABOVE: *Cornel Lucas took this iconic shot of the 18 year old Rank Starlet which now hangs at the National Portrait Gallery.*

OPPOSITE: *Over the top,* moi?

BELOW: *Always happy to celebrate any 'special relationship.*

I haven't given up wearing jeans altogether but I do pick the places where I will wear them: in Saint-Tropez I wear them to the market or shopping at the grocery store and, if it's really cold, on a boat. When I'm filming, I'll throw on a pair in the early morning, but in general I will only wear jeans for the purpose that they were originally designed – functionality.

However, I didn't hate them so much not to have, in 1979, my own jeans line. When 'Joan Collins Jeans' were launched, I thought they would be interesting as designer jeans were not common then as they are now. So off I went to flog 'em in various department stores in the provinces. They created quite a stir, as they fitted perfectly and were very flattering. Sadly, however, the line didn't last, so a rare pair of 'JC Jeans' now apparently goes for a pretty penny on eBay.

I knew the day would arrive when fashionistas would decide in their infinite wisdom that the much-derided eighties fashion was in vogue again. In 2009 *Harper's Bazaar* flatteringly chose me as the 'inspiration' for power dressing, which had a big-time reinvention with many major designers.

With Valentino on his yacht. When he dressed me for Sins *he was concerned that I was too buxom for his clothes. 'What shall we do about the boom booms?' he despaired. He eventually made me a corset to wear over my chest – which the director immediately made me remove!*

I'm really glad they've seen the light, because I've always thought eighties clothes had a really bad rap. When I started on *Dynasty* in 1981, I had no idea what effect the outfits were going to have on a female population of the Western world who were thirsty for empowerment and feminism was the order of the day. During the early part of the decade, the French and Italian designers were pushing their latest 'new look' of tiny fitted jackets with big shoulders, sleek knee-length pencil skirts and moderately high heels that a women could easily walk about in, unlike today's teetering, ridiculously high monstrosities

Bearing in mind Coco Chanel's axiom that a woman's knees and elbows are the least attractive part of her anatomy, eighties skirts skimmed the knees and the dresses had sleeves. The sleeves were a major feature of eighties dresses, suits and evening gowns. They were often big and too puffy, but were usually stunning and covered up what most women over forty want to hide – their arms.

OPPOSITE: *A sisterly cover also used on* Vanity Fair.

Eventually, the sleeves and shoulders became gaudier and more excessive, until eventually they reached such gigantic proportions that sometimes in *Dynasty* I had to go through the set doors sideways. When I met the queen mother at a Royal premiere during that time, I sported a shocking pink satin gown adorned with huge bows on each shoulder and, when I turned sideways, my face was half hidden!

I also loved wearing those slinky evening gowns or heavily beaded numbers, some of which were so heavy it took two dressers to help me into them. These dresses were also passed on to other actresses to wear in later episodes. A beaded gown I wore in one episode was slightly altered and worn again by one of my screen daughters several episodes later. And in the 1995 movie *Casino*, Sharon Stone wore two of my gowns from *Dynasty*. 'They just had to take them out a bit on the hips!' she joked.

The trouser suit was also a great statement look in *Dynasty*. Worn with heels and jewellery, it was utterly feminine, exuded dominance and was at the same time comfortable and easy to wear. In those yet nascent days of the metrosexual male, many men accepted being bossed around by a female in a power suit with better grace than in an overtly sexual outfit. In other words, you would be taken seriously if you dressed like a grown-up.

The eighties were a time of total excess, and art soon began to imitate life – or was it the other way around? The Reagan years in the White House featured lavish white-tie galas, and First Lady Nancy Reagan wore Galanos couture and looked fabulous. And Princess Diana, sometimes affectionately called 'Dynasty Di' by the press, did her bit for the eighties look with some gorgeous clothes. There is no doubt that most eighties fashion was flattering, feminine and fabulous – take a look!

Some different looks for any and every occasion throughout the years.

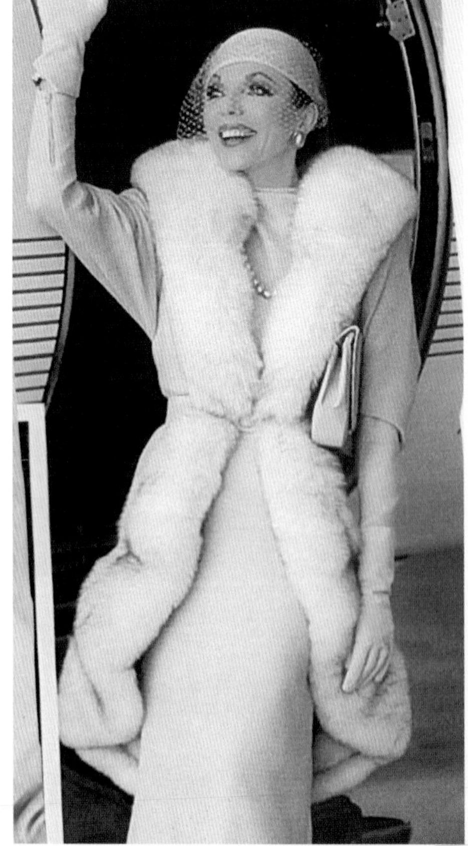

LEFT: *What we called the 'Bette Davis' dress, designed by Nolan. It was copied from one she wore and I wore it to honour him at his memorial party in 2012.*

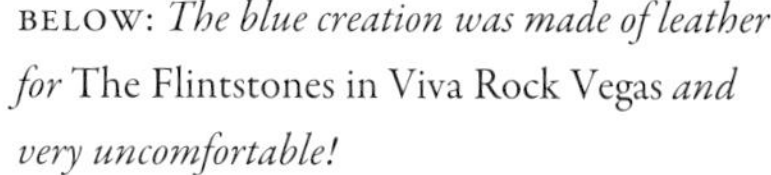

BELOW: *The blue creation was made of leather for* The Flintstones in Viva Rock Vegas *and very uncomfortable!*

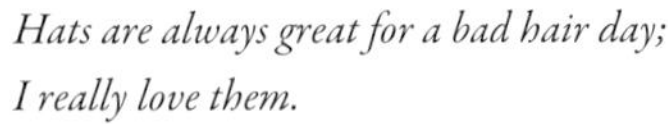

Hats are always great for a bad hair day; I really love them.

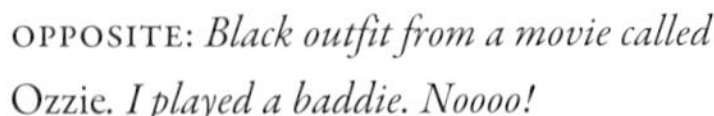

OPPOSITE: *Black outfit from a movie called* Ozzie. *I played a baddie. Noooo!*

Chapter Ten

RED CARPET

Of all the red carpet events the Oscars are the *raison d'être* of Hollywood's social season. Although the event is usually on the last Sunday in February or the first Sunday of March, Oscar buzz begins in late October when the first of dozens of DVDs pop through the letterbox destined for the illustrious elite: the voters who call the shots in the race to win the Academy Awards.

The Oscar, which was allegedly named when Bette Davis observed how closely the statuette's buttocks resembled those of her husband's Harmon Oscar Nelson, is without doubt the most coveted and prestigious of movie awards in all categories. Best Picture, Actor, Director and every possible technical achievement from lighting to sound to makeup and special effects enter the fiercest contest to win their division since Joan Crawford and Bette Davis tried to out act each other in *Whatever Happened to Baby Jane?* As a member of AMPAS (the Academy of Motion Picture Arts and Sciences), I am lucky enough to receive these DVDs to consider who or what I shall vote for every year. Some years there's a glut of good films, but sometimes the pickings are really slim.

OPPOSITE: *Berlin 1999, holding the Golden Kamera Award for 'Best Actress of the Century'! Oh really?*

I've been taking my Oscar voter responsibilities very seriously since I first went to the Awards ceremony in 1958 with Joanne Woodward and Paul Newman. Joanne, who was nominated for *The Three Faces of Eve*, wore a green taffeta gown that she had made and sewn herself. After she won Best Actress some Hollywoodians went into a frenzy – attacking her for wearing a homemade dress. Joan Crawford sniped, 'With that dress she's set Hollywood back twenty years.' Marlon Brando also won that year

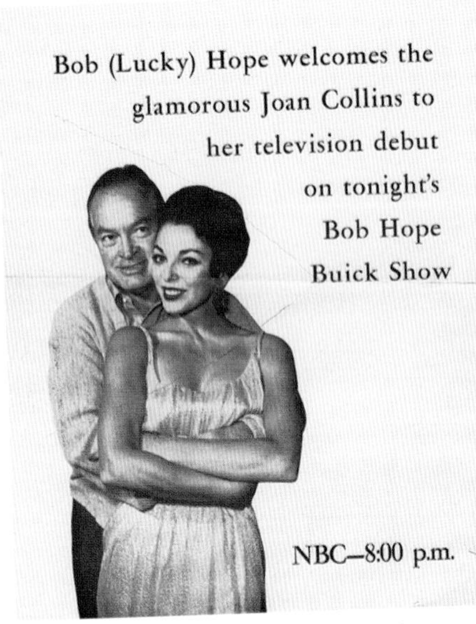
Bob (Lucky) Hope welcomes the
glamorous Joan Collins to
her television debut
on tonight's
Bob Hope
Buick Show
NBC—8:00 p.m.

My very first US TV appearance with Bob Hope.

and he clowned with Bob Hope, pretending to fight over his statuette. That was quite a turnaround for Marlon, who a few weeks earlier sat in my living room eating ice cream out of the carton and declaiming Bob Hope as 'a big fake who would go to the opening of a petrol station'.

I attended the ceremony several more times, once even performing a song with Dana Wynter and Angela Lansbury called 'It's Great Not to Be Nominated'.

I was in the audience on the famous night in 1974 that a streaker dashed across the stage as David Niven was making an introduction. Niven, with his usual quick, wit quipped, 'Isn't it fascinating to think that probably the only laugh that man will ever get in his life is by stripping off and showing his shortcomings?'

In 1975, Ron Kass, my then husband, was nominated as a co-producer for a documentary he made and we attended the awards ceremony in the pouring rain. Sadly Ron didn't win.

I was also a presenter a few times – once with Arnold Schwarzenegger. When announcing the award I laid my hand on his bicep and it was like touching a huge steel bar. 'Ooh, that's hard!' I squealed. Arnie, always with an eye for the ladies, reciprocated by patting my bum!

In the two weeks before the awards in this town (everyone calls Hollywood 'this town' but no one knows why), the beauty salons, tanning parlours and Botox clinics fill their appointment books with a who's who list that will rival the red carpet – actresses, starlets, wives and girlfriends of executives anxious to look as good as it gets on the evening.

OPPOSITE: *I wore this gorgeous Italian couture gown for one of the red carpet premieres for* Dr Doolittle.

Representatives of top couture designers flood in from New York, Europe and the Middle East with their most dazzling gowns to tempt the sometimes jaded palettes of the female nominees. If the actresses need to look good in an award-winning dress, they cannot be more than a size four at most, and the competition is fierce to achieve the best look. Some of the high-profile designers even pay high profile actresses to wear their gowns or their jewels!

Part of the thrill of Oscar week is the swag. 'Gifting suites' pop up all over town in the top hotels, offering free holidays, beauty treatments, costume jewellery and watches. The experience is akin to a giant, town-

wide Easter egg hunt – you can score or you can fail dismally. Once, Jackie and I passed by one of these and a huge bag was pressed upon us. When we got home we found it contained mostly hair products, face cream and body lotions, of which we have far too much already.

Weeks before the Oscars are announced the parties begin, some still hoping to grab the last-minute voters but most of them just to celebrate being nominated. The bibles of the business, the *Hollywood Reporter* and *Daily Variety*, send out free copies every day for six months to the Academy voters and are chock-a-block with blatant advertisements and announcements in support of the individuals hoping to participate in the cut-throat competition. By the time the Oscars come around, the Golden Globes, the Screen Actors Guild Awards, the BAFTAs and countless other awards have been handed out and are already gathering dust. Traditionally, the recipients of the latter are the favourites to win the elegant little golden statuette.

At the Oscars in 1975, when Ron Kass was nominated.

In the week before the Oscar ceremony, Hollywood is obsessed with high excitement – even the most seasoned stars and executives feel the buzz. 'Oscarexia' goes into top gear as a small army of the 'glam squad' stylists, diet experts, nutritionists, makeup artists and hairdressers bring out their wares.

During the days before the ceremony many of the streets leading to Hollywood boulevard are closed to all vehicles. As the red carpet is being put in place, fans and gawkers from all over the world start gathering behind the bleachers of the Kodak Theater, hoping to get a glimpse of their favourite stars along the red carpet. The telecast airs in over 200 countries. It creates 7,000 jobs and $130 million in revenue; 157 members of the media are allowed about a square foot each on the carpet in which to manoeuvre for their star-studded interviews and sound bites.

There are so many parties that it's impossible to attend all of them and you have to choose carefully so you don't look like rent-a-guest. On Oscar weekend

Mary and Irving Paul Lazar
cordially invite you to
Academy Awards Night
Monday, March 30, 1992
Spago
5 o'clock · Cocktails
6 o'clock · Showtime
Black Tie
Dinner

With Irving 'Swifty' Lazar at one of his exclusive Oscar parties.

the party pace is even more frenetic and we often hit a few of them. There's Barry Diller and Diane von Furstenberg's exclusive Saturday brunch filled with movers and shakers of the mogul and star-maker variety, along with a sprinkling of stars. Everyone sits on cushioned benches outside on the lawn; the grass is carpeted over with Persian rugs and the whole effect is tastefully Pasha-like. Harvey Weinstein's bash at the fashionable Soho House brings out an eclectic mixture of stars from Jennifer Lopez to Drew Barrymore to January Jones; and the *Hollywood Reporter*'s 'Big 10' bash, the newcomer on the party scene, brings out the new breed of stars, the faces changing every year.

But the biggest, most lavish, most amusing event of Oscar night is definitely the Sunday night *Vanity Fair* viewing party given by Graydon Carter at the chic Sunset Tower Hotel which I have been attending since it started. When Percy and I first went to the *Vanity Fair* party together shortly after our wedding, we were photographed in a group in which I was chatting to my friend Wendy Stark and Percy was talking to Barry Humphries's wife, Lizzie Spender. When a British tabloid ran the picture

they cut me out leaving just Percy and Lizzie seemingly with eyes only for each other. The headline blazed, 'Only married a month, and already cracks in the marriage.' Ah the power and pettiness of the press!

The precursor to the elegant *Vanity Fair* party was fabled agent 'Swifty' Lazar's Oscar party at Spago on the Strip or the Bistro (both now defunct). He would cut the guest-list down with the zeal of Genghis Khan if anyone table-hopped too much or chatted too loudly during the telecast.

BELOW: *A favourite question with the media on the carpet is 'Why are you here?' I usually have a salty answer but don't vocalize it.*

Vanity Fair has kept his tradition alive. With only twenty tables for ten people, this party is the most exclusive in Hollywood. Some people actually leave town if they haven't been invited so they aren't embarrassed that they haven't been asked. The dinner guests are usually an eclectic mixture of stars (Michelle Williams, Jane Fonda, Sidney Poitier, Sofia Vergara) and producers, studio executives and directors, fashion people like Tom Ford, Carolina Herrera and Valentino, and socialites like Lynn Wyatt and Betsy Bloomingdale.

After the Oscar show, which we watch on huge television screens, all the tables are moved and magically the place is turned into a huge ballroom with tiny tables and several bars and comfortable sofas on which to lounge whilst watching the action. And action there usually is as the stars arrive fresh from the Oscar ceremony and the Governor's Ball – some tearily clutching Oscars and being immediately lionized, some putting on a brave face.

Usually by 1 a.m. we fold our tents and clutching our Zippo lighters, engraved with a witty quote and left at each place setting, we head home after a great night and an exhausting week, although many other revellers celebrate into the wee hours of Monday.

In 2011 I had a particularly memorable *Vanity Fair* party, for reasons that are not necessarily pleasant. I squeezed myself into my gown – a beautiful creation of purple and lilac appliqué flowers and crystals by Georges Hobeika. Admittedly it was an extremely tight gown, but it fitted well so I resigned myself to not being able to eat much. Percy and I limo'd with my sister Jackie to the event at 4.45 p.m., a tradition which we had been keeping for several years.

OPPOSITE: *Another red dress, another red carpet.*

The dining room had been built over the pool and the views over Hollywood were spectacular as dusk fell. It was still so bright at 5:30 when the telecast began that some of the guests wore sunglasses. The ceiling was a masterpiece of huge white balloons and the walls of the entire place were lined with photos of Audrey Hepburn, Cary Grant and other iconic stars and film posters. When I asked a waiter where the ladies room was, he pointed and said, 'Right next to your poster of *The Opposite Sex*, Miss Collins.' I couldn't help but take a picture and post it on Twitter.

Skin-tight Oscar dress lands Joan in hospital

SEE PAGE THREE

The party teemed with exquisitely dressed women, and some of the men looked good too. The biggest star there to me was the fabulous Sidney Poitier, who seldom goes to events but was gracefully chatting and schmoozing with everyone.

The photo booth at the Vanity Fair bash is always fun.

Percy and I sat with my sister Jackie, George and Jolene Schlatter of *Laugh-In* fame and Leonard and Wendy Goldberg, producer of *Charlie's Angels*. Major studio execs and socialites filled the rest of the room to the brim, giving me pause to wonder who would have first billing if it burned down. The tables were beautifully appointed and the placement was clever.

The stars, winners and losers, of the night arrived from the Governor's Ball around 9 p.m., after we'd been socializing for about four hours and my couture dress was getting progressively tighter, although I felt better when Valentino admired it.

But by 10.30 with about 800 people milling about, I started feeling slightly dizzy so Percy and I walked outside to get some fresh air. Next thing I knew I was lying flat out in the basement of the hotel, on a stretcher, surrounded by some rather attractive firefighters who were asking me questions like, 'What's your name?' (as if they didn't know) and 'How old are you?' (which I refused to answer). Apparently I had fainted in Percy's arms and he, in a panic, had asked security to call an ambulance (which *was* roomier than our limo and, thanks to the sirens, much swifter). I was whisked to A&E where, after an hour of tests, the doctors discharged me with admonishments not to wear such tight dresses and to eat, in future, if I was expected to last more than seven hours at the fabulous *Vanity Fair* party. Not quite how I expected to end this glamorous night, but it didn't stop me from attending the following year – in a much looser dress.

EPILOGUE

I'm often surprised by some people's reactions when I say that I like to shop at supermarkets or department stores. They seem to think that actresses live in a bubble of personal assistants, toadying gofers, managers, stylists and hot and cold running helpers to do everything. Some do, however, but they are rare. Many starlets and stars cannot even do their own hair and makeup. The larger your 'entourage', the faster your coffers will dry up!

Boy, am I glad that I am no longer the flavour of the month as I was in the eighties and nineties. Then there were relatively few paparazzi and even the most daring still kept a respectable distance. I did have my fair share of nasty encounters but absolutely *nothing* compares with what today's celebrities and actors have to deal with. The voracious public appetite for sensational photos and stories about the several hundred people now having their moment in the spotlight seems never ending. Some celebrities revel in it: the pregnant girls baring their nude bumps, often with baby daddy proudly showing that he had something to do with it; the endless stream of look-a-like ladettes filling the pages of celebrity magazines with shorter and shorter skirts, tinier and tinier tops, higher and higher heels and a distinct lack of knickers; the dizzying array of reality stars whose only talent seems to be for exhibitionism at any cost.

ABOVE: *At the Glamour Awards 2013*

HOORAY FOR HOLLYWOOD
PARTY AT JACKIES 1994
GLAMOUR

Many stars and celebrities today are considered animals to be stalked by the endless swarm of paparazzi, who have zero qualms about following them or failing to respect their personal space. The tragic victims of this inquisition are often the stars' children who have to face the relentless flashlights, which must be extremely disquieting and disconcerting, not to mention bad for their eyes! I saw a young actress on a documentary called *$ellebrity* holding her three-year-old, who was screaming pitifully at the paps, 'Stop taking my picture! Stop it! Please!' But did they stop? No way. 'Celebs with kids sell,' one of the photographers said. 'It's like big game hunting. It's my job and they deserve what they get 'cause they're celebrities. They've asked for it.' Celebrities are not human beings to these predators, just grist for the mill of popular media.

Furthermore, to call them photographers in most cases is fanciful. The advent of the cheap digital camera has allowed the field of paparazzi to expand and include anyone and everyone with a little money to spend on a camera, including some who dress like tramps. Similarly, the rise of the camera phone has opened up a whole new world of opportunities for the amateur paparazzo to catch celebrities shopping at supermarkets, sleeping on planes, looking tired or out of shape, and to tweet or Facebook it immediately. There is absolutely no privacy for the big stars of today unless it's behind the closed doors of their homes. Before these devices, it was talented professional photographers, with means to purchase and develop film and with the knack of charming their prey and developing a relationship with them in order to capture them properly, who dominated celebrity journalism.

OPPOSITE: *Jackie throws another fabulous party in 1994 with all the usual suspects!*

Today fame is mostly ephemeral unless you have an enduring talent like Barbra Streisand or Meryl Streep. So many major stars from movies and television, who are still living, are gone from public consciousness. I don't want to do a laundry list of 'Whatever happened to . . .' but in these days of longevity it's sad to see some actors and actresses, magnificent in their prime, reduced to penury. Some stars are living almost hand-to-mouth, forgotten by the fans and media who once idolized them and no longer relevant to the employers who could give them a job. When they are recognized, it's tragic for them to see the dismay on the faces of their formers fans. Everyone gets old . . . it's better than the alternative . . . but the majority of people age in relative anonymity without facing the relentless scrutiny of the media.

One recent case of this 'fall from grace' is that of Burt Reynolds. Throughout the seventies, he topped the poll of the most popular actors in the world and his movies made millions. By 1996 he was filing for bankruptcy. He reportedly owes millions to the Inland Revenue Service and creditors, and by August 2011 was facing eviction from his home, having disposed of his properties, horses, cars, artwork and royalties. He is in poor health and works little but still the paparazzi are avid for pictures of him looking ravaged.

Contrast his fate to that of one of the most popular actresses of the 1970s: Ali MacGraw of *Love Story* fame. When her star began to fade she moved to New Mexico where she lives quietly and happily. Some stars reinvent themselves – Shirley MacLaine told me that when she was in her fifties she put herself up for roles of characters ten or twenty years or older than her, which thanks to her talent she could believably play. Meanwhile, Robert De Niro went from tough, dramatic actor to comedic roles in the Fokkers series and *Analyze This*, almost spoofing his tough dramatic actor characters.

'Twas ever thus, of course, but this longevity coupled with the current short-term memory of viewers wreaks havoc on one's relevance. Today, a few years is very long lifespan for a star these days, whereas not a decade ago, people generally were familiar with names from fifty or more years ago. A child of the seventies would have grown up seeing Charlie Chaplin movies whereas today the array of digital and televised content is so vast that it's rare for someone to know the work of a star from further back than the beginning of this millennium. It's strange that some actors only find themselves in demand either at the rise of their careers or the end of their life.

Although one star who shone brilliantly until the end of her life was Elizabeth Taylor. I first became aware of Elizabeth Taylor when I saw her in *Lassie, Come Home* when she was about ten years old. I had just started collecting autographed pictures of movie stars and I wrote off for one – not for Elizabeth's but for Lassie's! But I never received it (what a bitch!). And when Elizabeth became a teenager in *A Date with Judy* everyone at school tried to emulate her.

I met her many years later in Hollywood (not Lassie, Elizabeth) in the hair and makeup department of MGM where I was shooting the *Opposite*

David and Victoria Beckham at the Vanity Fair party 2012.

Sex (in which I played Krystal – Yes, I did!). I was in awe of the constellation of superstars who sat casually in hair rollers sipping coffee and gossiping. Grace Kelly, soon to leave to become Princess of Monaco, was regal and cool, but Elizabeth Taylor was animatedly showing off photos of her children and acting just like a normal mum.

I though she was gorgeous, down to earth and a touch bawdy, which caused the aristocratic Kelly to raise a delicate eyebrow but elicited gales of laughter from Ava Gardner and me. Shortly after, Elizabeth and I double-dated at the La Rue restaurant and chatted away. She told me that she always made the producer or director give her an 'end of picture' present. 'You *must* do that too!' she insisted, 'Careers don't last, y'know, they go up and down. You need to get a present when your career is up and when it's down you can recall how good it was from the amount of presents you have!'

In Fetish, *I play a fading actress who can't cope with the loss of fame.*

I didn't have the chutzpah to ask for presents like Elizabeth did. *No one* could get away with it like she could, or could ask for them in a most disarming and childlike way. When we made *These Old Broads*, her last movie, one of the producers rushed into my trailer in a complete flap.

'I don't know what to do!' she wailed. 'Elizabeth has asked that we buy a real chinchilla rug for the scene where she's lounging on the sofa!'

'How cozy,' I replied.

'Cozy? Not only do we have to buy it, but she then wants to keep at the end of the shoot, as a gift! We simply can't afford it – what do I do?'

'Tell her you can only afford to hire it – she'll understand,' I said. And of course she did and told the producer she was only joking. Elizabeth had a wicked sense of humor but she'd have kept the rug if they'd given in to her!

I decided to appear on the boards in panto in Birmingham in 2011 – it was huge fun, especially with Julian Clary and I outdoing each other in the dressing up box.

Throughout the years our paths have continued to cross. I'd dated her first ex-husband, the dissolute Nick Hilton (aka Conrad Jnr); then she had dated my ex-boyfriend Arthur Loew Jnr. I had been the 'utility infielder' ready to take over from her in *Cleopatra* when she was at death's door with pneumonia. I'd also been at a dreadful dinner party during the making of *Cleopatra* with a group of horrified acquaintances in the Roman villa she had shared with husband Eddie Fisher, whom she insulted and berated mercilessly. Everyone there knew about 'Liz 'n' Dick'. Everyone of course, except Eddie.

With Elizabeth and another icon, Liza Minelli, who has managed to survive a long career.

Although Elizabeth and I were not bosom buddies, or part of the Hollywood 'ladies who lunch' club, we nevertheless saw each other quite often at various parties and had close friends in common. After her divorce from John Warner, she moved back to Hollywood and started socializing and our paths rejoined. When she started dating my friend George Hamilton she was somewhat overweight, no doubt after the boredom of being a senator's wife. George immediately took her in his capable hands and put her on a strict diet and started telling her how to dress and style her hair. I was extremely flattered when she told me that she loved my short bouffant 'Alexis' coiffure in Dynasty, which had just become a hit show. She was very upfront about telling me she was copying it and I considered it a huge compliment that someone as iconic as 'La Liz' would want to replicate my coiffure.

Then, when I got the quickie divorce from the even more quickie marriage to husband number four, she sent me a little handwritten note that simply said, 'I'm still ahead by three!'

When we made *Broads* she seemed frail. However, she was cheerful despite the fact that she was in constant pain and had been for most of

I love doing my one-woman show, in which I talk about my life and times.

her life. On set, she spoke to me candidly. 'There's never been a time of my life when I wasn't famous. I've never been able to go outside without photographers following me.'

Despite all her glamour, beauty, wealth and fame, she was totally relatable one-on-one, even though she was admittedly quite shy. Her vocabulary could be salty and because of her marriage to Burton she knew some unusual profanities!

The media had a field day over *Broads*, with rumors of infighting and shenanigans on set, attributed to various so-called 'friendly sources'. Unfortunately, my alter ego 'Alexis' was being used liberally to dramatize these lies in print so I was getting the brunt of the blame.

'Why,' I wailed to Elizabeth despairingly, 'do they make up these stories about us? Why do I always come out as the nasty one causing trouble?'

'Because you're the prettiest,' she said. Her fabled smile lit up her face as she had lit up the screen and the warmth of that compliment, coming from one of the most famous and beautiful women in the world, made me forget the ugliness.

Elizabeth Taylor was the last legendary movie star and she lived life with passion. She had great highs and enormous lows, and her name and presence will survive when most of today's megastars are forgotten. Not since the death of Princess Diana did I see such a justifiable tornado of press and media coverage because there never was and there never will be another star like her.

As I look back at my life I realize that I too have had great highs and enormous lows, but through all these my innate optimism and passion for life helped me through the troughs and tempered the heights. As Robert Louis Stevenson so aptly said, 'Do not judge each day by the harvest you reap but by the seeds that you plant'. And my passion still burns brightly for my husband Percy, for my children and for their children and for my brother and sister, and mostly for this beautiful world I am lucky enough to enjoy.

OPPOSITE: *My biggest achievement is my beautiful family.*

For my family, and for Percy - for always

Constable & Robinson Ltd
55-56 Russell Square
London WC1B 4HP
www.constablerobinson.com

First published in the UK by Constable,
an imprint of Constable & Robinson Ltd., 2013

A copy of the British Library Cataloguing in Publication Data is available from the British Library

ISBN 978-1-4721-0235-5 (hardback)
ISBN 978-1-4721-0739-8 (ebook)

Designed by Carrdesignstudio.com
Printed and bound in the EU

1 3 5 7 9 10 8 6 4 2

Picture Credits

The publishers would like to thank the following sources for their kind permission to reproduce the photographs and illustrations in this book. Every effort has been made to obtain the necessary permissions with reference to copyright material, both illustrative and quoted. We apologise for any omissions in this respect and will be pleased to make the appropriate acknowledgements in any future edition.

42 – BFI Film Stills Archive; 56 – Annunziata Asquith; 61 – (Katy at Cabrillo image) Eddie Sanderson; 67 – Eddie Sanderson; 70 - BFI Film Stills Archive; 84 – (Joan Collins and Taki image) Richard Young; 127 - BFI Film Stills Archive; 132 – Harry Benson; 140 – www.brianaris.com; 145 – Eddie Sanderson; 148 – Charles Griffin; 188 – Getty images; 189 – (Michael Jackson, Elizabeth Taylor and Joan Collins image) Richard Young; 191 – (Joan Collins and George Hamilton image) Scott Downie; (Nigel Hawthorne and JC image) Stefan Rousseau; 192 – Alan Davidson; 198 – Eddie Sanderson; 200 – Press Association; 202 – Press Association; 203 – Richard Young; 204 – Press Association; 213 – (Top image) Mirrorpix; 234 – Charles Griffin; 272 – Sacha Newley

Constable & Robinson would like to thank Mark McMorrow and the Joan Collins Archive for their help in creating this book.